SUZANNE O'SULLIVAN

Dr Suzanne O'Sullivan has been a consultant in neurology since 2004, first working at The Royal London Hospital and now as a consultant in clinical neurophysiology and neurology at the National Hospital for Neurology and Neurosurgery, and for a specialist unit based at the Epilepsy Society. In that role she has developed an expertise in working with patients with psychogenic disorders alongside her work with those suffering with physical diseases such as epilepsy. This is her first book.

SUZANNE O'SULLIVAN

It's All in Your Head

Stories from the Frontline of Psychosomatic Illness

VINTAGE

3 5 7 9 10 8 6 4 2

Vintage
20 Vauxhall Bridge Road,
London SW1V 2SA

Vintage is part of the Penguin Random House group of companies
whose addresses can be found at global.penguinrandomhouse.com.

Penguin
Random House
UK

First published in Vintage in 2016
First published in hardback by Chatto & Windus in 2015

www.vintage-books.co.uk

A CIP catalogue record for this book is available from the
British Library

ISBN 9780099597858

Typeset in AGaramond Regular by Palimpsest Book Production Limited,
Falkirk, Stirlingshire

Printed and bound by Clays Ltd, St Ives plc

Penguin Random House is committed to a sustainable future for our
business, our readers and our planet. This book is made from Forest
Stewardship Council® certified paper.

MIX
Paper from
responsible sources
FSC® C018179

For E.H.

CONTENTS

1

TEARS

While I was convinced the woman was afflicted not by a bodily disease, but rather that some emotional trouble grieved her, it happened at that very moment I was examining her, this was confirmed. Someone coming from the theatre mentioned he had seen Pylades dancing. Indeed, at that instant, her expression and colour of her face was greatly altered. Attentive, my hand laid on the woman's wrist and I observed her pulse was irregular, suddenly, violently agitated, which points to a troubled mind.

Galen, *c.* AD 150

I qualified as a doctor in 1991. For fledgling doctors their first great dilemma comes when they are asked to choose their specialty. Some parts of the decision are easy. You either want to operate on people or you don't. You can react quickly in an emergency or you can't. Some want to be a scientist in a laboratory. Others would prefer to spend their time with patients. Medicine has room for every type of person. It is sometimes harder to make the more refined career decisions that follow. You know that you want to be a surgeon, but which bit do you want to operate on? Are you fascinated by the heart, where a single missed beat can put life in immediate peril? Or do you want to experience the highs and lows of the fight against cancer cells?

Despite all the possibilities, I knew from an early stage in my training what my decision would be. I wanted to be a neurologist. When I made that choice I thought I knew what it meant and where it would take me. I wanted to emulate the people I had learned from, the individuals who had inspired me. I enjoyed the detective drama of the job, unravelling the mysteries of how the nervous system communicates its messages, and learning all the things that can go wrong. Imagine a man who cannot move his right leg and cannot feel his left leg – where's the lesion? What's the disease? Or a woman who is otherwise well but finds she can't write and can't identify her fingers. Ask her to say which is the index finger and she will not get it right. What part of the brain, when damaged, causes that? Neurological disease manifests in elusive and strange ways. There is a sort of epileptic seizure that is triggered by brushing your teeth. There are strange temporary paralytic disorders that strike after eating salty food.

I started my first training post in neurology in 1995, expecting to look after people who had diseases of the brain and nerves and muscles; conditions like multiple sclerosis, stroke, migraine and epilepsy. I could not have predicted how far I would find myself drawn into the care of those whose illness originated not in the body, but in the mind.

Examples of how the mind affects the body are everywhere. Some are so commonplace that they are not regarded as anything out of the ordinary. Tears are only salt water produced by ducts in the eye. They are a physiological response to a feeling. I cry if I feel sad, but happiness can have exactly the same effect. Sometimes tears are triggered by a memory or a piece of music or a painting. They occur in response to anger or laughter. The instantaneousness of it all has always amazed me.

The body has a multitude of ways through which it can express emotion. Blushing occurs when the blood vessels of the head and neck dilate and become infused with blood. It is an instantaneous physical change seen on the surface but reflecting a feeling of embarrassment or happiness that is held inside. When it happens I can't control it. That point is important. My blushes betray a feeling and, even when they increase my embarrassment, I cannot stop them.

Sometimes the body's reactions are more dramatic than a brief blush or the odd tear. Even quite exaggerated bodily responses to emotion are easy to accept if the circumstances are right. In the early nineteenth century in *Naples and Florence: A journey from Milan to Reggio* the French novelist Stendhal described how he felt when he first encountered the great frescoes of Florence. 'I was seized with a fierce palpitation of heart, the wellspring of life was dried up within me, and I walked with a constant fear of falling to the ground.' Perhaps what Stendhal described seems extreme to some of us, but to others it may seem absolutely obvious that, on the day one first encounters the frescoes of Giotto, one's legs will weaken and one's heart will miss a beat.

There are many modern examples of the tendency to collapse in response to excitement. Think of young people fainting at pop concerts, for example. Of course, many such collapses are easily explained by the physiology of the body. A young girl is overcrowded in intense heat, her blood vessels dilate to cool her, venous pooling draws her circulation downwards away from her head and, for just a moment, her brain is deprived of oxygen, she collapses and consciousness is lost. She has fainted due to nothing more than the body's physical response to a physical trigger.

And yet when scientists examined just this phenomenon, they demonstrated that not every swooning, swaying teenager could be accounted for in this way. In 1995 the *New England Journal of Medicine* published an article in which young people who had collapsed at a music concert were interviewed. Of the 400 brought to medical attention, forty were examined. Sixteen of those forty lost consciousness in a faint that was felt to be entirely explained by physical triggers – heat and dehydration leading to falling blood pressure, circulation drawn away from the brain and subsequent collapse. Others had panicked when they found themselves trapped in a crowd, leading to hyper-ventilation that constricted the blood vessels going to the brain and, again, a brief blackout followed. But the doctors also observed that not every collapse could be attributed to heat or dehydration or the crush of the crowd; some had occurred in the context of only one trigger: an overwhelming surge of emotion. An emotional collapse, with no physical cause to account for it.

Most of us readily accept these common phenomena. We are familiar with the shake in our hand as we pick up the pen to sign the marriage register or the bead of sweat on our brow as we stand up to give the presentation we do not want to give. These are the body's physiological responses to stress. They serve a purpose even if that purpose is not always obvious. They belong to the impulse that made the caveman's heart beat faster so that he could run away from the woolly mammoth. But what if this type of normal physical response to emotion ceases to work properly? After all, every function of our body that supports us can malfunction. Any cell that is alive can overgrow so that tumours form. Or they can stop growing, as with hair loss, for example. Any chemical that is produced can be overproduced, or underproduced, as happens in the overactive or underactive thyroid gland. In just the same way, sometimes the physical response of our organs to stress goes too far. When that happens, something that was normal is no longer so and illness occurs.

The word psychosomatic refers to physical symptoms that occur for psychological reasons. Tears and blushing are examples of this, but they are normal responses that do not represent illness. It is only when psychosomatic symptoms go beyond the ordinary and impair our ability to function or endanger our health that illness results. Modern society likes the idea that we can think ourselves better. When we are unwell, we tell ourselves that if we adopt a positive mental attitude, we will have a better chance of recovery. I am sure that is correct. But society has not fully woken up to the frequency with which people do the opposite – unconsciously think themselves ill. Certainly, there are several medical disorders that are already commonly associated with stress. Most of us know that stress puts our blood pressure up and makes us more vulnerable to stomach ulcers. But how many are aware of the frequency with which our emotions can produce serious disability where no physical disease of any sort exists to explain it?

Psychosomatic disorders are conditions in which a person suffers from significant physical symptoms – causing real distress and disability – out of proportion to that which can be explained by medical tests or physical examination. They are medical disorders like no others. They obey no rules. They can affect any part of the body. In one person they might cause pain. Think of the child who gets a pain in the stomach when they are being bullied at school. In someone else they might affect the heart. It is not unusual for somebody going through a period of stress to be troubled by palpitations. These sorts of symptoms are quite common but psychosomatic illness can also manifest in more extreme ways: as paralysis or convulsions or almost any sort of disability. They are disorders of the imagination restricted only by the limits of the imagination. Think now of any physical symptom and, at some time, in some person, the mind has reproduced it.

On any average day perhaps as many as a third of people who go to see their general practitioner have symptoms that are deemed medically unexplained. Of course, a medically unexplained symptom is not necessarily psychosomatic. Some of these people have transient illnesses that do not reveal themselves in common investigations. Lots of viral infections, for example, do not show up on routine tests. They come, they go, we never know exactly what they were but, once we feel better, the exact cause doesn't really matter. Other people are clearly unwell and this is demonstrated through abnormal results of physical examinations or abnormalities on tests, but still the cause is not determined. There will always be diseases that stretch the limits of scientific knowledge. Every year scientists discover the cause for previously unexplained medical complaints, so some will get their diagnosis in time. But amongst those with unequivocal, but undiagnosed, physical symptoms is a large group in whom no disease is found because there is no disease to find. In those people the medically unexplained symptoms are present, wholly or partially, for psychological or behavioural reasons.

Psychosomatic illness is a worldwide phenomenon with little regard for any culture or system of health care. In 1997 the World Health Organization carried out a collaborative study to look at the frequency of psychosomatic symptoms in the primary care setting in fifteen cities across the world. Included were cities in the USA, Nigeria, Germany, Chile, Japan, Italy, Brazil and India. At each centre the frequency of 'medically unexplained symptoms' (i.e. where a psychosomatic cause is suspected) were quantified. The study showed that while the severest form of psychosomatic disorders are rare, the milder forms are not. The conclusion was that as many as twenty per cent of those attending their doctor had at least six medically unexplained symptoms, a sufficient number to significantly impair their quality of life. Interestingly, in this study, rates of medically unexplained symptoms were similar in both developing and developed countries. Differences in availability of health care did not affect the prevalence of the disorder. Sufferers in every country were high utilisers of medical services and had a high rate of disability resulting in lost work hours.

Disorders that are this common – that occur in twenty per cent of patients worldwide – must have a financial impact on the health service. This is very difficult to quantify. Those who have tried to do so have come up with some quite startling figures. In 2005 a study carried out in Boston revealed that people with a tendency to develop psychosomatic complaints cost the health care system twice as much as those who do not. These results were extrapolated to estimate the yearly cost of psychosomatic disorders in the USA – $256 billion. To put this into perspective, in 2002 diabetes, a common disease with multiple life-threatening complications, had a yearly cost of $132 billion.

Psychosomatic disorders are not neurological disorders. They belong to the fields of psychology and psychiatry. I am not a psychiatrist, I am a neurologist. At first my interest in, and exposure to, psychosomatic disorders may seem to make little sense. Until, that is, you realise that it is precisely because I am not a psychiatrist that I have come to see so many patients who suffer in this way. After all, if you collapsed or suffered a severe headache why would you ask a psychiatrist for help? Psychosomatic disorders are physical symptoms that mask emotional distress. The very nature of the physical presentation of the symptoms hides the distress at its root, so it is natural that those affected will automatically seek a medical disease to explain their suffering. They turn to medical doctors, not to psychiatrists, to provide a diagnosis. Those with abdominal pain see a gastroenterologist, those with palpitations a cardiologist, those with visual blurring an ophthalmologist, and so on. And because every type of specialist sees a different form of psychosomatic illness, and labels and treats it differently, it can be very difficult to fully appreciate the extent of the problem.

The two most common psychosomatic symptoms are fatigue

and pain. They are difficult symptoms to assess because they cannot be objectively measured, they can only be described. Psychosomatic illness for a neurologist, however, will often manifest as a loss of function, such as paralysis or hearing loss. These sorts of deficits are subjectively experienced by the patient but there are ways in which they can be objectively verified and quantified, at least in part. The neurologist can fairly reliably differentiate disability due to organic physical disease from that which has a psychological cause. As a result the neurologist is faced with a diagnosis of psychosomatic illness more often than other specialists, and that is how my interest arose.

Up to one-third of people seen in an average general neurology clinic have neurological symptoms that cannot be explained and, in those people, an emotional cause is often suspected. It is very difficult for a patient to be given the news that their physical illness may have a psychological cause. It is a difficult diagnosis to understand, let alone accept. And doctors can be reluctant to offer it up, partly for fear of angering their patients but also for fear of what they might have missed. Patients often find themselves trapped in a zone between the worlds of medicine and psychiatry, with neither community taking full responsibility. Those who struggle with the diagnosis may seek the opinion of doctor after doctor in the hope of finding a different explanation – and validation of their suffering. Repeatedly normal test results begin to seem a disappointment, so desperate is the patients' search for another answer. Some find themselves pushed into a corner where they accept the role of the undiagnosed, someone who cannot be helped, because anything is better than the humiliation of a psychological disorder. Society is judge-mental about psychological illness and patients know that.

When my medical career began my own views on psychosomatic illness were little different. Compared to *real* illness these patients did not make the grade. My interest grew slowly, at first through gradual exposure and later more quickly when I found myself thrown in at the deep end in a new job.

Like most doctors my first experience of psychosomatic illness came when I was a medical student. When you meet the first patient who is physically ill, but with no disease to explain it, you dismiss them. You are there to learn about disease and they have nothing to teach you about that. Then you qualify and become a junior doctor and you act as a sort of triaging service. You are often on the front line, trying to make a diagnosis and then presenting it to your senior doctor for their approval. You prioritise the patient you view as the sickest. The person in the waiting room with chronic unexplained pain finds themselves at the bottom of your list. If nobody else has been able to explain the pain it is unlikely that you will. You grade illness not by how distressing the patient finds it, but by your own ideas about what constitutes a serious illness. On this matter doctor and patient do not always agree.

Once I had started my training in neurology my relationship with psychosomatic disorders began to grow. I became increasingly aware that a large number of people coming through the door of our clinic had symptoms that were more likely to be related to stress than any brain or nerve disease but I, like so many of my colleagues, saw my role as one of ruling out neurological disease.

After I had done so I absolved myself of further responsibility. The rotating nature of training jobs meant that I might see a patient once and never again, so it was an easy stance to take. *Good news, we have not found a brain tumour, your headache does not have a serious cause.* And goodbye.

Then I met Brenda. She was unconscious that first time and for most of our meetings that followed. Brenda had come to the casualty department following several seizures. The on-call doctor had seen her and arranged for her to be admitted. We were on the ward when she arrived. Everybody stood back in fright as a trolley came speeding up the corridor towards us. Brenda had been stable in the casualty department but, as the porter transported her to the ward, her next seizure had started. The porter and the nurse who was with him had broken into a run. On the ward an oxygen mask was quickly clamped to Brenda's face, while two nurses attempted, and failed, to roll her on to her side. The trolley had come to a stop by the nurses' station and all the other patients and their families strained to see what was going on. A nurse appeared with a syringe filled with diazepam and handed it to me to give to Brenda. I tried to catch Brenda's flailing arm but it kept slipping from my grasp.

Another doctor came to help and we managed to pin down the arm even as it fought against us. I slowly administered the injection. We stood back and waited for it to take effect, but nothing happened. I could feel the heat of all those eyes on my back and it was a great relief when the registrar shouted for the anaesthetist to be called. Brenda had been convulsing on and off for ten minutes by the time the intensive care team arrived; the only drug that could be given safely on the ward had been given twice and failed. The whole ward breathed a sigh as we watched the porter and anaesthetist turn Brenda's trolley around and wheel her quickly away again.

I barely recognised Brenda when I saw her the next day. She was in the intensive care unit, intubated, her breathing under the control of a ventilator. A second tube threaded itself through her nose down into her stomach. Her eyes were closed with tape and her hair was pulled back tightly. Her seizures had not come under control so she had been put into a medically induced coma. Every time the intensive care doctor tried to withdraw the sedation and wake Brenda the seizures immediately started again. Over the next two days epilepsy drugs were given at escalating doses. In those two days Brenda became increasingly unrecognisable. Her skin became waxy and pale, her stomach dramatically distended, but her seizures were not improving.

On the fifth day we all stood around Brenda's bed watching her. The neurology consultant had asked to be present the next time the sedation was being withdrawn. It took only ten minutes for the first signs of Brenda's waking to show. She coughed against the breathing tube and her hands began to clutch at anything within reach.

'Brenda, how are you feeling? You are in the hospital but everything is okay,' the nurse squeezed Brenda's hand.

Brenda's eyes flickered open and she pulled at the breathing tube again.

'Can we take it out?' the nurse asked, but the intensive care doctor said not quite yet.

Brenda stared into the eyes of the nurse, recognising immediately the kindest person in the room. She coughed and tears began to run down her face.

'You've had a seizure but you are perfectly fine now.'

Brenda's left leg was beginning to shake.

'The seizure is starting again. Should we re-sedate?' someone asked.

'No,' the consultant answered.

By now the shaking had spread to the other leg and had become more violent. Brenda's eyes, which had been open and alert, were slowly closing again. As the shaking moved up through her body the machine that measured her falling oxygen levels began to beep behind her.

'Now?' a tense voice asked, syringe filled and held in preparation.

'It's not a seizure,' the consultant said.

Glances were exchanged.

'Take out the ET tube,' the consultant, again.

'Her oxygen saturation has dropped.'

'Yes, because her breath is held. She'll breathe again in a moment.'

Brenda's face reddened, back arched and limbs shook violently. We all stood around the bed, our breath held too, in sympathy.

'It's not an epileptic seizure, it's a pseudoseizure,' the consultant said and, as she said it, to our immense relief, Brenda took a large gasping breath.

Half an hour later Brenda was awake and sitting up in bed, with large tears coursing down her cheeks. That was the last time I saw her and the only time I ever saw her fully awake. Brenda and I never spoke.

Later that day when I was back in the hospital coffee room with the other junior doctors I told them about Brenda. 'You know that woman who has been anaesthetised in intensive care for most of the week? She doesn't have epilepsy, after all. There was nothing even wrong with her!'

It would be several years before I fully realised the danger that Brenda had faced. It would take longer still for me to really understand the disservice I had done her with my words. During my subsequent training I did become more understanding of psychosomatic disorders. But I would need to complete my training to mature as a doctor.

In 2004 I was appointed to my first consultant post and with this came the greatest change in my medical practice. As a senior registrar I thought I had known responsibility, but when the final decisions became mine alone I saw that I hadn't really. The weight of decision-making is very different when there is nobody above you to say what you did was right or wrong. Only the patient getting better or worse will tell you that.

The specific job I had chosen helped too, even though, at first, I did not fully know what I had taken on. I was trained in two specialities, neurology and clinical neurophysiology. Neurology qualified me to care for patients with diseases of the nervous system, and clinical neurophysiology taught me how to carry out specialist investigations on the nerves and brain. My first consultant post straddled those two areas and saw me running a service whose main purpose was to investigate people with epilepsy who were not getting better with standard treatment. It transpired that approximately seventy per cent of the people referred to me with poorly controlled seizures were not responding to epilepsy treatment because they did not have epilepsy. Their seizures were occurring for purely psychological reasons.

Suddenly I was seeing a greater number of patients whose illness could be more fairly classed as psychological than neurological. And each person I encountered had a story to tell, and too often that story was one of a journey through the hospital system that led them to no satisfactory understanding of what was wrong. Few received treatment and few recovered. I witnessed suffering that had lasted for years, and it was clear to me that it would no longer be acceptable for me to tell my patients which diseases had been ruled out and to consider that my job was done. If I was ever going to make anybody better I would have to start being more proactive. For the first time I saw clearly the seriousness of this disorder, how people struggled to recover – and how they rarely did.

Since those early days I have met many people whose sadness is so overwhelming that they cannot bear to feel it. In its place they develop physical disabilities. Against all logic, people's subconscious selves choose to be crippled by convulsions or wheelchair-bound rather than experience the anguish that exists inside them. I have learned a great deal through working with people who battle on despite the hardship and judgement that the world throws at them. I have found myself astounded by the degree of disability that can arise as a result of psychosomatic illness. In the beginning I sometimes fought against feelings of suspicion towards my patients, questions about their insight and their motives. So dramatic were some of the disabilities that it was not always easy to hold on to a belief in their subconscious nature. I have shared my patients' struggle to accept the power of the mind over the body. I have felt their frustration at how the system fails them and their anger at how they are perceived. In this book I will tell the stories of some of the brave people I have encountered. I have been very careful to protect the identity of my patients. All names and personal details have been changed completely, without altering the vital components of the stories. I hope to communicate to others what my patients have taught me. Perhaps then, future patients – people like you and me, our friends, families and colleagues – will not find themselves so bewildered and alone.

Before I begin, I need to clarify some terminology. So far, for simplicity I have used the term *psychosomatic* to refer to any physical symptom which cannot be explained by a disease and is suspected to have a psychological cause. But to say somebody has a psychosomatic disorder is not a distinct diagnosis, it is an umbrella term that encompasses several different diagnoses. That is also the case for the term *medically unexplained symptoms* – this is shorthand that the medical community uses to refer to symptoms that are thought to be stress-related and which cannot be accounted for by any physical disease. I will continue to use the terms psychosomatic and medically unexplained symptoms in this umbrella sense throughout the book. I will also use the term *psychogenic* when I am referring to symptoms where there is a strong conviction that they have arisen in the mind, as a result of stress or psychological upset.

However, the terms psychosomatic and psychogenic will not always be appropriate. These labels make assumptions. Each contains the prefix *psycho* which presupposes that a symptom arises in the mind, usually through emotional or mental distress. For some patients, particularly those who are wholly unaware of a psychological trigger, these terms are both alienating and potentially incorrect. In their place I will sometimes use the term *functional*. This is a purely descriptive term that implies that a symptom is medically unexplained but which makes no judgement about any particular cause.

To further clarify the difference in these labels, imagine a woman who suffers a serious sexual assault and soon after develops unexplained paralysis of her legs. In light of the known trauma, once medical disease has been ruled out, the paralysis could reasonably be described as either psychosomatic or psychogenic. On the other hand if a woman develops medically unexplained paralysis where there was no known preceding trauma, her paralysis would be better referred to as functional in the first instance. This term says that her neurological system is not functioning as it should, that no disease has been found, but it does not presume to know why. Many doctors use these labels almost interchangeably, but to the patient the distinction means a lot.

The *Diagnostic and Statistical Manual of Mental Disorders* (*DSM*) is the bible by which psychiatrists diagnose psychological and psychiatric illness and in it the term *psychosomatic disorder* does not appear. The conditions I describe in this book now more accurately fall into the *DSM* classification of *somatic symptom and related disorders*. Within that category there are several subclassifications. Each of those are designed to help the doctor make a diagnosis, but they are labels that cannot be offered easily to a patient. Included under this heading the *DSM* describes the following distinct conditions: somatic symptom disorder, conversion disorder, psychological factors affecting medical conditions, and unspecified somatic disorder.

A *somatic symptom disorder* is defined by the prominent presence of somatic (bodily) symptoms that cause significant distress and disruption to normal life for which there is no, or little, medical explanation. Pain is the most prominent symptom. It can be accompanied by almost any other sort of symptom, tiredness or diarrhoea or pretty much anything. The behaviour surrounding the symptom is key, not the symptom itself. There is disproportionate worry, anxiety and excessive energy spent on health concerns. It isn't enough just to have pain, what's important is how the person is disabled by that pain. They may stop exercising first. When the pain continues they stop working. Then they begin to avoid the normal activities of daily life.

There is an important distinction to be made here between the terms *somatisation* and *somatic symptom disorder*. Somatisation refers to the tendency of a person to have physical symptoms in response to stress or emotions. So, for example, if I get a headache when I am under pressure then I might be said to be *somatising* or to be a *somatiser*. But somatisation does not necessarily lead to a somatic symptom disorder. To somatise is a common, almost normal, feature of life. It is a basic mechanism through which the body demonstrates mental distress. If the symptoms are transient and not excessively disabling then they do not indicate illness and do not constitute a somatic symptom disorder. Only when they are chronic and disabling can this diagnosis be made.

A somatic symptom disorder is a rare and devastating medical problem which represents one extreme of a spectrum of diagnoses. It describes the person who is chronically severely disabled with multiple symptoms and has little chance of recovery. At the other end of the spectrum are the *unspecified and brief somatic disorders* that dip in and out of a person's life, wreaking havoc for shorter periods and to a lesser degree. Illness of this sort is common. An example of this would be somebody who develops joint pain that cannot be explained, it causes disability, interferes with life but isn't accompanied by multiple other symptoms and eventually disappears.

A *conversion disorder* is the neurological form of a somatic symptom disorder. Most of the same rules apply – it is still a condition where disability outstrips any disease that can be found – but in this particular case, the symptoms are neurological. So rather than pain being the most disabling symptom, there is loss of strength in a limb, or convulsions, or loss of sensation.

Conversion disorders are also known as *functional neurological disorders* and, in a small number of cases, as *dissociative disorders*. Conversion disorders were once also referred to as *hysterical conversion* or *hysteria*. When I use the term hysteria I will be using it in the historical sense, not in the way we use it now. Currently hysteria is used to describe an outburst of irrational emotion but in the past it was a medical diagnosis of unexplained, largely neurological symptoms. In this book the words hysteria and conversion disorder will be used to refer to the same illness in different eras.

It is important to point out that in a somatic or conversion disorder an organic physical disease may or may not be present. Such disorders do not presuppose *no* disease. Sometimes there is a medical diagnosis of a disease but the disability is out of proportion to it. That is where the classification of *psychological factors affecting medical conditions* comes into play. Imagine somebody who suffers with asthma. Their asthma is well treated and stable and for that reason lung function tests are normal and, when the doctor listens to their chest, there is no wheeze and the air can be heard going into the lungs. There is a disease present which is deemed under good medical control but the person still feels disabled by shortness of breath. If the asthma is well controlled and fails to explain the ongoing symptoms then those symptoms may be fairly considered as potentially psychosomatic or functional. Or, imagine somebody who has an underactive thyroid gland, a disease that causes fatigue. They are taking hormone replacement tablets and blood tests show that the treatment has returned their thyroid hormone levels to normal. We might expect that person to have minimal symptoms of thyroid disease. If that person suffers with ongoing crippling tiredness which the thyroid disease does not fully explain, then that tiredness might be called psychosomatic even though there is a known underlying medical problem.

In actual clinical practice all of these diagnostic terms are used in a fairly indiscriminate manner. It would not be unusual for a single patient to see several doctors and receive a different diagnostic label from each; conversion disorder from one, functional neurological disorder or psychosomatic disorder from the next. Sometimes a doctor uses the term that they perceive to be the least pejorative, or the one that the patient is most likely to understand and to accept. To a degree I will reflect that practice in the stories I tell.

Finally I need to clarify the terms *disease, organic* and *illness*. A disease is a biological dysfunction of the body. It implies a physiological abnormality or anatomical structural abnormality. The terms *disease* and *organic* refer to pathological disorders of the body, as opposed to disorders of the mind.

Illness is not the same as disease. Illness is the human response to disease. It refers to the person's subjective experience of how they feel but does not assume any underlying pathology. Illness can be either organic or psychological. A person can have a disease but not be ill. For example a girl with epilepsy has a disease, but if she is not having seizures and the epilepsy is asymptomatic she is not ill. A person with a psychosomatic disorder, on the other hand, is ill but does not necessarily have a disease.

Everybody's experience of illness is their own, and that is where illness becomes distinct from disease. I recall a non-medical friend of mine wondering why it was not possible to define all the characteristics of a single disease. Then a map or a formula could be created for all the common ailments and doctors might even find themselves obsolete – tap your symptoms into a computer program and a diagnosis pops up on a screen. That friend had failed to understand the human condition. He could not see the ways in which the individual patient impacts on their own disease. A person's personality and their life experience moulds the clinical presentation, the response and the outcome of any brush with illness. If you take one hundred healthy people and subject them to the exact same injury you will get a hundred different responses. That is why medicine is an art.

Many of the people I will tell you about in this book suffer from illnesses so severe that their lives have been destroyed. But most of them do not suffer from a disease. That distinction will prove very important to them. It will decide how their disability is perceived, both by themselves and by those around them. That, in turn, will determine everything that happens from that point onwards.

For most sufferers acceptance of the diagnosis is dependent on how the illness is viewed. Those who can accept it have the best chance of recovery. But for that to happen, some of the common preconceptions and judgements levelled at those with psychosomatic illness need to change. Those preconceptions and judgements mould every patient's story, and form a crucial part of this book.

2

PAULINE

At one time or another, we will try to silence painful emotions. But when we succeed in feeling nothing we lose the only means of knowing what hurts us and why.

Stephen Grosz, *The Examined Life* (2013)

Pauline was easy to spot. She was half the age or less of any other patient in the ward. The cot sides of her bed were up and each was covered with a layer of soft padding. To the right of her bed there was a wheelchair. In a high-backed chair to her left sat a woman who was staring intently at me. I saw her whisper something to Pauline and then their two similar faces turned back in my direction. Similar but different, in Pauline's face I saw only fear, but in the other I saw hope. Curtains were partially pulled around the bed, shielding the women from the neighbouring patients. Or the other way round, I didn't yet know which.

I had received a call the previous evening asking me to see Pauline as soon as possible. She had been admitted to the ward with pain and swelling in her leg. She had undergone a series of investigations but no explanation had been found. This was Pauline's third admission with the same problem. That morning the team looking after her told her that they had exhausted all possible tests in the search for a cause. Pauline was told that nothing further needed to be done and she could go home.

'It is not possible for us to find an explanation for everything. There is nothing more that I can do for you,' the consultant had said.

One hour later Pauline was in the bathroom when she lost consciousness. A nurse had heard a loud noise and had run in to find Pauline lying on the floor, convulsing. The emergency medical team was called and Pauline was resuscitated and carried back to her bed. In the hour that followed she was witnessed to have two more convulsions. After the on-call neurologist had seen Pauline and heard her story, I was next on the list.

Before going to talk to her I went in search of her medical records. I found them on the bottom of the trolley, where files are kept that are too bulky to be stored elsewhere. Pauline's notes came in two large volumes. These were the sort of notes that more commonly belonged to the elderly or people troubled by a lifelong incurable and serious condition. But Pauline's notes were different, they spoke of a lifetime in hospital but they did not contain any definitive diagnosis or satisfactory explanation of any kind.

I read through the file thoroughly, starting with her first admission to hospital and leading to the present day. How an illness evolves is of great importance if you are ever to find a cause. Only when I was familiar with the version of the story that existed in the records did I approach Pauline. I introduced myself and started as I always did.

'How old are you now, and when were you last completely well?'

'I am twenty-seven,' Pauline answered, 'and if you really want me to go back to the very beginning I haven't been well since I was fifteen years old.'

So I asked her to start there, at the point where one life ended and another began. This is the story she told me.

'I was just like everybody else – normal.'

'You were more than just normal, darling,' Pauline's mother rested her hand on her daughter's arm. 'She was very sporty, good at everything, in the top set at school. She could have been anything she wanted to be.'

'That was twelve years ago. Now look at me.'

In the year leading up to her GCSEs Pauline had begun to complain of feeling generally unwell. She was tired and plagued by aches and pains. Her doctor had run some tests, told her that she might have a urinary tract infection and put her on a course of antibiotics. That seemed to help for a while but the problem soon recurred. Pauline received four courses of antibiotics in only three months; each time she improved for a brief period but then deteriorated again.

'After the first infection I started to experience burning pain every time I used the toilet. Antibiotics only ever helped for a week or two. And when the infection came back I could barely get out of bed, I felt so weak.'

In the end Pauline was referred to a urologist, a bladder specialist. Numerous tests were done but all the results were normal. A camera was passed up into her bladder in the hope that an explanation lay there. There was nothing out of place. In the end the urologist put Pauline on a low-dose antibiotic which she was told to take every day to prevent future infections. She had taken the antibiotic almost continuously ever since.

'I got a bit better after that,' she said.

Pauline had got better but she had missed so much school that she could not sit her exams and was forced to resit the year. That meant that she was in the same class as her younger sister. Her old classmates had moved ahead of her. It was difficult, but Pauline was resourceful and able to make new friends and seemed to settle into her studies again. Pauline was soon at the top of her class.

'I didn't feel the same as I had before the infections but I acted the same so nobody could tell.'

'She was a driven child,' her mother told me.

For one whole term Pauline remained in school without missing a single lesson.

'I was always tired but I fought it. I could even play netball, that's how good things got for a while.'

Pauline's recovery was incomplete and short-lived. During the Christmas holidays she began to notice that her joints felt increasingly painful and swollen. She went to see her doctor and he wondered if this might be a side effect of the antibiotic. Pauline stopped taking it on his advice. Almost immediately she contracted another urinary tract infection. The antibiotic was restarted and Pauline was referred to a rheumatologist.

'When they saw how bad things were for me they thought I might have juvenile arthritis and started me on a course of steroids. But when the tests came back everything was normal, nothing was wrong,' Pauline recounted.

'I'm sure that when they said that everything was normal that they did not mean that nothing was wrong,' I ventured.

'Are you *sure*?' Pauline replied.

No, I wasn't.

While taking the steroids Pauline's weight increased dramatically, but her joint pain did not get better. She had difficulty walking and spent most of her time at home. Isolated, in pain, concerned about her appearance, she became depressed.

'Her depression was a wonderful opportunity for all the doctors to say that her illness was all down to that,' her mother told me, 'but she wasn't depressed when it all started. That came after.'

Pauline stopped taking her steroids. She also stopped eating. Her weight fell rapidly. At the same time her joint pain also got a little better.

'It was odd,' her mother said, 'when she stopped eating it almost seemed that she was improving in other ways. She even had a couple of weeks when we thought she would get back to school.'

But it was not very long before it became plain that Pauline's weight loss was in itself a problem. She became worryingly underweight. Her periods stopped. Her hair began to fall out. Yet it was difficult for Pauline to start eating again when this was as close as she had felt to being pain-free in over a year. Seeing how Pauline improved just as a result of a change in diet, her mother wondered if she had a food intolerance. She took Pauline to be tested for allergies. After a series of tests Pauline was told that she could not eat wheat, dairy products and a variety of fruit and processed foods.

'I was a bit doubtful,' Pauline said, 'I'd been eating most of the things they listed all my life. But I didn't have much choice so I followed the diet they gave me and I put on weight, which was good. The pain did come back but it wasn't quite as bad as it had been.'

Although Pauline gained weight she never fully returned to how she had been. She had missed so much school by then that her mother was concerned that she would struggle to catch up with the other children. A private tutor was hired. Pauline studied at home and only went back to school to sit her exams. She did well, her scores placing her in the top ten per cent of her class.

Pauline remained on a restrictive diet. She was taking regular painkillers. She could no longer play sport, but she could usually walk. She had also started going out with friends again, and even had her first boyfriend. It was a short-lived, lukewarm affair, but Pauline was happy to have had her first relationship. It made her feel normal again for a while.

Pauline was keen to take her A levels but was scared too. She did not want to get caught in the cycle of missing classes and catching up and falling behind that she had known for the previous two years. The decision was made to continue with tutors at home. She was glad of the decision in the years that followed. Her joint pain came and went in bouts. Every now and again she thought she saw a pattern develop, but almost as soon as one had been discovered, it disappeared.

Sometimes the pain was so severe that Pauline could not walk. She described how she would crawl on her hands and knees to the bathroom if there was nobody there to help.

'Sometimes I didn't drink anything all day just so I didn't need to make the trip.'

In time Pauline's mother had to leave work to care for her. 'I couldn't bear to be apart from her at that time. If I left the house for too long I had visions that I would come home to find her dead in her bed, or collapsed on the floor. That's how weak and pale she looked, like a girl who would die at any moment. And she was only eighteen years old.'

Pauline lived with her mother and her two younger sisters. Her parents had divorced when she was twelve. After the divorce she had regular contact with her father at first. Their meetings had only tailed off as she had grown older and had wanted to spend weekends with her friends instead of with her younger sisters and father. In time her father had started a new relationship and he had remarried shortly before Pauline's first illness. Her mother had remained single. When Pauline was first hospitalised with the urinary tract infection her father had rushed to be by her side. When Pauline's mother had to give up work her father supported the family financially and paid for tutors. But as her father's life moved forward and as Pauline's illness became more and more normal to the whole family, his visits had become less frequent too.

'Everybody forgot about how much pain I was in after a while. I didn't want to be the girl who was always complaining so they began to think I was better. My sister saw me taking my painkillers one day and asked me what they were for.'

Diet and rest had only partially controlled Pauline's pain. As she got older, it got worse. Simple painkillers were no longer effective and she had been prescribed morphine. Even that did not fully eradicate the pain, but to Pauline pain had become a normal part of life.

'I could have lived with the pain if it were not for what happened next.'

During the summer holiday in the lead-up to her final A-level year, Pauline's next illness struck. Her mother heard her calling out from her bedroom and came into the room to find her lying on the floor, doubled over and clutching her stomach. An ambulance was called and she was rushed to her local hospital. The admitting doctor diagnosed her with acute appendicitis and she was taken directly to theatre for an emergency operation. Her mother and sisters paced the floor of the hospital waiting to see if she would recover. They were by her bedside when she woke from the anaesthetic and cried out that the pain was no better. Two days later the surgeon told her that they had been mistaken in the diagnosis. When they had microscopically examined the appendix they had removed, they discovered that it showed no signs of inflammation and no evidence of appendicitis.

That was the beginning of a chain of events that would last over a year. A relentless and fruitless pursuit of the cause of her abdominal pain had begun. At first the doctors thought she might have a stomach ulcer caused by years of taking painkillers. A camera at the end of a long flexible scope was passed down into her stomach. No ulcer was found but her stomach lining seemed inflamed so she was given antibiotics and antacid drugs. They helped, but just a little and not for long. Next they wondered if the pain might come from chronic constipation caused by morphine and poor diet. A barium enema failed to provide an explanation. So a camera was passed through her back passage and into her bowel. Polyps were found, small out-pouchings of the bowel wall. Pauline was told that polyps were unlikely to be the cause of her pain but they might be a precursor for bowel cancer and they would need to be monitored for the rest of her life.

If Pauline had not noticed constipation before, she noticed it now, and it alternated with crippling abdominal pain and diarrhoea. Soon she had undergone multiple scans, one of her gall bladder, another of her liver, and then her ovaries. Whenever she thought the doctors had exhausted the operations they could do, it turned out they had not. She agreed to each operation thinking that she would do anything to get better and believing that it was not possible for things to be any worse. She was wrong. On the day that her younger sister sat the last of her A levels, Pauline awoke from her latest exploratory operation and discovered just how bad things could get.

'My mum was there when I woke up. I didn't notice anything wrong at first. After a while the nurse came and asked me if I had been to the toilet since the operation. I hadn't so she told me to give it a try. Mum pulled the bedclothes aside and I moved my body in the way that you do when you think your legs will follow. But my legs did nothing. Mum and I started laughing. That's how ridiculous it was. We thought the anaesthetic hadn't worn off fully. We stopped laughing when we saw the look on the nurse's face.'

From that day on Pauline had been in a wheelchair. She had lost all strength in her legs. A neurologist was called and he had arranged for her to have a series of tests.

'What was the outcome?' I asked Pauline.

'He couldn't explain it. I was a medical mystery once again.'

'Did he suggest any cause? Any treatment?'

'No, he just left her like that,' Pauline's mother answered.

Her voice was edged with frustration. When Pauline spoke it was more dispassionate. Sometimes it felt as if she was telling me somebody else's story.

After that the investigations stopped for a while. Pauline saw a physiotherapist and learned to move her legs a little but could never stand or walk. The joint and stomach pains continued and Pauline survived on a cocktail of drugs. The family home was converted so that Pauline had a bedroom and bathroom on the ground floor.

Life moved forward in many ways. When sports and other activities were no longer possible she found new ways to socialise and make friends. Always a keen reader, she set up an Internet-based book club specifically for people with disabilities who could not travel to meet in person. She began writing and kept a vivid diary of her experiences which she shared online. She eventually sat her A levels and easily qualified to study English literature at her local university. And she met her second boyfriend.

Mark was a student physiotherapist at the hospital that Pauline attended. They had become friendly during her treatments. One day Pauline was waiting outside the hospital for her mother to come and collect her when Mark appeared beside her. They started talking and discovered that they shared a love of books and films. By the time Pauline's mother arrived they had arranged to meet that weekend to see a film. They had been together ever since.

Pauline was twenty-one when she met Mark and started university. She had been ill for six years but at last she felt that she was experiencing some of the things that she had missed out on. While her pain and disability continued, everything else improved.

'While I was at uni I barely needed to see my doctor. I knew he had done all he could and it felt as if the problem, whatever it was, had burnt itself out.'

Pauline spent four years as a student. She required a small amount of help to allow for her disability – she was given extra time in exams because she could not write for prolonged periods, and friends brought her notes if she could not attend a lecture – but she did not allow her health problems to hold her back. She became a vital member of her university. She was secretary of the student union. She was the girl on campus that everybody recognised. For practical reasons she remained living at home with her mother but she socialised regularly and lived her life as any other student did. Pauline was no longer dependent on her mother, so her mother could return to work. Both her sisters had left home to go to university in other cities. Mark qualified as a physiotherapist and two years into their relationship he moved in with Pauline in her family home. They planned to get their own flat and marry when Pauline had finished studying and they both had jobs.

'I think that almost having it all made it worse when I began to lose everything again.'

Pauline sailed through her final exams and found a job in a junior position at a publishing company. She and Mark began flat hunting. She was close to many of her goals when she fell ill again. It started when several people in her office caught a flu bug. Pauline was also affected but worse than most.

'I have always had a weak immune system. I catch every bug going.'

She took a few days off work and stayed in bed. The day

before she was due to return to work she noticed that one leg was unusually painful.

'I always have pain in my joints but this was a new pain.'

Her doctor feared that her immobility had led to a clot forming in her leg and advised that she go to the local casualty department for some tests. Pauline was admitted to hospital and, while awaiting the investigations to explain her leg pain, she developed the familiar symptoms of a urinary tract infection. Passing urine became so difficult that the nurses inserted a catheter that would empty her bladder until she felt better. She had suffered yearly bladder infections despite taking daily antibiotics but she had never been catheterised before. Initial tests did not reveal any definite infection but three days later she was found to have a high temperature and her condition acutely deteriorated. Further microbiology tests showed that she had a hospital-acquired infection which was resistant to normal antibiotics. She was moved to an isolation room and was subjected to high doses of toxic drugs. It took a week to bring her temperature back down.

Pauline and her family were greatly relieved when she recovered. She was moved back to the general ward and the nurses removed her catheter. Four hours later Pauline was crying out in pain. Her bladder felt full to bursting but no amount of straining on the toilet would empty it. The nurses reinserted her catheter. The same thing happened the next day. Multiple further tests were ordered but it became obvious that this was another problem that would remain unexplained. Ultimately Pauline met with a bladder-care nurse who removed the indwelling catheter and taught Pauline how to empty her own bladder using a small rubber tube. After that Pauline never used the toilet in a normal way again.

In the six months that led up to my meeting with Pauline the quality of her life had once again stalled before slowly declining. Pauline felt that she was on the brink of losing everything that she had fought so hard for.

'For years I had limited sensation in my legs. It was all so cruel, the only feeling I ever experienced was pain. Not pain from the outside. You could burn me with a match and I wouldn't blink. The pain was on the inside.'

Twice more Pauline went to the casualty department with calf pain that no amount of morphine would quieten. Each time she was doubled over by it. Twice she was sent away. 'Your tests are normal. There is nothing we can do.'

'Something had to be wrong. There had to be something causing the pain, but I got the feeling that they thought I was imagining it,' Pauline said.

I agreed with her. To be in pain is not normal and there is always a reason.

The third time that Pauline presented with calf pain she was finally readmitted. The doctor had wanted to discharge her again but her mother had refused to take her home.

'If I have to bring my daughter back to the hospital in this state one more time and nothing is done, I will make a complaint.'

Four days later the consultant told her that she had no choice but to go home; he had exhausted everything he could do for her. That was the day her convulsions began.

'I knew I wasn't ready to go home,' she said.

Pauline had packed her belongings and was in the bathroom when she collapsed. She had been sitting in her wheelchair and brushing her teeth when she started to feel unwell. The room was suddenly spinning and she sat back in her chair to steady herself.

'Suddenly my vision closed in as if I was entering a dark tunnel. I knew something terrible was going to happen. I tried to call out, but I couldn't.'

After that Pauline remembered nothing for a while. Time passed in which she did not play a conscious part. When she awoke she was still in the bathroom but no longer in her chair. She was lying on the ground and strangers towered over her. Somebody had opened her pyjama top and she was aware that she was bare underneath it and she felt warm hands touching her, applying sticky pads. There was a sharp pain in her arm as a doctor she had never seen before stabbed at her with a needle. The floor underneath her felt wet. She would realise later that she was lying in her own urine, that her bladder which so staunchly disobeyed her conscious commands had emptied itself while she was unconscious. In the crowd she sought a familiar face and found a nurse who had cared for her on the ward. Reflexively she tried to push her attackers away and begged the nurse to help cover her up.

Once she was fully awake Pauline was carried back to her bed. But almost as soon as she arrived there she felt it begin again.

'I felt I was being sucked down into the bed. It was as if my life was being drained out of me. As soon as my vision began to get dark I knew I was going to lose consciousness and I willed it to stop. I tried to tell the nurse but no sound came out. I could feel my body stiffening. Someone put an oxygen mask on my face. It hurt. I knew the doctors thought I was unconscious but I could feel everything they did and hear everything they said. One nurse said she couldn't feel a pulse. Eventually my whole body began to shake and then I blacked out. I don't know how long it lasted but when I woke up my mother was with me. I was so relieved to see her.'

Pauline's mother had come to take her home. She was there when the third convulsion struck.

'She just went very pale and very still. Then she sort of flopped back on to her bed like a rag doll. She started to shake. The shaking was just in her arms at first but it spread and became more and more violent. She wasn't breathing. It felt like it lasted for ten minutes but I think it was probably shorter than that. At the end she let out a horrible gasping breath. When the shaking stopped she just lay there. It was if she was asleep but it wasn't a normal sleep. Nothing I did or the nurses did would wake her up.'

Pauline could not remember that attack, nor any that followed during the evening and night before we met.

'I forget everything after the third seizure,' Pauline reported. 'Was my mother with me last night? I don't know.'

And now I have forced Pauline to recall everything, to tell me in detail about what had led her here. And all the questions have been answered. No, there is no family history of epilepsy. Yes, my parents are divorced but it was a long time ago. I love my job, I can't wait to go back.

At times her mother became upset. 'Can't you read all of this in her notes? Is my divorce really important here? Is a bladder infection that happened when she was sixteen really relevant to what's happening now?'

'I think that everything that has happened is of great importance and I can understand the story better when I hear it from Pauline rather than just read it in the notes.'

There are always two realities, the one which exists in the notes and the one which lives in the patient's memory. I needed to know both and I knew that neither version could be wholly relied upon.

'Is this going to be yet another undiagnosed problem that I will have to live with?' Pauline asked.

'No, I believe that there is a very good chance that this will be different. We have very sophisticated tests to diagnose the cause of seizures. I am hopeful that this is something that we can diagnose and from which you can recover.'

At the end of the conversation I explained to Pauline that it was too early for me to say for certain what was wrong but that I would transfer her to the neurology ward under my care where she would undergo some further investigations. I ended the conversation as I always did:

'Is there anything important that you think I have left out or anything further that you want to ask?'

Pauline said there was nothing else, but just as I left she called me back.

'Have you seen anybody like me before?'

Too many to count, I thought. But other people's stories would be of no help to Pauline at that moment.

'I have seen people with similar problems to yours but no two people are ever the same.'

As I walked away I felt the guilt that I always feel when I have not been completely honest. I was certain that I knew what was wrong with Pauline but I had withheld that information. That I had been down this road before, and that it had not always ended well, was also withheld. But I knew that I was not the only one with secrets. Pauline's story had not been complete. It was our first meeting and it remained to be seen whether we would find a place where we could each be entirely honest with the other.

There is only one way of knowing with absolute certainty why a person has lost consciousness, and that is to witness the event. Otherwise a diagnosis is based entirely on interpreting the story that the patient and the witness have provided. That way is confounded by errors. People are not good witnesses. Distressed, frightened people are more unreliable still. Descriptions of seizures are influenced by what people expect to see as much as by what they have really witnessed. In the imagination of every mother watching her child convulse her child becomes deathly pale and moribund and foaming at the mouth. One minute always feels like an hour. And yet most of the time that description is all that doctors have to go on.

It's rare for a doctor to have the opportunity to witness their patient's seizure. Most seizures that recur do so infrequently, often only once a month or even once a year, and each attack only lasts for a minute or two. Admit that person to hospital to witness their seizure and you will have a long wait, and when it finally happens, blink and you'll miss it.

But there are circumstances in which it is possible to see a blackout and, in doing so, to make a definitive statement about the cause. For example, sometimes blackouts have a trigger. In epilepsy this might be flashing lights or sleep deprivation. If this is the case, and a diagnosis is needed, the patient can be brought to the hospital and exposed to the offending trigger so that a seizure happens in a safe environment in front of trained witnesses. Similarly, people who faint might notice that sudden changes in posture provoke their symptoms, so they are placed on a tilting table to induce an attack. Controlled monitored exercise might be used to provoke cardiac symptoms if that is the suspected cause of the collapse. In a small number of unfortunate people their collapses are so frequent that even a short hospital admission will allow you to see the attacks for yourself.

Where triggers are less clear, video-telemetry units are an invaluable facility for observing seizures. In them, patients ostensibly sit around waiting to collapse and staff sit around waiting for it to happen. Of course it is actually more sophisticated than merely waiting and watching, and it is all thanks to a trainee German doctor called Hans Berger.

At the end of the nineteenth century, Berger was riding his horse in a military exercise. For an unknown reason the horse reared and Berger was thrown to the ground. He landed perilously close to the rolling wheels of an artillery cannon. The horse that pulled the cannon came to a halt just in time to stop Berger coming to a grisly end. Berger was greatly relieved by his escape. That evening he received a telegram from his sister wishing him good health. She reported that she had been overwhelmed by concern for him that day and had felt compelled to send him her good wishes. Berger could not believe that his sister's impulse to send a telegram was just a matter of coincidence. It seemed clear to him that in his moment of greatest peril, he had somehow communicated his distress to his sister many miles away. He would make it his life's work to understand how this telepathy had occurred.

In the nineteenth century it was already widely known that the organs of the body produced electrical activity. Berger took this knowledge and tried applying an electrical discharge to the head in the hope that it would reveal the mechanism for psychic energy. This gave no useful information. So instead he attempted to measure the existing natural animal electricity present on the surface of the head using a galvanometer. He made a startling discovery: even through the skull he could make reproducible recordings of electrical activity that, he surmised correctly, must be coming directly from the brain. He was never able to prove the existence of telepathy but by 1929 he had published his first scientific paper on the recording of brainwaves in a human via the scalp, and had invented the electroencephalograph, or EEG.

Understanding the characteristics of the electrical activity of the brain would prove very useful. Most importantly Berger showed that the brainwaves were ever-changing and each change in pattern reflected a change in the state of awareness of the subject being tested. Drowsiness, light sleep, deep sleep and waking all had a pattern of their own. Brainwaves, as measured by an EEG, could therefore determine if a person was awake or asleep, conscious or unconscious, at any given time. An EEG came to be the definitive means of assessing consciousness and is used to this day as one of the primary tools in understanding why a person has suffered loss of consciousness or coma.

In a video-telemetry unit patients are restricted to a single room where they are under constant video surveillance. Small painless metal discs attached by paste to the head make a round-the-clock recording of the brainwave, or EEG pattern. A cardiac electrode takes a similar recording of the heart rate. A group of nurses rotate to watch the video stream of the patient at every moment of every day, with only the bathroom remaining private. When the convulsion or blackout under investigation finally occurs the nurse is ready to run into the room to assess the patient, check their blood pressure and blood sugar and keep them safe and reassured until they recover.

Through this type of monitoring, based on the principle that all our brains generate an electrical pattern and that the brainwave pattern reflects the level of awareness of its owner, it is possible to determine the cause of a large number of seizures with a high level of confidence. There are many reasons that a person might have a seizure or lose consciousness and video-telemetry monitoring distinguishes one cause from another.

If a healthy person faints, because they are dehydrated or overheated, for example, the first physiological change will be a fall in their blood pressure. Their heart detects the problem and tries to compensate with an increase in heart rate. The person feels weak and dizzy and they know something is wrong. They may be aware of their heart rate increasing. The blood literally drains from their face and they appear pale. If the increased heart rate is not enough to compensate for the fall in the blood pressure then, just for a moment, vital blood is drawn away from the brain. As the brain becomes deprived of oxygen the brainwaves slow dramatically and the patient loses consciousness. In a healthy person the blood pressure usually recovers quickly and, when it does, oxygen is restored to the brain. The normal waking brainwave pattern is immediately restored, the patient awakes and no harm is done.

But not all faints occur in healthy people for simple reasons. Some occur in people with heart problems. In those collapses the first change may be that the heart rate slows down dangerously. So the heart changes first this time and, if it is not beating sufficiently to support the blood pressure, that drops. With the fall in blood pressure the brainwaves slow and with that the patient loses consciousness. Only when the heart starts beating at a normal rate again does the patient, and their brainwaves, recover.

Or the cause of a blackout might lie not in the heart or blood pressure, but in the brain itself. This is the case in diseases like epilepsy. The sequence in epilepsy is different again. First the epileptic seizure produces a burst of unwanted electrical activity in the brain. The patient only loses consciousness as that electrical discharge spreads and takes over the brain. The heart rate and blood pressure may or may not be affected as the patient blacks out.

Blood pressure falls – heart rate increases – brainwaves slow; heart slows – blood pressure falls – brainwaves slow; brainwaves change – consciousness is lost; each of these patterns combined with a video recording of the collapse suggests a specific diagnosis that is usually reliable. The overarching principle on which each diagnosis rests is always that you cannot be unconscious – neither asleep, nor anaesthetised, nor in a seizure – if your brainwaves do not change.

These are the principles that I will use to determine the cause for Pauline's seizures.

Three days after Pauline and I met she was transferred to the neurology ward. On each of those days she had multiple seizures. On her first day and night in the video-telemetry unit she had six more. The following morning I reviewed the video and watched each seizure in turn. Each collapse was the same.

Pauline is lying in bed chatting to her mother. She suddenly stops talking. Her mother doesn't notice at first and continues with the conversation. Pauline is sitting very still, staring into the distance, when her mother realises something is wrong. She reaches to press the nurse call button and just as she does Pauline folds in on herself and drops loosely back on to her pillow. As the nurses run into the room Pauline begins to shake. At first it is a shivering but quickly it builds in intensity becoming more and more violent with every second. Soon her arms are flailing so wildly that the nurses cannot get near enough to help. Her arms are hitting against the padded sides of the bed. Pauline's mother is a foot away from her daughter, her hands covering her face.

In one minute the shaking stops. Pauline's whole body sinks back into the bed as if deflated. The nurses take the opportunity to roll Pauline on to her side. They have barely done so when the shaking begins again and it is just as violent as before. Another nurse enters and ushers Pauline's mother from the room. The shaking starts and stops five more times before it is over. At the end Pauline lies still on her side where the nurses have placed her. Her eyes are closed and her breathing is rapid. The nurses try to wake her to check that she is alright but for ten more minutes they cannot rouse her. When she does wake her mother is back by her side. Pauline doesn't say anything, she just starts to cry. Her mother comforts her.

I watched the video of each seizure and I reviewed the brain tracing and heart tracing for each and then I made an appointment to meet with Pauline and her family.

When we met again Pauline's mother was with her and this time Mark was also there. They sat like sentinels on either side of her, each holding a hand. I asked Mark to move to sit beside Pauline's mother. I didn't want my attention divided.

Before Pauline had moved to the video-telemetry room I had explained the purpose of the test in detail. Pauline understood the changing nature of brainwaves but I explained it again because it was of vital importance to what I would say next.

'I have reviewed each of your seizures carefully. I have looked at the video and at the brainwave tracing and the heart rate for each. The first piece of good news is that I have not seen the pattern that I expect in an epileptic seizure so you definitely do not suffer from epilepsy. The heart tracing was normal, so the heart looks healthy which I hope will also be a relief to you.'

'That's good news isn't it, darling.' Pauline's mother squeezed her daughter's hand. Pauline and Mark stared blankly in my direction. I saw no sign of relief.

'When I looked at the brainwaves during your seizures I saw that they showed the pattern I might expect in somebody who is conscious, a waking pattern.'

Mark tried to interject and I heard myself speak louder and faster.

'This is a very difficult thing to understand so please just let me finish and then ask as many questions as you want. The brainwave pattern looked normal and there is only one reason that a person can be unconscious, completely unaware of their surroundings, with the brainwaves still looking normal, and that is if the loss of consciousness is caused by something psychological rather than a physical brain disease.'

Mark shook his head and pressed his lips tightly together. I was aware my voice had become more emphatic.

'Let me first explain that all of our bodies produce physical symptoms in response to emotional distress. But we have become so used to the common ways that this happens that we have stopped noticing it. If I am nervous my hands shake – that is my body changing physically in response to an emotion. When we are frightened our hearts race. When we are upset tears flow from our eyes. These are all examples of the ways in which each of us have experienced physical symptoms when there is nothing physically wrong. These sorts of physical responses to distress are normal everyday responses to normal everyday fears and upset. But for some people physical reactions to emotion can be more dramatic and more disabling than these simple examples. One extreme way that the body can respond to upset is to produce blackouts and convulsions. This sort of convulsion is known as a dissociative seizure.'

I couldn't hold back Mark's questions any longer.

'You're saying that she's not really unconscious.'

'No, Pauline's unconsciousness is real. Think of the example

I gave of the heart racing in response to fear. The heart rate has really doubled, I can feel it in my chest and you could measure it. It's not imaginary. But it's not happening because I have a heart disease. My heart is healthy. My heart is just responding to distress.'

'You think it's all in my head.' As Pauline spoke she stared past me.

'No, Pauline, I know your seizures are real. They are real, but they are arising in the subconscious rather than being due to a brain disease. Dissociation means that a sort of split has occurred in the mind. Your conscious mind separates from what is happening around you. That detachment means that one part of you doesn't know what the other is doing. But it's not deliberate. You cannot make yourself unconscious any more than I can deliberately blush or produce tears.'

I wanted Pauline to look at me, but she wouldn't. I couldn't read her response.

'Pauline, is anything I'm saying making any sense to you? How do you feel about what I've said?'

She shrugged her shoulders. 'I just feel tired.'

'Do you understand what I'm trying to explain?'

'I understand. I just don't see how any of this applies to me. I'm not stressed. My life has never been better.'

Pauline is right, of course.

'I know. The examples I've given you are all ones in which stress is felt and the physical symptoms are experienced alongside it. Dissociative seizures are often different. Often the physical symptom is there in place of the emotional upset. So, for example, if there is a memory or emotion that is too painful for a person to experience, that emotion is converted into a physical disability as a sort of protective mechanism. In a convulsion it is as if your brain is shutting down for a minute to keep you safe.'

'Safe from what, though?'

'I don't know the answer to that. But even if it isn't possible to know the answer now it may be possible in the future.'

For a moment I thought of how Pauline's illness had behaved. How it struck her down when she was facing a challenge or when her life was about to change.

'So I'd rather have a convulsion than face something unpleasant from my life? Why would I do that to myself?'

'It's ridiculous, is what it is.' Mark was furious now.

'I know this is all very hard. You are not doing this to yourself, Pauline. If everything else I say seems ridiculous, then just remember one thing: the seizures are real, whatever they consist of. They are real and disabling and out of your control and they must be taken very seriously. The cause only helps to indicate a treatment; it shouldn't detract in any way from how awful these seizures have been for you.'

'What is the treatment?'

'I would like to refer you to a psychiatrist.'

'After all you said, you are just saying I'm mad.'

'No. These seizures are your body telling you that something is wrong. The psychiatrist might help you work out what that is. I think that these seizures are curable, Pauline. I think a psychiatrist might help you to see that.'

'Isn't there a medication that would help?' Mark asked.

I knew that Pauline was already taking seven medications.

None had resulted in any great improvement in her life. Two were there purely to counteract the side effects of the other five. Pauline was twenty-seven years old. I needed her to recognise a pattern that wasn't working and find a new one.

'Medication won't help dissociative seizures.'

'You think they're curable.' Pauline's mother interjected this time.

'I absolutely believe that these seizures can go away completely and I hope the psychiatrist will help speed up that process.'

We sat in silence for a while and when it seemed all the questions had been asked I ended the consultation as I usually did, 'Is there anything else you would like to ask? Is there something that you think that I have left out?'

'Nothing.'

As I said goodbye I felt that I had failed to connect with Pauline. She had agreed to see the psychiatrists but her acquiescence had felt empty. I was relieved when two days later Pauline kept our agreement and had her psychiatry assessment.

Few people will ever endure the scrutiny that Pauline had endured. Most of us get to put our childhood selves behind us but Pauline had been called upon to recount her story over and over, not just the story of her illness but of her life. The psychiatrist had been thorough. Pauline had told more of her story. Some of the information was new but much I had already gleaned from Pauline's notes the first time we met. Perhaps if you have a lifetime of illness in twelve years you forget some of your own story. Or perhaps Pauline had withheld information because she did not want me to be prejudiced by things that had happened in the past. Or maybe the subconscious was at play again, choosing what to tell me and what to hide.

It was true that Pauline had had a happy childhood but it was no more free of traumas than anyone else's. When she was nine years old she had developed an eating disorder. At that time a family dispute was tearing her father's family apart. Her immediate family became estranged from her paternal grand-parents, aunts and uncles. Pauline took it badly. She stopped eating and only recovered with the support of her family and the help of a child psychologist. It was a short-lived illness.

Trouble resurfaced when she was twelve years old and her parents divorced. Pauline stopped eating again briefly. The psychiatrist thought that Pauline must have feared losing her father, just as she had lost his family before. Her mother prom-ised her that would never happen and Pauline appeared to recover when that proved to be true.

Another striking omission from Pauline's story was that I was not the first doctor to raise the issue of psychosomatic symptoms with her. When her legs had become paralysed at the age of twenty-one a diagnosis of hysterical paralysis was offered as an explanation. Pauline had rejected it outright. She had seen the psychiatrist once and had never returned, nor had she accepted the advice that was given in that single session. I had known this when Pauline and I met but I didn't raise it with her. For Pauline and I to work together I needed to give her space and time to decide what she wished to discuss and when.

The psychiatrist thought that Pauline needed help but was concerned about her ability to accept treatment. In particular she wondered how her relationships might hinder her recovery. Was it possible that she was too well looked after? Would others miss her if she was not always dependent on them?

The psychiatrist had also discovered that, while Mark and Pauline's relationship was loving, it had never been consummated.

'I wonder if she is so focused on, and in control of, her own body that she could not possibly allow another person inside her in such an intimate way. She controls her intake of food in the same way. That sort of control is difficult to relinquish to others,' the psychiatrist told me.

I went to see Pauline after her session. For the first time her mother was not with her. The sight of her alone caused a hollow feeling inside me that I did not fully understand.

'How did it go with the psychiatrist?'

'It was okay.'

'I hope it made some sense to you,' I said ineffectually. 'Was there anything new you wanted to ask me? Did she raise anything that wasn't clear?'

'No.'

I needed to move Pauline forward but without alienating her.

'I think you had a chat about your leg weakness?'

'Yes, she says you think that's imaginary too.'

'I hope you know that I don't think anything is imaginary.'

There was a pause. I wondered what she might be thinking.

'Did the psychiatrist tell you what happened when I was nine?'

'She told me you were unwell for a while but we didn't discuss the details.'

She turned her head and looked away from me and towards the window.

'Did she say why?'

'Only that there were some problems in the family.'

The conversation had become stilted; I was not sure where it was going.

'Now that I'm officially mad everyone will think I was abused but I wasn't.'

Was this a statement? Or a question? Or an invitation?

'Why do you think we would think that?'

'I read it on the Internet. Dissociative seizures happen to girls who have been abused as children.'

'Sometimes, yes, but just as often it's nothing to do with anything like that.'

'It's not like that for me.'

'I know.'

I followed her gaze to the window but there was nothing for her to see there but grey sky.

'My uncle was accused of abusing a girl who lived next door to him. Dad wouldn't let us see him after that, even though they didn't prove it. Dad's family were furious. They said Dad should have taken his brother's side, not some stranger's.'

'That must have been very difficult for you.'

'He never touched me.'

'Good.'

I waited a while, not sure if our conversation was over.

'Do you think that my other medical problems are like the convulsions?'

I had been waiting for this question. I was glad it had come.

'I think there is a strong possibility that your other symptoms are psychosomatic, yes.'

'But you're not a gastroenterologist or a rheumatologist. Are you even qualified to say that?'

'No, I'm not, but I have read your test results and I have read what your other doctors have written in your notes. None of your other symptoms were ever explained and this would explain them. And, if I'm right, something could be done about those too.'

Pauline looked directly at me again. She was crying.

'For twelve years, Pauline, you have been in and out of hospital, having invasive tests, trying new tablets that never work. Every time you've had an operation, instead of getting better, you've ended up with a new problem. You go into hospital with a stomach pain and you come out in a wheelchair. I am asking you to try a new approach because the old one isn't working. The very least I can promise you is that it will not make things worse.'

'I want to talk to Mark.'

I could not shake the feeling that Mark inadvertently bound Pauline to illness, and this made me afraid that she would refuse to see the psychiatrist again. If you have asthma and the first inhaler doesn't work, you don't abandon the diagnosis, you ask for something stronger. And yet psychiatrists seem to get only one chance. It was hard to ignore the idea that six years ago Pauline might have chosen a wheelchair over a psychiatric diagnosis. I knew this thought was unfair to Pauline – if such a choice had ever been made, it had not been a conscious one. Pauline was right, nobody would choose what she had suffered. This was an illness out of anyone's control.

Pauline was due for discharge. Her tests had been completed.

We had a diagnosis. She had seen the psychiatrist. There was no reason for her to stay. She had only to agree to the next step. I told her she could go home the following day and that after that she would be seen by the psychiatrist and a series of psychological and physical therapists who would help her move forward.

But Pauline and I would have one more eventful night ahead of us before that happened. Just after midnight my phone rang. It was the on-call neurology junior doctor. 'Just a courtesy call to let you know that Pauline has threatened to kill herself. We've locked away her medications and given her a one-to-one nurse and have called the on-call psychiatrist, but we thought you'd want to know.'

'Thank you.' I did want to know. But there was nothing I could do. I went back to bed but I didn't sleep.

The following morning Mark greeted me at the entrance to the ward. There was no preamble.

'She has polyps and gastritis and recurrent urinary tract infections. Are you saying she's making those up too?'

I suggested that we speak again once I had seen how Pauline was doing and had talked to the doctors who had seen her the previous night. Mark's agreement came through gritted teeth. When I received the outcome of the previous night's consultations I was relieved to learn that Pauline's distress was felt unlikely to be linked to a real intent to harm herself. I would ask the liaison psychiatrist to see her again before I would allow her home. But first I went to see Pauline. Mark and her mother were present, positioned as sentinels once again.

'How dare you say that all her medical problems are

psychological? The only distress Pauline has ever had in her life has been because of her illness. If these convulsions are due to madness, it is all due to the pain she has suffered. Did you ever think of that?' said Mark.

It occurred to me for the first time that there could be things that Mark did not know.

'I'm sorry this has been so difficult. I know there are points on which we don't agree so I think it would be more useful to Pauline if we stick to addressing those things that are definite.'

'Pauline needs to pass a catheter to empty her bladder. That's definite. How could that be psychological?' A little spray of spittle accompanied Mark's words. Pauline's and her mother's eyes were cast downwards.

'We can't unravel all of this here and now.' I turned to Pauline. '*Pauline*, I don't have all the answers but I know one thing and that is that your convulsions did not occur as a result of a brain disease. That is what I know for certain and that is where I think we should focus our attention.'

The room fell completely silent. Pauline would not look at me. Her eyes were fixed on Mark who was gripping her hand. I looked at how their fingers intertwined. I could hardly tell one hand from the other and I thought of my discussion with the psychiatrist. Here was a girl who had, in a sense, lost one side of her family, and now illness bound her tightly to those who remained. I thought of her threat to harm herself and saw a girl who knew only one way to be heard.

'If you are feeling better later it will still be possible for you to go home. Do you think you will be able to come back to see the psychiatrist again and have the treatment she suggested?'

Now all three faces turned in my direction, one blank as usual, one adversarial, but I thought I saw something hopeful in the third, in the face of her mother.

'I feel that at least some of what you are suffering can be relieved. I ask that you just give the treatment programme some consideration.'

Did her mother give an almost imperceptible nod?

It has been through trying to treat people like Pauline that I have come to realise that not all suffering is the same. It is not necessarily the greater suffering that receives the greatest consideration and sympathy. Illness is not scored in that way. Deadly disease obviously scores higher than others. After that there is an unofficial ranking system for illness in which psychiatric disorders are the out-and-out losers. Psychiatric disorders manifesting as physical disease are at the very bottom of that pile. They are the charlatans of illnesses. We laugh at them. If all of Pauline's problems are indeed psychosomatic in origin then no matter how hard I tried to convince her, she knew she would be judged and she was right. Pauline and her family were fighting to preserve her dignity.

I had tried to make Pauline see that physical manifestations of unhappiness are something we all experience, it is not a personality flaw or a sign of weakness, it is a part of life. Life is hard sometimes. It is harder for some than for others. We all manifest that hardship in different ways: some cry, some complain, some sleep, some stop sleeping, some drink, some eat, some get angry and some suffer as Pauline does. But I made a mistake with Pauline. Over time, the more patients I have met like her the more I have come to understand it was not Pauline or her family who needed to be convinced of the reality and legitimacy of her suffering, it was the world outside.

After talking to the psychiatrist again Pauline was allowed home. I was on the ward as she left. Mark had gone to get their car and Pauline and her mother only nodded in my direction as they left. But, just as I thought I would never see either of them again, Pauline's mother suddenly turned around and came back towards me.

'She hasn't had a single seizure since you told her the diagnosis, you know. I don't think she's realised it yet.'

After her first night on the neurology ward Pauline's seizures had indeed completely disappeared. But what Pauline's mother had not yet registered was that the leg pain for which Pauline had been admitted had also just as silently melted away. As I watched them leave I suddenly felt hope for Pauline, if only she could bring herself to make it to the next stage.

3

MATTHEW

> In every voluntary movement it is the idea that triggers the corresponding contraction of the muscle; therefore it is not inconceivable that the idea should hinder the movement.
>
> Josef Breuer, *Studies in Hysteria* (1895)

In the legal system the burden of proof requires evidence to support the truth. But in the case of psychosomatic disorders the diagnosis often rests on the lack of evidence. The diagnosis is made when disease is sought but not found. It can be very difficult for a patient to accept that they suffer with a conversion disorder (a medically unexplained neurological symptom) when that assumption is based almost entirely on what is missing. It requires great trust between patient and doctor. Every week I tell somebody that their disability has a psychological cause. When they ask me how I have come to that conclusion all I can provide is a list of normal test results, evidence for the diseases that I have ruled out. When a person is paralysed or blind or suffering with convulsions it is not difficult to see why they find that a very unsatisfactory explanation.

'I am completely sure that you do not have multiple sclerosis.'

'How sure are you?'

'All of the tests are negative. You do not have multiple sclerosis.'

'What percentage are you sure?'

'I am absolutely sure.'

'You can't be one hundred per cent sure. Nothing is ever one hundred per cent.'

I could feel Matthew's desperation tugging at me. He was willing me to say any number that was less than one hundred. And I could see that even if I said that I was ninety-nine per cent sure, I would have offered him some doubt, however small. A part of his brain was hoping for just that. And in the face of his question I was forced to question myself. Was I as sure as I said I was that Matthew did not have a disease? Should I simply have agreed with him that nothing was ever unequivocally certain? I was very convinced that his disability was *functional*, that there was no organic cause underlying it, but was I one hundred per cent convinced? Of course, I know what was holding me back from offering Matthew any of my uncertainty. He was struggling with the diagnosis. Any shred of possibility that a physical disease had been missed offered him hope that his illness was not psychological and he might cling to that. If I allowed him any glimpse of my doubt I could be sending Matthew on a quest for a disease that might easily take up a lifetime.

Matthew was a product of the Internet age. When he came to me his research had utterly convinced him that he had multiple sclerosis. Throughout our first conversation he kept using the words 'my multiple sclerosis'. 'Is my multiple sclerosis more severe than other people's?' 'How will my multiple sclerosis affect my life insurance?'

Matthew's problem began with a feeling of pins and needles

in one foot. At first it affected him only if he sat for prolonged periods. Sitting at his computer in his office he would feel the tingling and would need to stand and move around to make it go away. In the evenings it would go but the next working day it was always back.

After having the symptoms for nearly two weeks Matthew went to see his doctor. He was assured that these sorts of symptoms were not uncommon and rarely meant anything worrying. The doctor examined him and told him that everything was okay. He was advised to take regular breaks at work, to avoid sitting for too long.

Matthew followed his doctor's advice but found it of little help. More worryingly, he noticed his symptoms change and spread. The pins and needles were now moving around his body, one day in an arm, the next over the bridge of his nose, then in the back of his head, then his lower lip. He no longer needed to be seated to feel the tingling. It could strike at any time and any part of him. Matthew went to see his doctor again. Again the doctor examined him and told him that he could find nothing wrong.

'I have often heard people describe symptoms like these,' his doctor said, 'and I have never seen them lead to anything serious. Stop thinking about it and it will disappear.'

Matthew was not satisfied. He took it upon himself to research the possibilities. The Internet advised him that diabetes could damage the nerves and lead to pins and needles. Matthew stopped eating sugary foods but got no better. Again he discussed his concern with his doctor who told him that his blood sugar was normal. He did not have diabetes.

Matthew read that trapped nerves were a common cause of his symptoms. Tired of his doctor's dismissiveness he went to see a chiropractor. The chiropractor wondered if Matthew might not have a disc out of place in his neck and suggested a course of treatment. This helped only briefly.

Matthew tried adjusting his life. First he began to exercise vigorously and regularly. He thought it was possible that he might have poor circulation and that exercise would correct it. When this did not help he tested the effect of avoiding exercise and resting as much as possible. The patches of numbness spread to his trunk.

Nothing Matthew did to help himself made him any better. By now he was finding it difficult to work. Sitting for prolonged periods was impossible. His workplace had assessed his office space and made changes but it made no difference. He cut down his working hours. He began to work from home. At the same time he intensified his research. That was when he discovered for the first time that multiple sclerosis could cause sensory abnormalities that moved around the body. In reading the stories of MS sufferers his own story was reflected back at him. At his request his GP finally agreed to refer him to a neurologist.

At last Matthew felt that he had made some progress and this made him feel better. But, at the same time, the potential diagnosis began to play on his mind and soon he felt worse. Matthew's symptoms had begun to evolve with everything new he learned. The tingling and numbness were constant now. He noticed pain and loss of balance if he walked any distance. He began to feel dizzy. Tiredness overwhelmed him. Two months had passed and by now Matthew was working almost entirely from home.

Then one day, before the date of his appointment with the neurologist, things abruptly came to a head. Matthew awoke to find that he had lost all strength in his legs. Numbness and pain were replaced by nothing, no feeling at all and no movement. His wife called an ambulance and he was taken to his local hospital where he immediately underwent a scan of his spine and brain. They offered no explanation. Matthew was admitted to hospital for further tests.

Over the course of the next few days Matthew underwent a series of investigations. A lumbar puncture took a sample of his spinal fluid and that was normal. Blood tests and electrical studies of his nerves and muscles showed nothing wrong. Matthew stayed in hospital for two weeks. During that time, even without a diagnosis, the strength in his legs improved slowly although not completely. When the neurologist had exhausted the investigation Matthew was given a wheelchair and a walking frame and sent home. The following day his distressed wife made an appointment to see their GP and one hour later the GP phoned me.

'This family is at breaking point. His wife is furious that her husband has been sent home with no diagnosis and no plan.'

'What were they told before discharge?'

'She says nothing.'

I arranged to see Matthew in the next available outpatient clinic. In the meantime I contacted his original hospital and asked for a copy of his records.

A week later Matthew's wife wheeled her husband into my office. Her expression was firmly set. I said hello and in return she offered a curt nod. Matthew was almost the opposite of his wife. He greeted me cheerily. He was seated in his chair, smartly dressed and with a sheaf of papers resting on his knee. He offered a warm handshake as his wife pulled up a chair and sat beside him. Once we were all seated I asked Matthew to tell his story from the start.

'I know I have multiple sclerosis,' he began.

'Let's not make any assumptions. For the moment just tell me how your symptoms started and how they evolved.'

Matthew took out his diary and opened it on the table between us.

'On the tenth of June, I got the first feeling of parasthesia in my right foot. I was at a barbecue at my brother's house. It was his birthday. We had been sitting in the garden for most of the afternoon. I suppose we arrived at about one and I noticed the problem at about four. Or maybe a little later, maybe five o'clock. I stood up to go into the house and my foot felt strange. It was a horrible sensation.'

Carefully Matthew detailed the events of that day and then of the gradual progression of events that led up to the day when he lost the power in his legs. Occasionally I asked an additional question. Every answer came in the affirmative.

Blurred vision? I have that, sometimes when I stare at a book all the letters come together.

Tiredness? All the time.

Bladder disturbance? Yes.

As I listened I tried to spot an anatomical pattern that would explain everything, but all I could see was that what Matthew was describing was impossible. There was no part of the nervous system that if diseased could account for everything that he described. But, at the same time, I wondered if he was simply elaborating on a simpler story. Maybe he had an organic neurological problem and it was being magnified and contorted somehow by the depth of his concern. So I kept listening. All the time Matthew's wife sat silently beside him while her husband listed each point documented in his diary. And Matthew was very specific.

'John always has a barbecue to celebrate his birthday, weather allowing of course. If the weather isn't good he might do something else. John lives in Kent.'

His language was peppered with medical phrases.

'I also have facial neuralgia and tinnitus.'

His story was detailed but he was strangely casual about his degree of disability for someone who three months previously was active and in full-time work.

'I have asked someone to come and put handrails up in my house. I think it will help me get around more easily.'

'What did the doctor say when they sent you home from hospital?' I asked.

'Nothing.'

After Matthew had finished telling me his story I asked to examine him. Although he was in a wheelchair he could walk short distances and moved, with difficulty, to the couch so that I could do this. When he was lying down I tested the strength of his muscles one by one.

I asked him to lift his leg off the couch. 'Keep your leg straight and lift it.'

Matthew couldn't. His whole face contorted with the effort. His right leg moved a few centimetres into the air and then he reached with his hands, cupped them under his thigh, to lift it further.

'Point your toe,' I asked him next.

Matthew's foot lay inert but his face told me that he was trying. When I pressed a blunt pin to his leg he could not feel it. When I applied a vibrating tuning fork to his skin he felt nothing below the waist. But the power to move or perceive sensations are things over which both the conscious and subconscious mind have some control so next I tested the things where this is not the case. Despite the lifelessness of his legs the reflexes reacted as they should. The tone of his limbs felt normal.

When I had nearly finished the examination Matthew stood again and I asked him to walk. He locked his knees tightly and walked with straight legs and with great difficulty. I asked him to try to take a few steps on his toes. Great effort was required but he managed a few short tippy-toe steps. And I asked him to sit on a chair and stand with his arms folded and after several tries he managed it. Matthew didn't realise yet that I had tested the same muscle groups in several different ways and that each time they had behaved differently. The same muscle that wouldn't allow him to move his leg as he lay on the couch had allowed him to rise from a seated position in a chair.

At the end of the consultation, as much as Matthew was convinced that he had MS, I was convinced that he did not. There were too many inconsistencies. Neurologists look for patterns. A disease of the spine causes one distinct set of symptoms, a disease of the nerves another. Brain disorders cause certain groups of muscles to be weak while others are surprisingly strong. Matthew's pattern did not fit with any anatomical location. I could not take dizziness and weakness of every muscle and numbness in the face and attribute them to a single diagnosis. And the examination presented other problems. The subjective part of the examination, concerning those things over which the subconscious has some control, such as strength and feeling, was abnormal; while those reflexes that are objective and less likely to be influenced by the mind, such as reflexes and muscle tone, were normal.

But Matthew was more than the sum of his medical history and clinical examination, he was a person with a life beyond his illness and in that life I saw other points of concern. Matthew had always seen his doctor regularly. In five years he had been prescribed five courses of antibiotics. He had had investigations for a number of medical problems in recent years. He had a scan to investigate back pain. He was being investigated both for constipation and diarrhoea. All of these tests were normal. The symptoms disappeared without ever being fully explained. And there were things about his personal life that also made me hesitate. Matthew worked in accounting and moved jobs regularly. He had been in his current job for nearly three years, the longest that he had stayed in a single position. What made Matthew move on so often? Did moving protect him from something? Did illness do the same? Was he hiding?

I had also reviewed the normal investigation results from Matthew's previous hospital admission and I could find only one coherent explanation, and that was that he had a conversion disorder, his neurological symptoms could not be explained by a neurological disease. But it was clear that Matthew was unlikely to accept the normal test results or my certainty that he did not have MS, so it seemed reasonable to give him the second opinion that he wanted and to reinvestigate. I thought of stretched resources and wondered if all that I was doing was reinforcing Matthew's worry about a disease having been missed. Matthew remained wheelchair-bound and unconvinced that he did not have MS, so I chose to put my reservations aside and keep an open mind.

As Matthew and his wife left I glanced once more through the discharge letter from his previous hospital. It read: 'I have told this man that I believe his symptoms are functional in nature. I have made a referral to a psychiatrist.' For all the details that Matthew had included in his story, he had left that one out.

The process of making a diagnosis of a functional or conversion disorder relies on ruling out disease. There are no exceptions to this. Sometimes when the doctor has listened to the patient's symptoms and examined them a psychosomatic diagnosis seems inescapable. Even when that is the case it is vital that all possibilities be considered and all appropriate tests be done – otherwise mistakes will be made. This is a lesson that Fatima helped me to learn.

I had not been a neurology registrar for long when Fatima and I met. She made an impression. She walked into the basement room wearing dark glasses. As soon as she sat down she asked me to turn off the fluorescent light that had flickered slightly as she sat down.

'Can you turn the lights off, please,' she asked. 'Light triggers my migraine.'

Even when the room was dark she kept her sunglasses on. Before we could talk she fumbled through her bag, found a piece of chewing gum and popped it into her mouth.

'Chewing is the only thing that helps my jaw pain,' she said.

It was a busy morning and I could feel my patience slipping away. She had barely begun to tell me her story and already I felt irritated. As I listened I wanted to say, stop, I've heard this one before. Fatima had suffered with chronic headaches, stomach pain and joint pain since her teen years. She took a cocktail of drugs to control her pain. Each medical problem had been thoroughly investigated. When she was twenty-seven the pain had moved and she had been admitted to hospital with crushing chest pain. Despite her young age she was investigated for a possible heart attack. Nothing was found in the tests but she continued to take aspirin to thin her blood and a cholesterol-lowering tablet. Just in case. She had kept the label of heart disease, even after it had been disproven and she had been discharged from the cardiologists.

Before we met I had read every page in Fatima's extensive notes. At the top of each letter was a list of medical problems. The most recent one read: migraine, arthritis, angina, irritable bowel syndrome, possible hypertension, abnormal liver function tests. Fatima was thirty-five years old. She did not smoke. She did not drink. I recognised the list, I had seen many like it before. It was the list that one junior doctor copies from the most recent letter in the notes into the letter they are currently writing. Lack of experience sees them underestimate the necessity of checking every fact. In that way a medical history can take the form of Chinese whispers. 'Chest pain under investigation' is slowly transformed into 'angina' with every retelling of the story. Fatima had been investigated for angina, but a read-through of her notes told me it had been ruled out, even though the diagnosis lived on in the legend of her letters. Soon, with little evidence for it, 'possible hypertension' would become 'hypertension'.

Fatima had come to me convinced that she had suffered a stroke. She had noticed that her right hand had become weak. She was clumsy, kept dropping things and was unable to write. She had stopped using her right hand as a result. When I asked Fatima to put her two arms out in front of her so that I could establish how severe the problem was, she lifted both her arms but quickly her right fell back down by her side. When I tried to test the strength of the arm by asking her to push against me she said she couldn't and could not even be persuaded to try.

'At least try just a little,' I said. I was becoming frustrated. I wanted Fatima to stop chewing her gum noisily. I wanted to turn on the lights and to ask her to leave and to call the next patient. A nurse came in and left two more sets of notes on my desk, a message to say that more people had arrived. I was falling behind.

Fatima wanted to have a scan. At that time people waited months to be investigated or to have tests. I didn't want to add Fatima to that burgeoning list.

'I don't think you've had a stroke,' I said.

'What is it then?' she asked.

'I think your symptoms could be psychological.'

'My doctor told me it was a stroke. So you're right and he's wrong. Is that it?'

'There is no reason for somebody your age to have a stroke.'

'I have high blood pressure and a heart problem.'

'I don't think you do.'

'I didn't come here for your opinion about my heart. I came for a scan.'

The door opened again. The nurse asked me how long I would be, the next patient had waited half an hour already. The nurse had broken the stalemate. I agreed to arrange for Fatima to have some tests done and I opened the door for her to leave.

Fatima was scheduled to have all her tests on a single day and three months later I saw her name on the list of admissions for that afternoon. My conscious memory couldn't quite place the details of her case but a feeling in my stomach when I read her name suggested that my subconscious had something to say on the matter. Before I could read through her notes and remind myself a nurse came to tell me that she was going to the reception to collect a patient. 'The porters phoned and need somebody to come and collect a lady who has prostrated herself across a row of chairs in the reception area!'

Fatima had arrived.

'Can't they just put her in a wheelchair and bring her up in the lift?'

'She's says she's too weak to sit up.'

Fatima had travelled by public transport but almost as soon as she had stepped into the foyer of the hospital she declared herself overwhelmed by fatigue and weakness and unable to walk even one step further. The porters had called for nursing assistance.

Fatima lay across three chairs in the foyer with her jacket over her head to protect herself from the artificial light. With the help of a porter the nurses encouraged Fatima to climb on to a trolley and together they wheeled her to the day unit. I watched as she arrived, her dark glasses in place, the back of her hand pressed to her forehead, little sighs escaping and her eyelids fluttering. Three nurses were required to help her from the trolley to a bed.

Over the course of the day Fatima had the tests that were planned for her and between each she returned to her bed and sat with a pillow over her head. When the investigations were complete the nurses asked me to see her to verify that she was safe to go home while we waited for the results.

'How have things been, Fatima?'

'My arm has been getting worse.'

I examined her again and the arm that I had seen her freely use all day to shade her eyes flopped repeatedly down by her side when I asked her to hold it in the air. I told her that I could find nothing new, that she was well enough to go home and I would see her again in clinic with the test results.

'I can't wait that long,' she replied.

For the second time our stalemate was broken by one of the nurses.

'There's a bed on the ward. She can stay one night and go tomorrow if you can get the results together by then.'

So Fatima stayed that night. The following morning I went to see the neurophysiologist who confirmed that the studies he had done on her arm showed no fault in Fatima's nerves that would explain her weakness. Her blood results were normal too. Finally I went to see the radiologist to look at the scan.

'Take a look at that!' He snapped the scan up on a screen in triumph.

There right in the middle of the scan, superimposed on the grey of the brain, was a white circumscribed ball of tissue that most certainly should not have been there. Fatima had a brain tumour and it sat in just the place that when compressed would lead to weakness of the arm.

I have thought of Fatima often since that day. I use the memory of her to remind myself that a clinical suspicion is only that, an unsubstantiated opinion. A doctor forms a medical diagnosis in part based on their knowledge of disease but much is also drawn from the qualitative nature of the story that a patient tells. Doctors struggle when a patient's complaints or level of disability seem to outstrip what they can find on examination. We expect people to complain only in proportion to our idea of their illness. A large disparity between the extent of the disease that can be found and the degree to which the patient appears to be suffering can lead to a breakdown in the working relationship, and this might see a patient neglected.

As I watch doctors mature through their careers I see how their behaviour changes, how an open-mindedness often slowly emerges. It is a characteristic that is more often than not learned through experience and, more importantly, getting it wrong. An experienced doctor will be right a lot more often than they are wrong, and their early clinical impressions will be correct most of the time. But in the field of psychosomatic illness mistakes will remind you that for a symptom to be medically unexplained somebody must have first tried to explain it. To consider every possibility and exclude physical illness is at the heart of the diagnosis of these disorders.

Matthew got his tests. He had a further MRI scan of his brain and spine, the standard tests for MS. We looked for white spots of inflammation on the scan and didn't find them.

But not every disease shows up on a scan, so I set out to check the integrity of Matthew's nervous system. He underwent an electrical study of his nerves. A tiny electrical stimulus was given to the nerves in Matthew's feet and arms. Metal electrodes were stuck at points on his skin that followed the path his nerve travelled as it carried messages to the brain. In this way we could literally watch as the electrical impulse moved from a point at the ankle, up the leg, up the spinal cord and into the brain. Although Matthew could not feel the stimulus, a clear electrical impulse was seen to arrive at every recording point and each arrived at the correctly appointed time. And even though Matthew could barely move his legs voluntarily, when the electrical stimulus was given, his foot twitched and jerked in a perfectly normal way. Then his visual nerves were stimulated to assess their integrity. Matthew was asked to sit in front of a television that showed an ever-changing pattern of squares. A small metal electrode placed on his scalp tracked the message that was picked up first by his optic nerve and then transmitted along the visual pathway to the visual cortex. The message arrived safely. His neurological pathways were intact.

When all the results were available Matthew and I met again. He was, as usual, well presented, sitting in his wheelchair, dressed carefully and clutching a sheaf of notes. He always looked as if he had just come from the office, although he had not been to work for months. His wife was with him again, a pace behind.

I knew Matthew's concerns and I tried to address them from the outset. I explained how we make a diagnosis of MS and explained then that none of Matthew's tests had shown any evidence of it. What fantastic news, I suggested, MS is a serious illness but it had been ruled out. I could see Matthew's face darken and just to his left his wife's shoulders heaved and I saw her roll her eyes.

'I know you are suffering, Matthew. I don't want to detract from that. You are suffering and something needs to be done. But you do not have MS.'

I explained the diagnosis of functional neurological disorder, that his leg paralysis could not be explained by any neurological disease. Although I had not gone as far as to call his paralysis psychosomatic I also told him that I was wondering about a psychological cause.

'How can you say that? Just because the tests are normal you assume I'm mad. That's what doctors say when they don't know what's wrong.'

'There is more than just the normal tests,' I answered. 'The weakness in your legs doesn't fit with neurological disease. Such profound weakness should come with other clinical signs, altered reflexes or wasted muscles.'

The practice of clinical medicine is holistic just as much as it is scientific. Matthew's scans were normal but there was much more to his diagnosis.

'You are afraid to admit that you don't know what's wrong.'

74

'I do know what's wrong, Matthew. I'm trying to tell you what's wrong.'

'But it feels so real, it can't be nothing.'

'It feels real because it *is* real. Your paralysis is not imagined but that does not necessarily mean that it is a primarily physical disorder.'

'I just don't feel confident yet that MS has been ruled out.'

Matthew had come prepared. He took the papers he had been clutching on his lap and placed them on the desk. He pushed some pages towards me. They were designed to show me that I was mistaken. He told me of the woman he had met on the Internet who was told she did not have MS but the doctor had been proven wrong. He told me that he had a friend who had headaches and was told that he was depressed but it transpired that he had a brain tumour. He showed me an article from a daily newspaper that extolled the virtues of a novel treatment for MS. I told Matthew again that all the appropriate tests had been done and that he did not have MS. I could tell that Matthew was stricken. His desperation was palpable.

'All of the tests are negative. You do not have multiple sclerosis.'

'What percentage are you sure?'

'I am absolutely sure.'

When I chose a career in medicine I believed I would diagnose disease and learn to treat it. Sometimes I would deliver bad news of something serious. But at other times I would get to give good news. I would tell people that the scans were all clear and they would be relieved and happy and shake my hand warmly. I was trained to deliver the difficult diagnoses but I was never taught to anticipate the impact that apparent *good* news could sometimes have on the patient.

People like Matthew have taught me that ruling out disease is not the same as ruling out illness but it often feels that way to the patient. Matthew's disability was not altered by the fact that I had found no evidence of multiple sclerosis. This new diagnosis was not only confusing, it also muddied his view of how he might get better. With a diagnosis of MS he knew what to expect but now he needed to learn to let go of one certainty and, in its place, accept a hard truth. I had put Matthew in a difficult position. What would he tell his friends about his illness? And his employer? How would they receive the news?

'Are there other tests I could have? You must be wrong sometimes,' he said.

I didn't answer.

He shook his head and continued to leaf through his papers. Scientific papers about MS. Newspaper articles. He asked to see his brain scan as if he would find something that the radiologist had not. I had reached the point in our discussion where I was struggling to find a way to move things forward and needed to remind myself that I would be ill-advised to enter a battle of wills with a patient. But Matthew and I were saved when something quite surprising happened. His wife spoke.

'For heaven's sake, Matt, how many times does she have to say it? You don't have MS. You came here for the doctor's opinion so why don't you try listening to her?'

She turned to me. 'Can we have a moment alone please?'

All I needed was a glimmer of acceptance and it seemed his wife might give me that. I left the room and returned five minutes later.

'Okay, let's say it's not MS,' Matthew started. 'Let's say that this psychosomatic idea is *possible*, how does it happen?'

'I'm not sure why or how it's happening. It's possible that this is a sign that there is some stress that you are suppressing and it is leaking out in the form of a physical symptom.'

'But how? What's stopping my legs from moving?'

'I don't have an answer for that.'

Matthew went back to rustling through his papers. His wife reached over and took them from him. Matthew's hands froze in mid-air for a moment.

'It would be a lot easier for him if you could explain it,' his wife said.

'There is some dysfunction in the way the message telling Matthew's legs to move is travelling from his brain to his legs but I don't know how that happens. I just know that it can happen and that it may help for Matthew to see a psychiatrist.'

In the same way that we rule MS in or out through a series of investigations, a psychological assessment need only be another exploratory test. Unfortunately many patients find it difficult to make that final step in the investigative process. To see the psychiatrist feels to some as if they are relinquishing their grip on physical disease, and with it losing all validation of their suffering. For Matthew to agree to see the psychiatrist required a sacrifice that would change the way that society would view his disability.

I was lucky that day.

'Okay,' Matthew reluctantly agreed.

Matthew wanted something very reasonable from me: proof. If I could provide evidence, or at the very least a coherent explanation for why his legs failed to move, then he could, in return, accept the diagnosis. Instead I offered him only my conviction and a list of normal test results.

The effect the psyche can have on the physical self has long been observed, but for all that time scientists and doctors have also been trying, and failing, to understand how it occurs. As long ago as 400 BC Hippocrates noted that emotion could trigger sweat and cause the heart to beat strongly in the chest. And it could lead to illness. Hippocrates believed that to treat the sick it was necessary to see the person as a whole, that treating the mind was as important as any treatment of the body; he cured illness by analysing dreams over 2,000 years before Freud was born.

Hippocrates is credited with the earliest descriptions of the illness known as hysteria. He considered it to be a disease of women said to originate in the womb. It was believed that the uterus was a mobile organ that travelled around the body causing disease; if the uterus was displaced upwards or down, or irritated in any way, this could lead to delirium and collapse. Hysteria was not a coherent syndrome with well-defined symptoms; descriptions of it were vague and variable. Seizures were a common manifestation, but shortness of breath, loss of voice, neck pain, dizziness or palpitations were also described. The ancient Greeks knew nothing of physiology and very little of anatomy so they did not distinguish psychosomatic illness from other disease. Hysteria was an organic illness, a disease of the body rather than the mind.

Mobile organs were not the only possible mechanism for illness in ancient Greece. The four humours – black bile, yellow bile, blood and phlegm – were believed to be pivotal in maintaining health and also causing ill-health. The balance of these essential fluids could both determine our temperament and control the stability of our physical health. Each humour was associated with one of four temperaments – choleric, melancholic, sanguine and phlegmatic – and the proportions of each fluid within a person was thought to determine the person's character. Where the balance was in favour of blood that person was sanguine, cheerful and optimistic. A balance in favour of yellow bile suggested a choleric person, more likely to be ill-tempered. The humours were constantly in flux so a person might be both ill-tempered and optimistic at different times.

By AD 200 Galen was still setting great store by the importance of humours but he also developed another hypothesis about how illness developed and spread. He set out the theory that organs could communicate with one another. He imagined nerves as hollow tubes that carried messages from one organ to the next, and the name that he suggested for the message that was transmitted was *sympathy*. Galen was the first to suggest that one organ might change or react in sympathy for another. He described how a disease of the stomach might travel in spirit form through a nerve to the brain resulting in a fainting or a seizure. Galen was correct in noting the importance of nerves in transmitting information, even if he had not understood exactly the purpose of this or how it was achieved.

In the Middle Ages, superstition and religion took precedence over medical theories. Hysteria all but disappeared as a condition of medical interest and importance and would not reappear in earnest until the beginning of the seventeenth century, when prevailing myths would have to be dispelled before new explanations for hysteria were sought.

In 1602 Mary Glover of London began to suffer seizures seemingly triggered by an altercation with a neighbour. Soon Mary was deemed possessed by the Devil. The neighbour was accused of putting a curse on Mary and was put on trial as a witch. A prominent physician of the time argued that Mary was not possessed but was suffering with the disease hysteria. His argument was rejected by the court. In England the last executions for witchcraft took place at the end of the seventeenth century, but until then witchcraft and the Devil provided explanations for illnesses that could not otherwise be explained. When witchcraft was no longer believed in, hysterical symptoms could not be attributed to such external factors either and it became necessary to provide an alternative explanation: if they weren't cursed or possessed, patients must be mad. Hysteria became an illness of the mind: sufferers were transferred into the hands of the psychiatrists of their day, the asylum doctors, also known as alienists; witch trials were replaced by madhouses. The eighteenth century saw asylums become the last resting place of the destitute and the hysterical. That move away from hysteria's organic beginnings meant that sufferers received no treatment and had no hope of cure – an asylum's purpose was containment.

Fortunately, as the eighteenth century progressed, the world was on the brink of change, entering a scientific era. Asylums would not go out of fashion for a long time, particularly for the lower classes, and the majority of doctors would still consider hysteria to be synonymous with insanity, but some modern scientists started to wonder if it was possible that hysteria did not originate in the mind, nor even in the head. This thought saw many new explanations for hysteria that would prove as varied and strange as the symptoms themselves. The finger of blame was pointed first at a host of disparate organs and later at the nervous system.

The first advance was in fact a step backwards as an ancient idea was brought to the fore again: the uterus as a source of hysteria. By now it was fully accepted that organs were fixed in place but it was still believed that the uterus, through the power of humours, had the ability to bring other organs into sympathy with it. The status that was given to the uterus is quite complimentary – beyond the brain or any other part of the body, it became the master organ. Either underuse or overuse of the womb could lead a woman to an attack of the vapours, an overwhelming feeling of weakness and fatigue.

The uterus was the preferred organ, but not the only organ implicated in this latest version of hysteria. An explanation was also needed for men who suffered with fits and malaise. Continental Europeans were particularly enamoured with the stomach as a source of hysteria, drawn to its dense confluence of nerves and influenced by the stomach sensation that many sufferers described just in advance of a seizure. The spleen was also a culprit, a blockage of which was believed to lead to any number of disabilities.

The concept of the master organ and its role in hysteria survived a hundred years, until a new type of specialist doctor started to emerge: the neurologist. In the early nineteenth century it was discovered that muscle fibres were excitable and contracted in response to a stimulus. Tapping on the knee was shown to elicit a reflex contraction. This reflex was believed to be mediated by the nerves in the spine. Suddenly the nervous system, and the spine in particular, were considered to be the centre of the body's communication system. Nerves had been shown to be both excitable and irritable and this led to a new explanation for hysteria – spinal irritation. Young women were noted to have a special sensitivity of the spine, which could communicate its irritation to other parts of the body resulting in pain or paralysis or vomiting just as easily as it could in fits. Spinal irritation became one of the first popular nervous illnesses. This idea led quickly to its successor, the reflex theory – if the spine could communicate its distress to the rest of the body, perhaps every organ could do the same. When many women are pregnant they vomit – was this evidence that the distress of the uterus had been communicated through the nerves to the stomach? Was it an indication that irritability could travel from the uterus to elsewhere in the body?

Up until this point, the 1850s, there was at least a shred of sense in these theories about hysteria. But in the late nineteenth century my favourite explanation was proposed – the theory of nasal irritation. The idea that the mucosa of the nose could be responsible for illness became very popular in the 1880s and it survived into the early twentieth century. The nose became implicated in afflictions as diverse as seizures and pains in the stomach. Cauterisation of the mucosa of the nose or the correction of a deviated spectrum began to be used as treatment. So legitimate was this condition that Sigmund Freud, who was said to suffer chronic ill health not entirely unrelated to the sort seen in his patients, sought frequent treatment of his nasal turbinates. And even with the remoteness of the nose from the sexual organs, nasal irritation did not forget those organs. Doctors felt that the similarity in the engorgement of the mucosal lining of the nose and the engorgement of the penis could not be dismissed as coincidence. The uterus was also inexorably linked to the nose, a blockage of one leading to a blockage of the other. Excessive use of either the female or male organs could be just the thing to cause the nasal mucosa to swell and for hysterical fits to begin.

The role of the master organ, spinal or nasal irritation – each of these theories was embraced by patient and doctor alike. Even though many doctors considered hysteria a feigned illness, a manifestation of either attention seeking or lunacy, they were happy to apply new labels since they pleased patients and required lucrative treatments. Seizures as a result of spinal irritation could be treated with cupping or the application of leeches over the back. Patients could be bled or encouraged to urinate to balance the humours. Sex, pregnancy, vaginal douching and hysterectomy took the place of consignment to an asylum. If a patient was offered either spinal irritation or madness as an explanation for their suffering, it is not hard to understand why they chose the former.

While each of these proposed mechanisms for hysteria has survived in small ways within modern society, they no longer exist in conventional medicine. However, at the end of the nineteenth century came a series of doctors whose theories about hysteria remain the basis of our understanding of psychosomatic illness today and provide the mainstay of current psychological treatments. First there was Jean-Martin Charcot, a French neurologist responsible both for piquing the world's interest in hysteria and for producing an epidemic of diagnoses of it. Then psychologist and doctor Pierre Janet produced an account of the subconscious which brought hysteria to the realm of the mind. Finally came Sigmund Freud, whose work took the ideas of both men and expanded on them to create his own concept of the conversion disorder. Although these three men were working about one hundred or so years ago, their contribution has been so lasting and their influence so great, that we will meet them and their ideas in more detail throughout this book.

The ways in which medicine has attempted to account for hysteria are fascinating not only for the theories themselves, but also for how they have echoed into the future. When the uterus was cast in the role of the master organ, or when the reflex theory was conceived, very little was known about physiology. Scientific advances have proved that these theories are unfeasible, but even so they have not been completely left behind. Even now a woman's physical and mental well-being is often considered closely linked to her uterus, and in particular to the stages of her menstrual cycle. We no longer believe in witches, but we do look outside ourselves for external explanations for how we feel, attributing blame to viruses or pesticides or electricity pylons. The multimillion-pound industry that is osteopathy has much in common with the treatments for spinal irritation. Reflexology and acupuncture are direct descendants of the reflex theory. It seems that only nasal irritation has been truly left behind.

*

Nowadays, I have at my fingertips a host of sophisticated investigations that the original nerve doctors did not have. You might surmise therefore that in the twenty-first century I would be in a position to understand the mechanism of psychosomatic illness, at least in part, and could provide the proof of diagnosis that patients like Matthew want. But the truth is that doctors still struggle to provide a coherent explanation for psychosomatic illness. There have been many advances in our understanding of biological disease but progress to explain how emotions can produce physical symptoms has been slow and incomplete.

The biggest leaps have been technological. Shortly after I qualified as a doctor the magnetic resonance imaging (MRI) scan was just coming into use in clinical practice. It brought a new language to how we described the brain. Computerised tomography (CAT or CT) scans showed us *density*; the MRI scan showed the *intensity* of the brain. Suddenly parts of the nervous system were visible that had been impossible to look at in a living patient before, and things were explained. The MRI scan produced such detailed pictures that it could easily detect the lesions of diseases like multiple sclerosis. The diagnosis of MS, which had previously involved a series of unpleasant investigations spanning months or years, could now be made with a single scan. In people with a lifetime of unexplained epilepsy the MRI could visualise tiny scars and birth abnormalities in the brain, thus providing a whole new range of explanations for the disease. That was in the 1990s, and several generations of technology have come and gone in the evolution of brain imaging since then. Many new diseases have been found where it was not the patient or disease that had changed but the technology.

Now there are dozens of ways for the brain to be viewed. We can look at its structure or the blood flow, at how the brain utilises fuel or at its electrical fields. The advent of the *functional* MRI scan has allowed us to look at what is happening in the brain at the time of a specific action. Rather than concentrating on the solid components of the brain it maps how the brain behaves while a person carries out a task. That task could be thinking or moving or experiencing an emotion. For example, the subject lies in the scanner and is asked to tap their finger. The functional MRI takes an image that detects a change in blood flow, comparing the brain before and during finger tapping. This gives us a picture of which part of the brain is active during the task and indicates the possible nerve cells where the finger tapping originates.

Such MRI techniques have been applied to patients with psychogenic paralysis, paralysis for which no organic disease can account and where there is a suspected cause of mental distress. The patient lies in the scanner and is asked to move the paralysed limb. While the patient tries to do this an MRI picture is taken. Then, the same technique is applied to healthy volunteers and to a group who are asked to feign paralysis. It is possible to see in the scans a clear difference in what is happening in the brain of a healthy volunteer and that of a patient with suspected psychogenic paralysis. In a healthy control subject the motor cortex shows intense activation, but in the patient with psychogenic paralysis there is less activation in the motor area, and instead a different part of the frontal lobe activates. But, much more importantly, there is also a difference between the brain activation of those patients with psychogenic paralysis and the volunteers who are asked to *pretend* to be paralysed. Those feigning weakness show a distinct pattern of brain activation of their own. So all three groups are different. The MRI has demonstrated that something in the brain is not functioning as it should in those with psychogenic paralysis and it has told us that psychogenic paralysis is not feigned. But the changes seen on imaging are not consistent in every patient, nor are they easy to understand. They provide an interesting part of a puzzle that will hopefully one day make sense but, for the moment, they continue to tell us almost nothing about why or how the paralysis has occurred.

The truth is that for all the advancements in our understanding of how the brain works and how our bodies respond to stress, our tests are still blunt tools. We still have very limited understanding of how thoughts or ideas are generated; we are no closer to explaining imagination and no closer to understanding or proving the reality of illnesses that arise there. So how can one ever be sure of a diagnosis which is offered in such an insubstantial way?

Often doctors do not confront patients with suspected psychosomatic disorders for just that reason. The diagnosis is too hard to prove and therefore will not be accepted. And what if the future brings some new test that will reveal that the original diagnosis was wrong? In some ways we have not moved on from the eighteenth century, the diagnosis may still be avoided for the comfort of both patient and doctor. And this is particularly the case where the symptoms are subjective and cannot be measured. If a gastroenterologist sees a patient with stomach pain the first step is to rule out disease and tell the patient what has not been found. You do not have an ulcer. You do not have colitis. But it is not easy to conclusively distinguish a pain that originates first in the mind from one that exists only in the stomach.

This is where neurology departs from other specialities. It has always had a close relationship with psychosomatic disorder, and has even given it its own particular name, conversion disorder, as if the conversion of distress into paralysis or seizures instead of pain or fatigue is in some way special, when it is not. One symptom is not any more significant than another. Conversion disorders are not any more common than other somatic disorders such as chronic pain. In fact unexplained pain is far more common. Yet the diagnosis of conversion disorders is more likely to be directly confronted. This is because the integrity of the nervous system can be assessed objectively. Essentially, neurologists have the tools to reliably assess the function of nerves and muscles and, in doing so, they are faced with a much clearer diagnosis.

The neurological examination is a sophisticated tool. Weakness that is psychogenic has quite a different quality to weakness caused by neurological disease. Different muscles are affected. Aspects of the examination can be assessed objectively, without the participation of the patient. The nervous system consists of a complex collection of nerve pathways that intersect and join together and divide again as they travel from the peripheries of our body to our spine and brain. The subconscious mind cannot authentically reproduce in the nervous system the complexity of the symptoms caused by a single lesion. For these reasons, conversion disorders are usually a poor mimic of neurological disease.

I once had a patient called Linda who had noticed a small lump on the right side of her head. She saw her GP and he said it was a lipoma, a harmless fatty lump that sits in the skin. But even with this reassurance Linda couldn't stop re-examining and checking the lump. Was she imagining it, or had it grown in size? Soon she experienced a sort of tingling down the right side of her body. The sensation in her right arm slowly disappeared and then weakness of the right arm and leg followed and she knew for sure then that the lump had reached her brain and was pushing inside.

When I saw her she was split down the middle by the harm that the lump had done. A line could be drawn that divided her exactly in two, on the right was the lump, on the right everything about her limbs was dulled, all movement and sensation. Because Linda didn't know that the right brain controls the left side of the body her subconsciousness had imagined her symptoms wrong.

Symptoms that arise through stress or anxiety are produced in the mind and are dependent on what the sufferer understands about the body and disease. The subconscious mind reproduces symptoms that make sense to the individual's understanding of how a disease behaves. In the absence of detailed knowledge of the body, disabilities that arise in the subconscious rarely obey anatomical rules.

It is just this rule-breaking that makes conversion disorders so out of keeping with neurological disorders, particularly when they are severe. But the neurologist has a second tool when there is doubt or to back up a conviction. Our brain and nerves and muscles all function through the passage of electrical discharges and there are reliable tests that can objectively measure this function in any part of the nervous system. Those methods that are used to scientifically explore psychosomatic disorders are equally useful in everyday clinical practice.

It is precisely because the neurological examination is so objective and the nervous system so amenable to measurement that neurologists find themselves confronted so directly by psychosomatic illness. It is hard for neurologists to ignore the possibility of psychosomatic factors, which in turn makes it harder to simply offer the patient a list of what has been ruled out.

But, even with all these techniques at our disposal, all we can prove is that the structure of the nerve pathways is intact. This may help us decide whose weakness is impossible but it still does not provide what Matthew wants – an explanation for how and why. Nor will it validate the reality of his suffering. Every week I hear the word *real* used over and over, as if something that cannot be measured cannot be real. But the world is full of things we cannot see but either know or believe to be real. Our thoughts are vivid and constant but nobody knows how they are generated; they can't be seen or smelled or touched but it wouldn't occur to us not to believe in them. Dreams are the same; we all have them but can only speculate about how or why they occur. A large proportion of the world believes in the concept of God. He is worshipped by intelligent, educated, rational people. Wars are fought for Him, with no scientific evidence that He exists.

There is nothing I can show Matthew, no shadow on a scan or irregularity on a blood test, that will allow him to believe that my diagnosis is correct. But I will ask him to believe me even without that proof, in the same way that I believe that his paralysis, that I cannot measure, is as real as any other.

Most of my patients will face the same uncertainty as Matthew. But methods do exist that provide patients with absolute proof of their diagnosis. Conversion disorders occur when distressing emotions or traumatic events cannot be voiced, and some treatments focus on finding a way to release that voice.

From the late nineteenth century hypnosis became integral to the assessment and treatment of hysteria. Under the influence of hypnotism patients were able to face the suppressed experience that they had been denying, their hysterical state was reproduced and their negative feelings purged. This catharsis, of facing and surviving the trauma, could lead to a full resolution of the patient's disability. In the early twentieth century it was discovered that a similar effect could be achieved with drugs. Barbiturate drugs were given in order to disinhibit the brain and reveal the hidden truth. Under the relaxing effect of sodium amytal the patient was able to see the traumas of the past more clearly, and then, in time, the negative feelings were discharged. Once sedated, the patient demonstrated a similar suggestible state to that seen in hypnosis. A suggestion to get better was slowly sown. Or the patients could be exposed to the thing they feared most in an environment that was safe.

The technique retained the label abreaction, referring to the emotional purge that is the basis for the treatment. In the mid twentieth century this technique allowed victims of World War Two to confront traumatic memories, desensitising them to the extreme reaction they had experienced in the face of particular fears.

Sodium amytal interviews remained in use into the late twentieth century. Its first use was in those with catatonia; people lost to the world, mute and motionless with no brain disease to explain it. Such catatonic patients have been coaxed to move, speak and reveal their secrets under the influence of barbiturate drugs. Many psychosomatic disabilities have reportedly been *cured* in this way. When the drug is given it travels to the brain causing a gradual disinhibition of the frontal lobes. These control our social behaviour; they stop us telling the inappropriate joke at the formal meeting, they control our impulses, warn us of danger. Drugs can chemically disconnect the frontal lobes leaving our brains uncensored. In one example this technique was used to assess the memory of a man who had attacked a young female acquaintance of his. Following the attack he developed a dense amnesia. He could not remember what he had done nor any detail of his own life. During an interview carried out using sodium amytal the man's memory returned. It emerged that he had been in love with the woman he had assaulted, but he perceived that she had rejected him. Immediately following the drug interview the man lost his memory again and went into a deep sleep, but over the course of the following week piecemeal fragments of memory returned until, eventually, he made a full recovery. There are similar accounts of paralysed people regaining the ability to walk. After the drug has left the brain not every patient remembers what occurred during the interview. By watching a playback of the video taken at the time they can see that they were able to overcome their disability, even if only briefly.

However, there are significant issues associated with the technique. Cases of long-buried abuse and neglect have been released using this method. Patients have suffered extreme reactions to such abrupt revelations of something suppressed for so long. But, more worrying still, the reporting of false memories has been attributed to both hypnosis and sodium amytal interviews, leading to false accusations of sexual abuse and rape.

Matthew would have to find a way forward without abreaction, with only the inadequate evidence of normal tests and my clinical opinion. I was greatly relieved therefore when I met him six weeks later and was greeted by a transformation.

I went to the waiting room and called his name. He was still in his wheelchair, well dressed as usual but this time he had no large file or armful of papers. He looked less like a man who had come to defend himself. I hadn't yet had the psychiatrist's letter and I was not sure what to expect but, even from a distance, he looked more content. His wife walked behind the wheelchair as Matthew came into the room and, although she didn't smile or acknowledge me, I thought I could detect a glimmer of something positive in her too.

When Matthew told me how he was doing there was only good news. Somewhere in the time since we had last met he had been converted, or had converted himself, to the idea of a psychosomatic disorder. His wife had encouraged him both to meet the psychiatrist and carry out his own research, and somehow he managed to bring himself to an understanding that there might actually be some truth in my odd diagnosis.

'How did the meeting with the psychiatrist go?'

'Well, I didn't like it at first but I realised he made a lot of sense. He said my paralysis was due to a functional blockage in my nerve pathways. There's a blockage in the message between my brain and legs. He called it a functional neurological disorder.'

'I'm pleased he's helped.'

'The psychiatrist explained things a lot better than you did. He said the nervous system is like a computer, that my hardware is intact and the wires are all in the right place, but I have a software problem that stops my legs receiving the instruction to move.'

Matthew had been given a label and an explanation that he could relate to. For any illness the first step to getting better is to accept the diagnosis and Matthew had learned to do that. That came with firm benefits for Matthew: now he could move forward to treatment, and he could do things to help himself. And he had a prognosis. He could anticipate recovery. He could contact his workplace and tell them he had a functional neurological disorder, that he had to undergo intensive physiotherapy but that he would get better.

'I know I can defeat this blasted thing,' Matthew said, rubbing his legs.

Matthew had found his way out.

Once the diagnosis was finalised Matthew's care could move

to the psychiatrists, who kept me updated. With intensive physiotherapy and occupational therapy Matthew was learning to walk again. He was keen to return to work and his employer allowed him to work from home until he had recovered. And with the intervention of the therapists little pieces of him had been revealed. He was one of three brothers and they were a successful family, but Matthew never quite felt that he made the grade. He was as successful as his brothers but felt he had to continually work harder to hold on to his success. He was a man on a treadmill looking for a way off.

Although I had passed Matthew's care to somebody else I continued to see him from time to time in clinic. Even those who embrace their diagnosis will occasionally have doubts and I am still needed when the dark days come and thoughts of physical disease sneak back in. Recovery is not linear, it comes with ups and downs. Every now and then Matthew developed a new symptom and when he did I was there to examine him and assure him, and myself, that no further tests were needed. Soon he was able to accept my reassurance even knowing I could not provide the proof.

'Are you absolutely certain?' he asked occasionally, from the need to be sure.

'I am one hundred per cent certain.'

And eventually Matthew didn't need me to remind him any more. Soon he could do it for himself.

'I'm going mad again, Doc,' he said every now and again and I could see that he had come to understand what his body told him and could even laugh about it now. His symptoms were still there but when he felt them he responded differently. He had come to realise that the message that they convey is not always what it seems. Now if they tried to interrupt his normal life he knew he didn't have to do exactly what they say.

4

SHAHINA

If you want to keep a secret, you must also hide it from yourself.

George Orwell, *Nineteen Eighty-Four* (1949)

Cassandra was the daughter of the King of Troy. She had been both blessed and cursed. Her blessing was one of prophecy, Cassandra could foresee the future. Her curse was that she was not believed. That is how people with psychosomatic disorders feel. Their suffering is real but they do not feel believed.

Telling somebody that their disability has a psychological cause creates in them a feeling that they are being accused of something; they are being told that they are lying, faking or imagining their symptoms. For my patients to recover I need them at least to consider a psychological cause for their illness and to agree to see a psychiatrist. Even when the patient succeeds in this, their families often don't. The most important and challenging aspect of my role is to support the patient and their family through the difficult journey they have to take. I do not always find that easy and I do not always succeed.

Shahina's illness had begun six months before we met, following an incident at university. Shahina had turned up late to her lecture that day, not realising how this small thing would change her life. All the outer seats of the long tiered rows were taken. Rather than pushing noisily past her classmates Shahina took off her coat and sat on a step behind a row of other late-comers. She laid her coat across her knees and sat back with her hands placed behind her on the floor for support. For the next five minutes the door of the lecture theatre swung open from time to time as other students ducked in.

Shahina was just leaning to one side, craning to see the lecturer, when she felt a crushing pain. She let out a loud cry and a titter went up from the students nearest to her. The red-faced boy who had stood on Shahina's hand muttered an embar-rassed apology. He bent down mindlessly to touch her arm, as if that would take back what he had done. Shahina pushed him away and a tear came down her cheek as she held her hand to her chest. For the rest of the lecture Shahina could not quite concentrate as she watched a large dark bruise develop.

Shahina's family had little sympathy for her that evening when she complained bitterly of the pain and refused to help with household chores. They reacted differently when they saw how swollen and bruised her hand was when she woke the following morning. Shahina's mother took her straight to the casualty department where it was discovered that she had a hairline fracture of a metacarpal bone. Her hand was splinted and her arm was put in a sling. Her abashed mother drove her home and took the day off work to care for her. For the next three weeks Shahina could not use her right arm. She typed with one hand and used a Dictaphone to record her lectures.

When Shahina was finally allowed to remove her splint, her

hand was thin and useless. Underuse had left it misshapen and a fraction of the size of its partner. The doctor told her not to worry and arranged for her to meet the physiotherapist, who advised on a series of exercises. She found the exercises painful but was glad to be able to do normal things again. The pain bothered her a bit, and her hand felt clumsy, but she enjoyed regaining her independence, fastening buttons, driving the car.

About two weeks after the splint was removed Shahina was sitting in a lecture when she felt an unpleasant cramp in her hand. Her pen slipped from her fingers and rattled noisily to the floor. She bent to pick it up but, just as she grasped at it, the cramp struck again. She found herself pawing uselessly at the pen as it slid between her fingers and rolled away. She had to leave it on the floor. For thirty minutes she found herself sitting mindlessly staring at her lecturer as his words floated by her.

When the lecture was over Shahina showed her friends her hand. The index and middle fingers were bending inwards. She could easily stretch them out flat with her other hand but as soon as she let go the fingers curled again slowly like a little animal avoiding danger. Her friends laughed when they saw it and for half an hour played the game of curl-and-uncurl with Shahina's fingers. Shahina also found it funny, but only for a while.

That evening when she tried to eat her dinner she couldn't hold a knife. Her parents were distressed to see their daughter suddenly disabled in this way. They phoned the physiotherapist and left a message requesting an urgent appointment.

Shahina saw the physiotherapist the next day. She stretched Shahina's hand, which helped, but the problem remained. The physiotherapist advised Shahina to see her doctor again, which she did the following day. A repeat X-ray revealed that her fracture had healed well. Despite the reassurance of the X-ray Shahina's hand did not feel any better. In fact she felt the X-ray had the opposite effect.

'It didn't feel as if I was being told that everything was okay. I felt as if I was being told that I was imagining it. The reassurances made me feel worse, not better.'

'You were telling them that you couldn't use your hand and they were telling you that you were fine?'

'Yes, I told them my hand was not working properly and they essentially told me I was wrong.'

For a month Shahina exercised her hand several times per day. The pain increased. Her mother arranged for her to see a private doctor who gave her a series of muscle relaxants and painkillers. This helped the pain but did not prevent her fingers from curling inwards. Writing invariably resulted in cramp so, on the advice of the doctor, Shahina began to record lectures with her Dictaphone again and borrow her friends' notes so that she could avoid writing for prolonged periods. And, at the suggestion of a family friend, she began to bathe her hand in ice every night before bed. All of this helped the pain but had no impact on what mattered most, her ability to use her hand. It took approximately one month for all four of Shahina's fingers to curl in almost completely, rendering her right hand all but useless.

When Shahina and I met in the outpatient department, one month later, her arm was in a sling. The sling gave her relief. If she allowed her hand to hang downwards she found it crippled by a throbbing pain that could only be relieved by elevating it again.

'If she lowers her hand you can almost see the blood rushing into it. Her hand is so lifeless that the blood just pools there with nowhere to go,' said Shahina's mother, who spoke almost as if her daughter's hand was no longer part of her.

When I examined Shahina, I found all four fingers curled inwards, the index and middle fingers were completely folded with the fingernails hidden deeply from view. The half-moon of the cuticles of the ring and little fingers were just visible. The thumb moved freely which meant she could still pull at zips and buttons as long as they were loose and easy to access. Writing was impossible, the scribbles of a child. She could use her thumb to type but it was slow and full of errors.

When I tried to straighten Shahina's fingers there was resistance. It was painful but possible to draw the fingers outwards so that the palm of the hand was fully bared. Four red welts were visible where the fingernails had burrowed into the skin. When I released the fingers they immediately sprang back into their coiled position.

'She can open her fingers sometimes,' her mother told me.

'I can pry them open for just long enough to cut my nails or wash my hand,' Shahina said.

'Have you ever seen anything like that? Do you know what it is?' her mother asked.

'It looks like Shahina has developed focal dystonia. It's a condition in which people's muscles go into spasm. It can be triggered by trauma but we need to look for other causes. I am concerned about how disabled Shahina is by the problem so I would like to admit her to hospital for tests. That is the quickest way to get an answer.'

'My daughter is precious; please don't make her wait too long,' her mother said.

When Shahina and I met again she had been admitted as an inpatient on the ward. Her hand was just as it had been when I saw her last. Blood tests, genetic tests and brain scans designed to look for an underlying neurological disease were all normal. An electrical study showed the muscles of the forearm in a constant state of contraction but did not say why. Patients who suffer with dystonia often have normal tests, so this did not imply any particular diagnosis. But Shahina's dominant hand was useless to her now, and she needed her mother to close her buttons and cut her food. Something needed to be done. A specialist neurologist in movement disorders came to see Shahina and recommended that she be given a therapeutic trial of botulinum toxin.

Botox isn't just for cosmetic use. It has long been used as a treatment for neurological disorders. In people whose muscles go into painful spasm, for whatever reason, it can paralyse the muscles so they relax. The paralysed muscle may then prove useless but if it results in an improvement in pain and deformity it can be worth it anyway. Botulinum toxin wouldn't tell me what was wrong with Shahina but it could relax the muscles in her hand just enough to give her some use of her hand and some pain relief.

I accompanied Shahina to have the procedure. A small needle electrode was placed into the muscles of her forearm. The electrode recorded the excess electrical activity that was produced by the furiously over-contracting muscles leading to Shahina's fingers. The computer converted the electrical activity to a noise, so that when the needle was inserted into Shahina's arm the room filled with a wild crackling sound. The doctor running the test leaned over and turned down the volume.

'Is that my arm making that noise?' Shahina asked.

'Yes.'

'Is that what it is supposed to sound like?'

'Not if you are trying to relax. If the muscles going to your fingers were able to relax there would be silence.'

Next the doctor took a small syringe filled with botulinum toxin, attached it to the needle and slowly injected. Shahina was watching the computer screen and I knew she was also listening intently to the noise it gave off. We were all listening. One minute is a very long time when you are just watching and listening but that is about how long we waited before we noticed the change. The static crackling that had been present since the needle electrode had been inserted was dying down. Shahina's gaze moved from the computer to her hand. Her eyes were transfixed as her fingers slowly unfurled.

'It worked!' she cried.

The doctor who had given the injection looked at me with raised eyebrows.

That afternoon I went to the ward to see if Shahina's improvement was sustained. I found her tapping away at the keyboard of her computer.

'It hurts and my hand feels a bit weak but look how good it is.' She opened and closed her fist. 'I'm cured, can I go home now?'

What I did next I would regret many times.

'I need to explain something to you, Shahina.' I sat beside her on her bed as I spoke. 'Botulinum toxin poisons the nerve ending and the result is that it relaxes the muscles. But it doesn't usually work instantaneously. It takes a day or two for it to take effect.'

Shahina looked at me puzzled. I could tell she had not understood the full implications of what I had said.

'But it worked straight away for me. That's a good sign, right?'

'Yes, which is all that really matters.'

'Okay, so I can go home.'

Shahina had offered me an opportunity to retreat and I ignored it.

'What I'm trying to say is that I don't think it could have been the botulinum toxin that made you better. The recovery was too quick.'

'But I got better right after the injection so it had to be the botulinum toxin.'

'Sometimes, when we desperately want to get better and we are offered a treatment that we hope will help, we get better just through the power of our minds and the strength of our will. And getting better in that way might tell us a little about what caused the problem in the first instance.'

Shahina was staring at her hand, watching her fist opening and closing in front of her.

'Shahina, the speed at which your hand responded to the toxin makes me wonder if there is a chance that the spasm in your hand might have a psychological rather than a physical cause.'

'You think I'm mad?'

'Of course not.'

'What, then? What does psychological mean? Either I'm doing it on purpose or I'm going mad! Which?!'

The mood in the room had turned quickly. People passing the open door heard the raised voice and looked in.

'Physical symptoms for psychological reasons happen to all of us.'

'I can't fucking believe it! I came to this hospital with muscle spasm in my hand and now I'm being told I'm doing it on purpose.'

A nurse came to pull the door closed. 'I'll give you some privacy, shall I?' she said.

'I'm very sorry that this is so upsetting for you, Shahina. Your hand is better. That's what matters.'

Shahina sunk into silence. Minutes passed before she spoke again.

'So what do I do now?'

'You're better so you can go home.'

'What are you even talking about when you say it's psychological? You haven't even explained what you mean.'

The next ten minutes were delicate. I felt the conversation could veer in any direction at any moment, that every word had to be the right one. I imagine Shahina felt it too, the vigilance in the room. I explained psychosomatic symptoms to her.

'I'm not saying that this is the case for you, Shahina, I'm just wondering. Does what I have said make any sense to you?'

'I don't know. No, it doesn't make sense. It sounds like nonsense.'

'Perhaps, in that case, it is best to put this idea aside for the moment. Your hand is better so let's focus on that.'

Though it was of course too late to brush what I had said aside, we both knew that.

'How can a hand go into spasm for psychological reasons?'

'We all get physical sensations through stress sometimes. Have you ever felt your shoulders tense up through stress? This could be something similar, but, of course, worse.'

'But I'm not stressed.'

'I know, but you had a trauma, a difficult time with the broken bone in your hand; maybe it's worth looking into how that affected you?'

'I don't want to see a psychiatrist.'

'That's okay; I don't think it's necessary at the moment.'

'Where does that leave me? Will my hand stay better? Will I need botulinum toxin again?'

'I think that since your hand is better now it will probably stay better.' I was offering hope because expectations matter.

'I'm sorry I shouted.'

'I'm sorry you've had such a hard time.'

I left understanding that Shahina would go home and that we would meet again in the clinic in the future. An hour later I was called back to the ward.

Shahina's mother stood squarely in the door. Shahina was sitting on her bed, packed bag beside her. Her father sat on the chair by the bed. A nurse joined me as I went into the room.

'I want to know exactly what you said to my daughter,' her mother said.

I explained that Shahina's tests were normal but that her response to the botulinum toxin had raised some concerns.

'My daughter has told me that you said she was doing this deliberately.'

Shahina's mother stood in front of me and I could not see her daughter.

I craned to talk to Shahina. 'I don't think you are doing anything purposefully, Shahina, I am just worried that there is something underlying your dystonia that we haven't fully explored. I may be completely wrong, I accept that, and I'm sorry if I am.'

'Sorry won't cut it,' her mother said. 'Do you really think a young girl could hold her hand in that position for weeks? There are welts on her hand. She's in pain.'

'Shahina's spasms of her hand are involuntary and very disabling, we all agree on that.'

'She has a broken bone on her X-ray. Can you acknowledge that?'

'Yes, the dystonia was clearly triggered by a trauma.'

'So you still admit she has dystonia?'

'Yes, Shahina has dystonia. The question we have been trying to answer is why.'

'I know my own child. She is a bright girl, halfway to being a lawyer. She works hard, she is never ill. I guarantee you that if she had any control over this it would not be happening.'

As the questions and answers passed quickly between us I suddenly felt as if Shahina had left the room, as if it was just me and her mother standing there. Shahina and her father had blended into the background.

'Shahina . . . ?' I tried to get her back.

'I am going to take my daughter home and when I get there the first thing I am going to do is write a complaint letter about you.'

At this cue Shahina's father picked up the suitcase and gently put his hand on his daughter's back to usher her along. Shahina stood up from her chair and took her handbag from her bed. I watched as she clutched that bag tightly in her right hand and walked out of the room behind her mother.

'She doesn't believe there's anything wrong with me,' I heard her say as she crossed the threshold.

'She's wrong,' her mother turned to answer and, in doing so, caught my eye. 'This is not the last you will be hearing of this.'

For a parent illness and disease jeopardise the opportunities they dreamed of for their child. They are angry at the disease that robs them in this way. When that illness becomes psychological, where does the fault lie? Who can they be angry at then? Themselves? Or has their child become stained with something so stigmatising that they cannot bear to look? With no other choice they redirect their attention somewhere else.

A week later the letter of complaint arrived:

I would like to complain about the treatment that my daughter received at the hands of Dr O'Sullivan. My daughter has been severely disabled with spasms of the right hand for some time. Despite the purely PHYSICAL nature of my daughter's symptoms, and based on no evidence that I can see, Dr O'Sullivan summarily accused her of having psychological problems!! My daughter, who is a law student and extremely reliable, says that Dr O'Sullivan approached her without warning and advised her that she was imagining her symptoms.

The letter continued in this vein. It was printed on the headed stationery of the law office where her mother worked. It ended by saying that Shahina had met with another doctor who had assured her that there was no possibility that the problem could be psychosomatic. It did not include any correspondence from that doctor.

After that I sent several letters to Shahina asking her to meet me again in the outpatient department. She did not respond. I had to wait over a year before I heard anything further about her progress. The news came in the form of a letter from another neurologist at a different hospital.

Dear Dr O'Sullivan

I would appreciate if you could send me any test results that you have for this young lady. She tells me you diagnosed her with focal dystonia and that you gave her botulinum toxin with good results. When I saw her first her dystonia had recurred and she responded well to a further administration of Botox. That improvement was not sustained however. I'm sorry to say that ultimately the dystonic contraction moved to her left arm and is now spreading to her trunk. She seems to be developing a generalised dystonia for which I cannot find a cause. I wonder what you thought when you met her? I am beginning to wonder whether some, if not all, of her problem may be psychological in origin.

It is not unusual for patients who reject the possibility of a psychological component for their symptoms to seek out other medical opinions that seem more palatable. Unfortunately if a treatment works more through its placebo effect than its biological effect the benefits of that treatment are not always sustained. That is not to say I have not wondered many times if the outcome for Shahina could not have been very different if I had managed to communicate my suspicions to her and to her family in a better way.

Over the years I have tried to learn how to temper a patient's response. The manner in which the diagnosis of a psychosomatic condition is delivered is of pivotal importance to what happens next. If the patient feels that they have been told that their symptoms are imaginary they will walk away. It is too often just that which prevents people getting the help that they need and deserve.

Even when a diagnosis of psychosomatic illness is delivered carefully anger is a common response and it is always flagrant. When it comes in the form of a letter it is filled with capital letters and underlining and exclamation marks. Even in the written word the patient is straining to be heard and believed.

Anger has a purpose. It tells others we are not alright. It also has a lot in common with psychosomatic symptoms. It can be misleading because often it is something else in disguise – hurt or fear repackaged. It is easily misinterpreted, both by those who feel the anger and those at the receiving end. And its effect may be detrimental. It is frightening. The person at whom the anger is directed may well be compelled to flee, possibly just when they are most needed. Anger can destroy the relationship between patient and doctor. The doctor escapes or avoids or ends up treating the anger and not the patient.

I have come to accept anger as a stage in a difficult process. An unpleasant truth is being forced out into the open and that does not come without consequences. Anger will often dissipate with time, but there are other defence mechanisms that are far greater barriers to recovery, including denial.

I see Shaun every three to six months. Usually, I wait to hear from him and when I do I send him a clinic appointment. Sometimes he phones me himself to say things are going badly. Other times I get a call from a doctor at another hospital to say he is in the casualty department. Those are the best scenarios; the worst are when I get a letter a week after he has been discharged from an intensive care unit: *this man was admitted in status epilepticus, we have started him on Phenytoin, we understand he is under your care with epilepsy . . .*

Shaun and I had met two years previously. When he fell ill he was a teacher. On the day of his first seizure he was at work. Halfway through the morning he had started to feel unwell. He was nauseated and felt weak and dizzy. A colleague suggested he go home and offered to drive him, but he insisted on driving himself. Shaun lived two miles from the school, and was almost in view of his street when he lost consciousness. He remembered nothing about what happened. He awoke, still seated in the car, which was stalled and half on the pavement. The road was empty of other cars. There were no witnesses.

Shaun saw his doctor who advised him against driving and referred him to a neurologist. With very little information to go on the neurologist did not feel confident that he could say why the blackout had occurred. Tests were arranged. The brain scan was normal. The EEG brainwave test showed some irregularities that were not felt to provide conclusive proof of epilepsy but were sufficient to make the neurologist suspect that diagnosis.

Shortly afterwards Shaun had a second collapse. This one was witnessed by his wife. She reported that Shaun turned deathly pale and collapsed like a rag doll to the floor. Soon this was a regular recurrence. Shaun was started on drugs for epilepsy. At first the drugs helped and Shaun's collapses disappeared for a full month. Everybody was very relieved, feeling sure that an uncertain diagnosis had proven right. But soon the seizures were back and worse than before. By now Shaun shook violently during the attacks, which lasted an increasing length of time. Soon Shaun's wife noticed that he would drift off mid conversation for seconds at a time, and she suspected that he was having other seizures that did not lead to collapse. Shaun was given a second epilepsy drug. Again his seizures disappeared but came back, this time after three weeks. At that point Shaun was referred for video telemetry. During three days in hospital Shaun had multiple convulsions and brief episodes of losing awareness. His wife was by his side every day and was with him when we met and I told him that he did not have epilepsy, he had dissociative seizures.

'It makes no sense,' his wife said.

'The test was conclusive,' I told her.

'If he doesn't have epilepsy, then why did the epilepsy drugs make him better?' she asked, reasonably.

'Drugs can make dissociative seizures better for a variety of reasons; because we desperately want to get better and believe they will make us better; because epilepsy drugs do more than control epilepsy, they can improve mood and make us feel generally better in ourselves.'

'A colleague at work whose child has epilepsy saw one of my seizures and said he was sure it was epilepsy,' Shaun said.

'Dissociative seizures are very easily mistaken for epilepsy. I have the benefit of your test results, so I am absolutely sure about the diagnosis.'

'Can an EEG ever be normal during an epileptic seizure?'

'Not in the sort of seizures you have.'

'So it can be normal in some sorts of epilepsy.'

'It's never normal in convulsions.'

'What sorts of seizures is it normal in, then?'

'I know it is very difficult to be given a change of diagnosis after months of being told that you have epilepsy. I don't want to dismiss these seizures because they have impacted on your life. But there is another perspective. You have lost your driving licence. And your job. You've been on toxic drugs that haven't helped. We know what is wrong with you now. This illness can be cured. It takes time but now we know what's wrong you can be treated and you can get everything you used to have back again.'

Would Shaun be willing to make the sacrifice required to get better? Would he relinquish the diagnosis of epilepsy and take on one that offered a chance for him to recover but was difficult to bear? Shaun agreed to meet the psychiatrist, after which I met him again.

'I've been talking to the other epilepsy patients, they have the exact same symptoms as I do. How can this not be epilepsy?'

I didn't answer, we had been over this before.

'Is it possible that some of my seizures are epilepsy, just not the ones you have seen?'

'How did it go with the psychiatrist?'

'It was fine. She said I'm not depressed but I knew that already.'

The psychiatrist had told me that Shaun was not depressed, nor anxious, but she also told me a story that Shaun had not. A year before his seizures began a teenager at his school had accused Shaun of hitting him. Shaun had pleaded his innocence. The pupil said they were alone when it happened. With no proof to vindicate Shaun he was suspended. An investigation followed taking three months. Shaun could not work during that time. The problem had only resolved itself when a friend of the pupil told another teacher that no assault had occurred. The story had been made up as an act of revenge for some slight that Shaun had committed but could not even remember. Shaun's tearful accuser eventually admitted the truth. Shaun got his job back. His fellow teachers, who had never believed the accusation and had supported him throughout, were jubilant at his return.

'He had three months of humiliation and absolute hell,' the psychiatrist told me. 'He believed he would be prosecuted, he would go to jail, never work again. He couldn't see a way out.'

But now Shaun believed absolutely that he had been through his greatest trial and had put it entirely behind him.

'I don't think he can accept how the accusation affected him and I don't think he's going to accept the diagnosis,' the psychiatrist said.

So far the psychiatrist's assessment was proving right.

'The other neurologist said I have epilepsy,' Shaun said.

'You were sent to me because your doctor was no longer sure about the diagnosis.'

'My first EEG was abnormal. The doctor who reported that EEG said I might have epilepsy.'

'EEG tests are open to interpretation, everybody's are different. It's easy for a small irregularity to be labelled as an abnormality, when really it is just evidence that we are all a little different on the inside just as we are on the outside.'

'Everybody's telling me something different,' Shaun said.

'I have the benefit of seeing your seizures in the video-telemetry unit. The other doctors only had the story to go on.'

'I've read about epilepsy, all my symptoms fit.'

Shaun was not the first and would not be the last to have difficulty believing the diagnosis. We would ride out his confusion together and I would wait to see where we ended up. Shaun stayed in hospital for one further week as his epilepsy drugs were withdrawn. On the day he was due to go home we met again.

'I'm not saying that I agree with you, but I'll do whatever you suggest. It can't do any harm.'

I was pleased.

I left Shaun and his wife with one final instruction: I told them that the seizures might stop after he went home, but they might not. If they continued they were not dangerous, so Shaun's family and friends should avoid calling an ambulance, if they could. Dissociative seizures are fed by the attention they receive.

'So we should do nothing when they happen?' His wife looked worried.

'Never be afraid to call for help if you need it, but it is better if you just let them happen.'

When I met the psychiatrist later I told her of the progress we had made.

'I think he's coming round to the idea,' I said, 'I'm really hopeful that he will do well.'

'I think you're wrong.'

She was right, of course.

In the twenty-first century psychosomatic illness is a socially unacceptable disorder. That was not always the case. There was an era when things were very different, when patients embraced hysteria as a diagnosis. That era was ruled over by Jean-Martin Charcot and it starred Blanche Wittman.

The nineteenth century had seen the birth of spinal irritation and the reflex theory, both of which were purely speculative theories, based on little physiological or anatomical fact. Both gained great popularity, particularly with the rich who could afford to pay for the recommended treatments. However, there were many doctors who still considered hysteria to be a sign of insanity. Hysteria in the poor in particular was still attributed to madness and the poor were consigned to an asylum just as often as they had been one hundred years before. There would be a sharp change in attitudes as a result of the work of Jean-Martin Charcot.

Charcot was one of the most powerful doctors of the nineteenth century and one of the most famous neurologists of all time. Amongst his other achievements he would spend decades trying to understand hysteria. He was the first doctor to subject it to rigorous scientific study. In doing so he would attract great minds to the disorder. He would not find the solution, and everything he believed about hysteria would eventually be discredited, but the attention he brought to the disorder was enough to see it transformed.

Imagine the scene. It is 1887 in Paris. Blanche stands at the front of the auditorium. She is by far the most conspicuous person present. She is the star of the show but she would be conspicuous even if she were not. There are more than thirty people in the room and she is one of only three women present. Even amongst those three Blanche is worthy of attention. Her white blouse is open to reveal her cleavage. Her skin is pure creamy white. Her brown hair, perhaps tied up neatly at the beginning of the day, is now loosened and is giving her a wild appearance. The other two women are nurses. They each wear bonnets tied tightly under their chins. Their tunics are dark in colour, and stiff, and buttoned up into a high collar. Nobody has come to see them, though.

Jean-Martin Charcot stands beside her. He is the most pre-eminent neurologist in Paris and Blanche is his patient. A dim light breaks through the high windows. The light sets Blanche's pale exposed skin in stark contrast to the audience of austere, dark-suited men around her. The men write furiously lest they miss any fragment of what is said. They are keen to see the specifics of what happens next. They have only ever heard the phases of *la grande hystérie* described.

But not all the eager voyeurs are doctors. Charcot's Tuesday lessons have gained such notoriety by now that they have become of interest to all of fashionable Paris. André Brouillet, the artist, bears witness. Charcot's son, Jean-Baptiste, is also in the audience. He is a medical student but in the future he will be better known as an explorer. *Le tout Paris* is present and when the lesson is over the greatest amongst them will be invited to retire to the drawing room of Charcot's home on boulevard Saint-Germain for an evening of more refined entertainment. Blanche will return to the locked hospital ward where she has been resident for eight years.

In the 1800s the Hospice de la Salpêtrière in Paris was an asylum. More than 8,000 patients were incarcerated there, from the lowest sections of society: prostitutes, beggars and the aged poor. Many were deemed mad through venereal disease, others simply mad. It was the least prestigious medical institution in Paris, which is what made it so singularly unexpected when one of Paris's most promising young doctors chose to take a permanent academic position there. In 1863 Charcot chose to dedicate his future to the Salpêtrière. He had seen the possibilities, even if others had not. What Charcot had recognised was that the infirmary created a perfect stable population for scientific study. Charcot had found the ideal environment to employ the new technique called the clinical-anatomical method.

In a time that lacked sophisticated investigations Charcot began to follow disease from its early stages to its very end. He did so by employing the technique of carefully recorded and thorough physical examination. He tracked each patient's progress and rigorously documented what he observed. In an elderly and sick population patients regularly died. When they did it allowed Charcot, who was initially a professor of pathology, to examine them post-mortem. He was then able to correlate what he had seen physically in life with what he found microscopically in death. Charcot was senior physician at the Salpêtrière for over thirty years. In that time and through this method he defined more neurological diseases than any other doctor before or since. Pre-Charcot, the tremor seen in Parkinson's disease could not be differentiated from that seen in multiple sclerosis. But his scrutiny of the patient's clinical condition, combined with his examination of the brain after death, allowed him to distinguish the two. What he discovered allowed doctors to clinically identify many previously poorly understood disorders – motor neurone disease, syphilis and polio amongst many others.

Charcot's detailed scientific study and clinical-anatomical method would change neurology to such a degree that the impact of his discoveries is still felt. Which is precisely why it is so surprising that when it came to hysteria Charcot's theories would prove to be so wrong.

Perhaps it was always inevitable that Charcot would be drawn to hysterical illness. The Salpêtrière housed a large number of hysterics and the majority of doctors working in the asylum were psychiatrists. Having proven its use in other diseases, he soon applied the clinical-anatomical method to hysterics in the Salpêtrière. He renamed their illness *la grande hystérie* and dedicated himself to it.

From the outset Charcot's practice differed from that of other doctors. He did not visit his patients on the ward. They were brought to him in his office. He sat behind his desk like an observer and barely touched the patients, but instead gave instruction. The patient undressed and he watched. His interns reported interminable silences during which he would only stare. Then he would ask the patient to stand or walk or lift an arm and he would stare again. It was likely in a setting such as this that Charcot met Blanche Wittman.

Blanche was admitted to the Salpêtrière in 1878. She was born in poor circumstances. Her mother died when she was young, her father was a carpenter who was institutionalised when Blanche was a child. To support herself Blanche was a laundress, a furrier's apprentice and a nurse. Blanche had her first convulsion at the age of fifteen. It was provoked by a sexual assault made by her employer. At the age of sixteen she was admitted to the Salpêtrière. She would never leave. The story of her life before the Salpêtrière is largely based on rumours, but her life after admission was lived publicly and recorded. She was scrutinised, photographed, painted, written about, studied and never forgotten.

For a decade before Blanche's admission Charcot had carefully documented the features of *la grande hystérie* in the expectation that he would be able to explain it as he had other neurological diseases. He subjected patients to close clinical scrutiny, carefully documenting every clinical sign they displayed. He began to notice distinct similarities. The hallmark of the illness was seizures, and each seizure presented with a very specific pattern that did not vary between individuals. He noticed that seizures were often triggered by trauma, either physical or psychological. These features were each important in the diagnosis but there was another feature that became the hallmark of the condition in his mind. The sufferers had a unique vulnerability to hypnotism and he considered this an important diagnostic feature of the illness.

Every week, on Tuesday and again on a Friday, Charcot gave lectures during which he demonstrated the clinical features of hysteria. He induced hypnosis in his patient. In this state the clinical features of hysteria could be produced and reproduced for any audience. Blanche and others were triggered to convulse as Charcot stood by their side detailing the stages to the astonishment of those watching. He showed the audience the depth of his patient's detachment from their surroundings by asking them to partake in activities to which they would never agree in their fully conscious state. Women undressed or crawled around the room on hands and knees like a dog.

Charcot also experimented with metallotherapy. It was widely believed by patients and doctors that magnets had great powers. Charcot demonstrated that magnets could shift symptoms from one part of the body to another or even from one person to the next. Convulsions could be transferred from the right arm to the left. Even more incredibly an affliction could be taken from one woman and given to the one beside her.

It was not only hypnotism that could be used to produce hysterical attacks. The symptoms could also instantaneously appear just through applying pressure to the ovary. Charcot did not completely disagree with the other theories still in play at the time. He demonstrated that such pressure did not only cause seizures but could also be used to terminate them.

Over many years Charcot carefully detailed and demonstrated the diagnostic manifestations that he considered absolutely typical of hysterical disease; the loss of normal sensation, the restriction of the visual field, headaches, dizziness and, of course, convulsions. But it was not so easy for Charcot to document his hysteria patients all the way to death as he had with other diseases, because hysteria was never fatal. Fortunately, however, the inmates of the Salpêtrière were rarely released, so it was inevitable that hysterics would eventually die for other reasons. When a patient died he could examine their brain for a pathological explanation of their symptoms. He never found one. He examined the ovaries and they too were normal. What is strange is that despite this lack of pathological evidence he held the almost unshakeable conviction that hysteria was an unequivocally organic disease. In the absence of an identifiable brain lesion he noted how stereotyped the disorder was between different patients, every seizure was the same and obeyed the same rules. Madness was rarely so uniform. He noted that sufferers often had a family history of hysteria or had a relative committed to an asylum. He became convinced that hysteria must be an inherited disorder in which *functional* lesions in the brain came and went. He imagined swelling of the brain that disappeared at death and, in doing so, escaped detection.

Hysteria responded to the attention paid to it by Charcot. There was a dramatic increase in cases and in 1890, under Charcot's protection, hysteria had reached epidemic levels in the Salpêtrière. By bringing the scientific study of hysteria to the fore, Charcot created a plague of hysterical seizures that quickly spread to all of France and then throughout Europe. In a single year Charcot alone saw more than 3,000 patients, 800 of whom were diagnosed with hysteria. The late nineteenth century was the age of hysteria. It was created by one man and would prove dependent on him. In 1893, after a thirty-year reign, Charcot died. It took less than one year for Charcot's version of hysteria to follow him. The rate with which the diagnosis was made plummeted and many hysteria patients that had been under his care went into remission. Charcot had made hysteria acceptable, even popular, but he had only succeeded in doing so by strongly reinforcing it as an organic disease of the brain. Others would take the next step, but with that hysteria would lose its acceptability once more.

I planned to meet Shaun again in the outpatient clinic a month after he went home, but circumstances demanded that we met again much sooner than that. Six hours after Shaun was discharged from the neurology ward I received a phone call from another hospital to tell me that he had been admitted there.

Shaun's wife had been driving him home when he had a seizure. She had pulled the car on to the hard shoulder and, when the attack did not show any evidence of stopping, she called an ambulance. Shaun was taken straight to the nearest hospital. The seizure was the longest he had ever had. The doctors in the casualty department had started him on emergency drugs, treating him for status epilepticus, a life-threatening, unrelenting epileptic seizure.

Medicine can be a wonderful career, one in which there are many instantaneous rewards. Then there are times when everything you have done seems to have been for nothing. This was one of those times. I sat imagining the discharge letter tucked into Shaun's pocket, the one that said 'I am happy to say that this man does not have epilepsy, his seizures are non-epileptic, I have stopped all his epilepsy medication.' I wondered if his wife had shown it to the doctors. She probably did, there had never been anything covert in Shaun or his wife's behaviour. So, if they had shown the doctors the letter, the doctors had ignored it.

I rang the junior doctor who was looking after him at his new hospital.

'You know he doesn't have epilepsy,' I told her.

'That's what his wife told us, but his seizure just wasn't stopping. He'd been fitting for over twenty minutes.'

Dissociative seizures are not dangerous, I have seen them last for several hours. Those hours should be spent sitting quietly, reassuringly, with the patient. I understood the casualty doctor's position. Imagine you are watching Shaun convulsing but I have told you not to intervene, how long would you last? In the car his wife had lasted ten minutes. In the casualty department the doctors had lasted twenty.

Shaun was discharged from hospital and I met him one week later in my clinic. His wife reminded me strongly that my instruction to *let him be* during a seizure was of no use whatsoever on the hard shoulder of the motorway. Intervening when psychosomatic symptoms occur perpetuates them, you are paying attention to something that wants attention desperately and that is ill-advised. But that is the advice I give from the safe distance of my office and it is not easy to carry it out in the world. I discussed the diagnosis with Shaun and his wife once again.

'But the doctors in casualty were convinced I had epilepsy,' he said.

'That was probably the only seizure those doctors had seen

in their whole career, Shaun,' I answered. 'They thought they were doing the right thing, they wanted to help you, but what they did was wrong.'

'I need you to explain the whole thing again. Why did the first doctor say I had epilepsy? Why are you dismissing the abnormal EEG? Why did the epilepsy drugs make me better?'

So I explained it again. Later I told the psychiatrist what had happened.

'It's not surprising,' she said. 'Shaun was incredibly proud of his career, it defined him. What happened at work threatened not only his whole life but his view of himself. Now you are threatening that again.'

Since then Shaun has been admitted to another hospital on three further occasions because of seizures, each time receiving epilepsy drugs he didn't need. Shaun and I meet every few months now, and each time our conversation follows a similar thread.

'I accept that my old seizures were not due to epilepsy, but I have a new sort of attack, I'm sure it's epileptic,' he says.

People with epilepsy sometimes develop psychogenic seizures. The mechanism is unknown but I think it is learned behaviour. If you have lived a lifetime of epileptic seizures, then when you are distressed, your body harks back to previous experience and calls on it for an expression of your distress. But there is no reason for somebody with dissociative seizures to develop epilepsy at a later date.

'No, Shaun, it's not epilepsy.'

'No? Okay. My wife found an article in the newspaper about a woman who had a disease called limbic encephalitis. She said it sounded just like me. Have I been tested for that?'

'Limbic encephalitis causes epileptic seizures. We have clear recordings of your seizures and they were not due to epilepsy. You absolutely do not have limbic encephalitis.'

'Have you ever heard of stiff person syndrome? It causes muscle stiffness and my muscles get stiff in my seizures.'

'But your tests were normal, they showed nothing like that.'

'My seizures are no better, do you think I should try more epilepsy drugs anyway? Just in case?'

'You do believe that your seizures are not due to epilepsy, don't you, Shaun?'

'Yes, of course I do.'

I welcome anger in comparison to denial. Anger tells me that the message has been heard, but denial says it has not. Where a diagnosis cannot be clearly demonstrated with positive tests, doubt has room to grow. Where the mechanism of an illness is so poorly understood, questions flourish. To a person struggling against the possibility of a psychological diagnosis, the unknowns create a hiding place. Denial of the diagnosis is far harder to counter than anger and far less likely to end in recovery. It is likely that Shaun's seizures will go on until they are replaced by another expression of distress, another illness.

5

YVONNE

Hear now this, O foolish people, and without understanding;
which have eyes and see not; which have ears and hear not.

Jeremiah 5:21

There is a very famous psychological experiment called the
Selective Attention Test featuring an invisible gorilla. In it an
audience is asked to watch a video of six players passing two
basketballs between them. Three players are dressed in black
and pass a ball to each other. The other players are in white
and they pass the second ball. The audience is asked to concentrate and count only the passes made by those in white. The
audience is motivated. They want to win, to get the answer
right, and so they concentrate. When the video comes to an
end the presenter asks the audience how many passes they have
seen.

'Fifteen!' the audience cries in triumph, pleased with themselves and certain they are right.

'And how many of you saw the gorilla?' the presenter asks.

A small number of hands shoot up but most of the audience
are just confused. What gorilla? What is he talking about?

The presenter plays the video again. This time the audience

are not counting. They are wondering what trick has been played on them. This time they can see it plain as day. The players are running randomly around, deftly passing the ball just as they did before, but there, right in amongst them, is a grown man dressed in a gorilla costume. He doesn't try to hide or run, he stops in the middle of the frame to beat his chest before he strolls away. Those who had not seen him the first time around cannot believe that he was ever there. 'That's not the same video,' one woman says. But it is. The crowd struggles to accept that they have only seen what they cared to see and their minds erased the rest.

The day I first saw the invisible-gorilla experiment my mind immediately went back to a patient I had known for a brief period many years before.

When I met Yvonne I was a nascent doctor. I was in my early twenties and just out of medical school in Dublin. I had yet to encounter the harsh realities of life and in many ways I was still a child. I had learned a lot but had a lot to learn. When it comes to psychosomatic illness there are struggles that doctors and patients share, and Yvonne would teach me a little something about that.

I first heard Yvonne's story from another doctor on a ward round. There were nine of us crammed into a small side room on the ward. We were a mixture of junior doctors, medical students and a nurse, overseen by a neurology consultant. The more junior we were the more we cowered behind others, afraid of being asked a question we couldn't answer. One of my friends, only a year ahead of me in their training, had admitted Yvonne the previous day and detailed for us what he had learned from her.

Yvonne was forty years old and worked in a supermarket. She was stacking shelves one Tuesday when the accident occurred. A row of workers were removing broken packages from the display and pulling the older stock forward so that would sell first. The perishable goods were kept refrigerated behind glass doors and Yvonne was working in that section, moving from fridge to fridge opening each door in turn. Around her other women were doing the same while they chatted and laughed.

Yvonne had almost finished her section. As she stood back from the fridge she was aware of another person on the other side of the glass door she was holding open with her right hand. As she closed the fridge door she automatically turned to face the person. As Yvonne did so her neighbour, not expecting the fridge door to close, released a small spray of window cleaner into the air. Yvonne felt the liquid splatter against her face. She closed her eyes reflexively and raised her hands in defence. At first she cried out in shock but very quickly the cries turned into ones of pain. Yvonne experienced an immediate intense burning in both her eyes and when she tried to open them she found she couldn't. Another colleague quickly led her to the bathroom and washed her eyes with water. When it became apparent that this was not enough to relieve her pain an ambulance was called and Yvonne was driven to her local hospital. In the casualty department a doctor and nurse examined Yvonne and then bathed her eyes carefully. Her husband was called and by the time he arrived at the hospital Yvonne was feeling better. Her eyes were red and full of tears but she could see normally and the pain had lessened. Her husband was allowed to take her home.

Yvonne left her family to fend for themselves and went to bed early that evening. She thought she would be better the next day and so was disappointed to find her eyes were still bloodshot. She prepared breakfast and made the children's lunches with the vague feeling that she could not look directly out of the window into daylight, preferring the darkness of the kitchen.

Usually on a Wednesday Yvonne would leave the house with the children because she did an early shift at work. That day her husband told her she should stay at home. Yvonne had never missed a day of work and was very reluctant to do so now. 'They won't thank you for it,' her husband had said and eventually Yvonne had agreed with him. Over the course of the day Yvonne noticed her vision blurring. By lunchtime, when her husband phoned her to see how she was, she was struggling to make out the numbers on the digital clock. She found herself rubbing her eyes repeatedly. When the family came home that evening they told her she looked tired. One of Yvonne's children offered to cook the family tea while her mother went to bed.

When Yvonne awoke and opened her eyes and everything was black, she thought she must have slept through to the middle of the night. But as she sat up she realised it was an impenetrable sort of darkness, there was no light at all and no shapes. She waited for her eyes to grow accustomed to the dimness and when they didn't she began to panic. She felt the bed beside her and realised her husband wasn't there. She tried to stand and her foot caught on something on the floor. Her heart began to pound in her chest and she felt herself pawing at her eyes as if that would clear them. She cried out for help and she heard the noise of people entering the room and realised she could not see them because she was completely blind.

Yvonne went immediately back to the hospital. The doctor who saw her examined her and bathed her eyes again but it did not give her any relief. Completely unable to see she was admitted for a series of tests. At the end of one week of investigations Yvonne had not recovered any of her vision and doctors said that they could not find a cause for her blindness. That was the beginning of six months of hospital admissions and appointments for Yvonne. They came to nothing. Each doctor told Yvonne that they could find nothing wrong and discharged her to the next doctor in line. As a last resort Yvonne was referred for an assessment by a neurologist. The referral letter made it clear that nobody really believed that Yvonne had a neurological problem but it was the only avenue that had not yet been fully explored. This was enough to make us suspicious before we had even started.

My friend flicked through Yvonne's notes as he told us about her, detailing every normal test and every failed treatment. Aside from Yvonne's symptoms he interjected to tell us how her life had been affected.

'Never went back to work after that and is receiving disability payments.'

Wry smirks were barely suppressed.

'Needs a full-time carer. Cannot do housework or engage in normal daily activities.'

Once we had heard the medical history in detail, we shuffled out of the room and the consultant led us to Yvonne's bedside. Seeing her for the first time I was surprised by how she looked.

Although she was only forty years old, younger than my mother was at the time, she looked so much older. It was hard to know why. It was not her skin, which was clear and unlined. Nor her hair, which was brown, untinged by grey. Was it something in her demeanour then? She was sitting on the bed, a tiny woman, shoulders hunched, her elbows pressed tightly to her sides, fingers intertwined and held in her lap. The belt of a quilted dressing gown was pulled just a little too tightly around her waist. Her blank eyes stared far beyond us. Her husband sat beside the bed. He was loose-limbed, one leg draped over the knee of the other as he reclined in the chair. His arms were folded over an expansive chest. His eyes were vigilant, capturing each one of us as we distributed ourselves around his wife's bed.

The consultant introduced himself and began by reviewing the accuracy of the details of the story we had heard. Yvonne's husband spoke for her, making frequent corrections. 'No it wasn't just window cleaner, it was a bleach-based detergent.' 'Yes, a work colleague had tried to rinse her eyes but had only wiped them with a wet towel. They had not used running water which would have been better.' He told us that he had contacted the company who made the detergent and they had said it could cause nerve damage if it was absorbed by the eye. He would like that documented. I exchanged a small smile with one of the other junior doctors. Yvonne had not been seen by anybody at work who was qualified in first aid, we were told. My friend smiled back.

Then the consultant spoke directly to Yvonne. He asked her if her vision was good enough to distinguish light or dark or to make out shapes. Yvonne answered that she could sometimes tell that a light had been switched on but that was all. To test her the consultant shone a bright torch directly into her eye and asked her if she noticed any change and she answered, perhaps, but she couldn't be sure. At first, as she answered the consultant's questions, Yvonne appeared to stare far to his right, as if she could not even tell where he was in the room. But as the conversation developed her eyes began to dart about, sometimes to his face or towards her husband and then quickly flitting back to a point in the middle distance.

We watched as the consultant worked through his examination. Yvonne's pupils reacted briskly and symmetrically to light just as they should. But when he asked her to follow the light with her eyes she couldn't do it. He took a small rotating handheld drum from his bag. It was painted in alternating black and white stripes and it spun on an axis around the handle. He held the drum in front of Yvonne and spun it quickly. Yvonne's eyes flickered minutely from side to side in response to it, her eyes involuntarily drawn to the spinning stripes.

Next he asked Yvonne to touch the very tips of her index fingers together in mid-air in front of her. Yvonne lifted her arms and brought her hands towards one another at about the level of her chest, both her index fingers pointed. But the left hand went higher than the right and the knuckles of that hand hit against the raised thumb of the other, the pointed fingers missing each other.

We had never seen this asked of a patient before so behind the consultant half of us were now standing with our eyes closed trying to do what Yvonne had failed to do.

In the final stages of the examination, just as the consultant lifted the ophthalmoscope close to Yvonne's eye for the final time, she blinked. I thought I heard a small thrill of a laugh somewhere in the room. Yvonne must have heard it too, as she was startled.

'Is there somebody else here with you?' she asked.

The giggles were less stifled this time.

Once we were outside in the corridor again one person whispered a shared thought.

'When's the court case?'

I was just about to laugh out loud at this but before I did I searched the faces around me for their approval and in doing so caught the expression of my consultant just before he spoke.

'You lot had better hope that poor lady is blind, and deaf too, and that she did not notice how you were behaving in that room. Can we show some maturity in future, please.'

We had enough sense to be just a little scared at that. We quickly straightened our expressions and became very quiet and extra deferential on the ward round from then on. But because we were still nothing more than glorified children we released our laughter when we were having coffee together later.

'We were like a herd of elephants going into that room,' said one, 'how could she not know we were there?!'

'There'll be no Oscars for that performance,' said another.

And we planned what we would do to *catch Yvonne out*. I said that the next time I was in her room I would allow a five-pound note to slowly drift from my pocket and on to the floor and we would wait to see how long it took for her to find it. Someone else planned to scream loudly and point at the window and see what happened. But of course we wouldn't do any of this. We were young people, just out of college, who had seen things that most people never see. In the previous year I had known people younger than me die. We had rushed to help people who were seriously ill and failed. And yet we were not ready yet to understand a different type of suffering.

Yvonne was in the hospital for a week waiting for her tests. It was my job to see her every day and make sure that she knew what was happening. I spent a little longer with her than the other patients because I was interested in her, although I knew that my interest could not always be called honourable. As the week went on the details of her story became clearer to me.

Yvonne spoke warmly of her family and her life, but even if she did not mean to tell it that way, I heard hardship too. She had grown up in rural Ireland. The first half of her life was spent in her parents' home, a loving but also a sheltered place. A place from where a young girl rarely went out alone. At the age of twenty she had married her first boyfriend, Gerald, who was ten years older than her. There was not much of a difference now that she was forty and he fifty, but a great difference then. Within ten months of the wedding she had her first child. By the age of thirty she had six children under the age of ten.

Yvonne had spent most of her adult life devoted to the care of her family. Her husband worked full-time so she alone wrestled with six young children. Yvonne and her husband's roles were well defined. He was the provider and he did his job well. She cared for the children and made a home for the family.

'We are a good team,' she said.

It was only when the oldest children had left home and

the youngest were all in secondary school that Yvonne first experienced what it felt like to have time on your hands. Encouraged by her eldest daughter she decided to take a job in a local supermarket. It was a big step for Yvonne, who was a woman who had spent most of her time alone or with children. She had been in paid employment only once, two years before she married Gerald when she was eighteen years old. Yvonne came from the first generation of her family to have the chance to finish school. She had taken a job working as an office girl at a nearby university. It was the most prestigious job she might have hoped to get and she was very proud of her success.

'I loved the feeling I was off to the office,' Yvonne told me, sounding happy, but then changed her tone as if correcting herself. 'The job was menial I suppose, but because I was working in the college it felt more than that.'

Yvonne had met Gerald at a dance on a rare night out with her friends from work. Within a year they were engaged. Yvonne gave up work straight after the wedding.

'Back then you had to give up work when you married. Besides, Gerald thought my time would be better spent looking after my own family rather than working my fingers to the bone and only helping some stranger fill their own pockets.'

Almost immediately they left Cork and moved to Dublin. Gerald was the youngest child of a large family and he would inherit no part of the family farm or home.

'Gerald was the cleverest, but being the youngest there was no bit of farm left for him. We had to leave,' Yvonne told me.

'You didn't want to leave Cork?'

'No, but it was the right thing to do. Gerald trained as an electrician and now he has his own business and we are more comfortable than we ever would have been had we stayed at home.'

'Dublin is home now, I suppose?'

'I suppose it is.'

When Yvonne decided to apply for a job at the supermarket Gerald had been against the idea. He worried that she would have less time for the family. She assured him that she would only work in school hours and that, when the family got home, they would not even know that she had ever been anywhere but there waiting for them all day long.

The job was simple and unexciting, easily within Yvonne's capabilities. But for all that it lacked in challenges Yvonne quickly learned to love it. It gave her money of her own and a few hours in the outside world. She was a quiet woman who did not find it easy to meet new people. At work she had colleagues and regular customers that she came to know. She relaxed in their company and began to enjoy herself. She made sure she kept up with things at home and life for the family continued much as it had before. Gerald grumbled occasionally but she gave him no grounds for real complaint. Things were going well for Yvonne, until the accident.

During Yvonne's stay in hospital I saw her children visit in the evenings, usually the older ones who no longer lived at home. The youngest ones visited only once accompanied by an older brother.

'I'm only in for a week. It's not that long,' Yvonne said. 'And sure am I not useless to them now in any case?'

'Is Gerald visiting today?' I occasionally asked. I had not seen him since the day of our first meeting.

'Gerald is run off his feet with the business,' she said, 'he built it from scratch and he doesn't like to leave things unsupervised.'

One day I saw a girl I took to be an older daughter sitting by Yvonne's bed reading the newspaper to her. I was writing notes on the ward and I could not help watching them together. It was a touching picture, the girl sat attentively, poured her mother's tea, adjusted the radio and nurse call button so that they were more readily in reach. They kissed affectionately when the girl finally stood to leave. Yvonne's hand lingered on the girl's arm as she pulled away.

For a few moments after the girl had left Yvonne sat quietly on her bed staring straight ahead. I was looking down at my notes as I wrote when a movement from Yvonne caught my eye. She had turned to the right and with her hand she reached mindlessly for a tissue whose corner was just sticking out of a box on the far side of her locker. How deftly she had done it, no feeling about, no hesitation. As soon as I saw it I had an impulse to laugh again, to go and tell my friends what I had seen the blind woman do, but then I realised she was crying and so I thought again.

Over the week, Yvonne came to recognise my voice and step, and greeted me warmly when I called to see her. I noticed a gradual but definite change in how Yvonne connected to me when we spoke. On the first day she had stared over my shoulder just as she had with my consultant, as if she could hear my voice but not locate it. But as the days went by I noticed increasingly that when she spoke Yvonne looked me in the eye. When she did so it was more than just a simple glance; I felt our eyes connect.

At the end of the week I joined the consultant to see her on the ward round. Gerald was with her again. Yvonne had undergone several more tests of her eyesight and each one had been normal.

The consultant told her the news and Gerald shook his head and muttered 'Not again,' then asked more loudly, 'Has every possible test been done?'

Yvonne had not yet had her last scan. There was a waiting list for everything and she was not deemed to be the most in need. The consultant suggested that Yvonne could go home and have that final test done as an outpatient. It would mean that she would wait longer to have the test done but at least, while she waited, she would be at home and with her family.

'Sure I'm no use at home like this. I'll stay for the test,' Yvonne said quietly.

Yvonne often talked about her children, how proud she was of them, how dreadfully she missed them. There are some patients for whom hospital provides company and support. That is particularly the case for those who live alone. For some, going home can be difficult. Yvonne did not seem like one of those people to me. But now she was turning down the chance to go home. She had surprised me.

Yvonne stayed in hospital for a full further week before all her investigations had been completed and we had the results to give her. On the day that she was to be discharged Gerald was with her again as the consultant gave her the final results.

The integrity of Yvonne's visual pathway was intact, her brain was normal and we could not find any neurological cause for her problem. The only possible explanation left for her loss of sight was functional blindness, caused by stress.

'My wife hasn't had a day of stress in her life. You're talking nonsense,' Gerald replied.

It was explained again that all the avenues had been explored more than once and that there was no other possible explanation, that it would be best to take the advice that they had been given if Yvonne wanted to get better. Yvonne had taken to staring into the middle distance again. The conversation ended with a reluctant agreement that Yvonne would meet a psychiatrist; if only 'to prove us wrong' as her husband put it.

After we walked away from Yvonne's bed I told the consultant that Yvonne had begun to look straight at me when I entered the ward. One day she had smiled and acknowledged my presence even before I had spoken to identify myself.

'Whatever else you do, give people the benefit of the doubt. The moment you say to that woman that you think she can see you have lost her,' was the advice I received.

When I returned to the ward to give Yvonne her discharge letter I felt impossibly confused. Had I been told to disbelieve her blindness but avoid confronting her? Or should I disbelieve myself and what I thought I knew?

Yvonne was alone by her bed when I entered the ward. I said goodbye and handed her a letter for her doctor.

'I have something for you,' she said as I was moving to leave. She handed me a card.

The picture on the front was of a flower-filled field overlooked by a single dominating tree. It was drawn in coloured pencil. The words inside the card said thank you, it was nice to have somebody to chat to every day.

'I made the card,' Yvonne said.

'You made it!' I could not keep the surprise from my voice.

'Yes, I borrowed the pencils and the paper from the woman in the bed next to me,' Yvonne replied.

Even with my consultant's warning ringing in my ears I heard myself say, 'But if you can't see how could you draw a picture?'

'I can feel the pencil marks on the paper,' she answered. She did not seem in the least affronted.

Gerald appeared then, picked up his wife's things and led her from the room on his arm. As they walked away I looked at the picture again. The leaves of the tree were green, the bark brown, the field was scattered with purple and yellow flowers. Not a single outline was broken, nor was there a single leaf or flower out of place.

One of the greatest challenges for most doctors is the struggle to believe in the truly subconscious nature of their patients' psychosomatic symptoms. If I cannot believe that then I am calling every patient I see a liar, whether I say it aloud or not. As soon as a patient is given the diagnosis, this is their first concern. *They think I'm doing it on purpose.* To believe in the subconscious nature of the symptoms is difficult but absolutely necessary for both patient and doctor.

Pierre Janet was a French philosopher and psychologist who was pivotal in the development of the concept we refer to as the subconscious. He was a protégé of Charcot, he learned from his master but also influenced him. For the majority of his career Charcot had asserted that hysteria was unequivocally an organic disease. Only in the very latter part of his life did Charcot begin to consider that his assertions about hysteria were wrong, that he had not found a pathological disease at post-mortem because there was no disease to find, that there might be a psychological cause for hysteria. His change of heart was said to be in part due to the work of Pierre Janet.

In the 1880s Janet was a young professor working in the Lyceum at Le Havre. He studied the techniques of Charcot, in particular his use of hypnotism. In the 1890s Janet moved to Paris to study medicine and began to spend as much time as possible at the Salpêtrière. Charcot admired the work of Janet. Shortly before his death Charcot opened an experimental psychology ward and offered Janet a small laboratory so that he could develop his research. Only weeks after their collaboration began Charcot passed away, but Janet was already in place at the Salpêtrière.

The death of Charcot and the work of Janet were turning points for hysteria. Almost immediately after Charcot's death his detractors found their voice. Those neurologists who had always secretly disagreed with Charcot rounded on his organic paradigm for hysteria, pointing out the lack of pathological evidence and the ludicrousness of hypnotism as proof of an organic disease. Several scientific papers were published to that effect. Quickly the world stopped viewing hysteria as a neurological disease and started seeing it as a psychological illness born in the mind.

Janet's work at the Salpêtrière would result in some of the

key concepts that still influence how we think about hysteria today, the most important and lasting of which were his delineation of the concepts of the subconscious and dissociation. Janet described consciousness as those sensory experiences and thoughts of which we are actively aware, those that are currently receiving our attention. He described consciousness as expanding and contracting, allowing things to move in and out of our field of awareness. He thought our consciousness could choose what we perceived and what we ignored. To understand Janet's idea, think of the chair you are sitting on. When you pay attention you can feel every contour of it against your body. Everything your skin touches produces a sensation. But our mind dismisses most of this as unnecessary noise and only pays attention to the things that seem important. Imagine that one moment you are aware of a sound and the next you are not. Further to this, Janet suggested that a neglected sensation could be lost from consciousness, not just transiently but absolutely and completely. In this way a person might completely lose the feeling in a limb because the mind was ignoring it. In extreme situations the field of consciousness could retract to such a degree that it could render a person catatonic – in a state of unresponsive mental stupor, unaware of anything.

Janet described the subconscious as the place where everything that one has learned and experienced is hiding, a place to store information that is not immediately available to the conscious mind. He proposed that consciousness existed in parallel with the subconscious and that each could be entirely unaware of the other. He demonstrated this through the use of hypnosis. Under hypnosis patients lost conscious awareness and their subconscious became suggestible. He showed that in the hypnotic state paralysis could be induced in the patient just through an idea. On waking the subconscious retained the idea that had been planted there but the conscious self was unaware of it. This observation was later used in abreaction – suggestions to influence recovery were sown under hypnosis, and unbeknownst to the patient those suggestions were retained by the subconscious when the patient awoke. It is also the basis for hypnosis as a source of entertainment as it is used today.

Janet went on to theorise that a split or separation could occur between the different parts of the mind, thus depriving a person of conscious awareness of reality. Memories and feelings could exist in parallel parts of the mind, neither knowing of the other. This he referred to as dissociation. Dissociation, he said, occurs when feelings, thoughts or memories become disconnected from one another. Janet believed that the split arose as a result of trauma. A psychological trauma caused the secrets of the subconscious to slink away so that they were no longer available to their owner.

On Janet's model, where two states of mind can exist but one doesn't know about the other, it would be possible for Yvonne both to see and be unaware of seeing at the same time. But it is a difficult concept to grasp. It is an idea for which there is no proof and on which there is still no consensus. When I am faced with a difficulty understanding how the subconscious can hide things in this way I look to everyday life for supporting evidence and I often find it. Have you ever had a cheating partner? The deception goes on for months undetected, but as soon as it is revealed you realise that you had known all along.

You had seen the receipts, heard the late-night phone calls, but had consigned your unwanted suspicions to your subconscious until forced to face them. We hide unwanted thoughts from ourselves all the time. And some of us dissociate occasionally, but only briefly. You cannot find your wallet. Eventually it turns up in your briefcase but you are absolutely convinced that you didn't leave it there. You take the train, sooner than anticipated you arrive at your destination and realise that you recall very little about the journey. You are watching the news and suddenly you have lost the gist of it and don't know what the presenter is talking about.

Our minds are constantly choosing what to perceive and what to ignore. You do not have to have participated in the invisible-gorilla experiment to recall a time when you stared right at something but didn't see it. Looking for a friend in a crowd, say. They are right in front of you, waving, but somehow you look right past them as if they weren't even there. 'You *must* have seen me. You looked right at me!' they say afterwards. But you didn't. For a moment, your mind employed selective attention and blocked something from your view.

Janet's idea accounts only for negative symptoms, lost sensation or lost memories, but the mind can do more than keep sensations and feelings from us – it can produce sensations from nowhere just as easily as it can hide them from view. I remember a time when I was invited to the home of an elderly friend of mine. As soon as I crossed his threshold a wave of odour hit me, a slap of wet dog directly in the face. The front door opened on to a single reception room littered with old newspapers and other detritus, in the kitchen the worktops were scattered with unwashed crockery. Two dogs sat on the sofa. My friend nudged the dogs from it and I was invited to sit.

Even now I can feel vividly the discomfort I felt that afternoon. My imagination was attributing life to that sofa that it did not contain. My skin was so invaded by itching that when my friend left the room for a moment I had to stand and shake out my clothes looking for imaginary insects. Even when I went home I could not escape the feeling of a thousand flea bites. Only when I had washed my clothes and showered did I feel any relief.

There were no insects in the sofa, nothing was crawling on my skin, nothing was nipping me. But the itch and tickle felt absolutely real. My mind had produced real physical sensations triggered only by an idea. Even with the evidence of my eyes that saw no fleas I simply couldn't shake the imaginary feeling of being bitten. And even though it was years ago, and all in my mind, I am experiencing it all over again now just through remembering it.

More than anything else it is through my experiences working with patients with dissociative seizures that I find the most compelling evidence for the subconscious nature of the illness. The behaviour of dissociative seizures scream of it.

I have seen the same pattern with dissociative seizures time and again. A patient suffers a series of seizures before we meet, maybe five or ten in a six-month period. That amounts to less than one hour spent in a seizure in six months' worth of hours. Then I meet the patient for the first time in the outpatient clinic and they collapse in front of me, or in the waiting room. I arrange for them to have an EEG and they collapse during the test. When a patient has a typical seizure during the EEG it is always a relief because it means that I can make an incontrovertible diagnosis. But could it possibly be only good luck that the patient collapsed at that moment, just when it mattered most?

Even when dissociative seizures occur rarely in a person's daily life they will often appear on the day of a hospital appointment. It is an odd coincidence for a person who has rare seizures to suffer a seizure during the brief time they spend with me, but that is exactly what happens. Patients with epileptic seizures do not typically have an attack in the clinic or during their tests. But it is a feature of dissociative seizures that they have a very high chance of happening right at the moment that the patient is at the hospital. The odds cannot support this as a chance occurrence.

In the first instance when a patient collapses right in front of you it is tempting to see it as a deliberate cry for attention. Or even an ill-judged attempt to impress you and to fool the system. At the beginning of my career I struggled to see it as anything but a conscious act by the patient. Deserving of sympathy, even so, but done with intent. It took time for me to realise how little sense my judgement made. When a patient has an EEG they understand its purpose, it is fully explained to them. Why would a person straining to deceive or attempting to engender sympathy collapse just then, just at the moment that they are guaranteed to be *found out*?

Imagine for a moment that you want to impress a new friend by telling them that you are an expert at playing the guitar. By wonderful coincidence they have a guitar somewhere nearby and would love to hear you play. Unless you believe absolutely that your claim is true you will be very reluctant to agree. To collapse in the epilepsy clinic in front of the epilepsy specialist doctor or in the EEG department is an act of innocence, not one of manipulation. It is a cry to be understood that comes directly from the subconscious. If a patient simply described their seizures to me but never let me see one, I could never prove the diagnosis.

To my mind, the very manner in which patients with psychosomatic illness pursue a diagnosis provides the most compelling evidence for the subconscious nature of the illness. When Matthew looked for a cause of his paralysis he did so exhaustively. Yvonne had subjected herself to the most minute scrutiny in the hope of finding an explanation for her loss of sight. Pauline had the same tests again and again because she could not believe that no organic disease had been found. A person who is feigning illness has no need of such a search. If I am *pretending* to be ill, the sophistication of modern medicine becomes a threat to me, and it was no threat to Yvonne or Matthew or Pauline. They could not stop their search because they were looking for something that they were certain was there.

I believe in and accept the unconscious, uncontrollable nature of a psychosomatic disability. But many in the medical community struggle with the notion as much as any other person does. As it is the doctor's job to allay the patient's fears and dispel any confusion about the diagnosis, a problem arises if the doctor is not convinced.

Shortly after I became a consultant I attended a paediatric epilepsy training course that I hoped would broaden my experience of diagnosing seizures in children. One session of the course was interactive. In a small group we were asked to watch videos of children having seizures and we were called upon individually to offer our diagnosis based on the video alone. Most of the other professionals there were not specifically trained in epilepsy as I was. What's more I was already regularly working in the field of diagnosing seizures from video recordings, although usually with adults, so I knew that I was likely to be more experienced than the rest of the group. For that reason I avoided offering the diagnosis too quickly.

Near the end of the session we were shown a video of a girl of about fourteen years old having a convulsion. It was not at all unlike the sort of seizures suffered by adults so I did not think the diagnosis presented much of a challenge. The doctor running the session went from person to person in the room asking for opinions on the cause of the seizure.

'Frontal lobe seizure.'

'Tonic-clonic seizure.'

I was at the end of the row so answered last. I was the only doctor to say that I thought the seizure was dissociative. I was asked to give my reasons and I gave them.

With unconcealed venom another member of the group turned to me and said, 'No way is that child faking her seizures.'

And there we have a problem. Whether I was right or wrong in my diagnosis, if that doctor thinks dissociative symptoms are faked how would he ever present that diagnosis to the patient in a palatable way? Or worse, how often would he miss the diagnosis? His words came from compassion for the child so could he ever make such a difficult call if, in his heart, he considers it such a damning judgement?

These days I'm more likely to be the teacher at such a session and I hit on the same problem all the time. Doctors are scared to make the diagnosis.

'What if it's wrong? Wouldn't it be better to treat the patient for epilepsy just in case?'

The mistake of offering a patient an organic diagnosis *just in case* has led to many people suffering lifelong seizures with no abatement. It happens for a number of reasons. Doctors are frightened to face the almost inevitable anger that will occur when a psychosomatic illness is mentioned. But protecting the patient from that upset is not in their interest in the long term if they are being denied a diagnosis. Also doctors worry about calling a symptom psychological and discovering later that there was an organic cause after all. Calling an organic problem functional is a mistake that is guaranteed to engender anger in a patient and their relatives, and can lead to a lawsuit.

In 1965 an eminent British psychiatrist called Eliot Slater published a paper in the *British Medical Journal* in which he described a ten-year follow-up study of a series of patients diagnosed with hysteria. He reported that over twenty-five per cent were ultimately found to have an organic disease that had not been detected at the time of their first diagnosis. He went on to say 'the diagnosis of hysteria is a disguise for ignorance and a fertile source of clinical error. It is in fact not only a delusion but a snare.' This paper influenced many doctors to stop making a diagnosis of conversion disorder. It played on their worst fears.

I doubt many of my contemporaries in medicine have read this paper but the attitude it portrayed lives on in them instinctively. Contrary to what many patients believe, doctors worry all the time that they might be wrong, particularly in this field. They worry that a new scientific study will prove every diagnosis of psychosomatic disorder to be incorrect in the future. So they avoid the diagnosis, refuse to acknowledge it and fail to see the harm that stance does. But in the fifty years that have passed since Slater published his paper there have been numerous similar studies, none of which are in agreement with his findings. His study is widely agreed to be flawed and modern technology has also helped to guarantee a more sound diagnosis in the twenty-first century. Equally eminent psychiatrists have shown that in a modern era, *where the diagnosis of conversion disorder is made in a sound manner*, the likelihood of an organic disease eventually coming to light is low. Only four per cent will later be demonstrated to have an alternative diagnosis – this is the same misdiagnosis rate as many diseases where there is not a single diagnostic test. So the diagnosis is correct ninety-six per cent of the time, but still doctors shy away from it.

Missing an organic disease – putting the patient's life in danger and often leading to guilt and self-doubt in the doctor – is the mistake most feared by the medical profession, but it is not necessarily always the worst one. It is quite common for psychosomatic illness to find itself incorrectly labelled as organic in the first instance. Doctors and patients often find it the more palatable option, even when incorrect. But the harm that can come from this sort of error is often underestimated. It can be immeasurable.

Firstly, there is a face-saving internal struggle involved before a patient can move away from an organic diagnosis to a psychological one, and often that struggle is just too hard and the patient simply cannot accept the new diagnosis. The longer a person carries the wrong diagnosis the worse the prognosis becomes. Once somebody has been given an organic explanation for their symptoms the chances of recovery quickly fall. Many studies have shown that if somebody is told, in error, that their seizures are due to epilepsy before the correct diagnosis of dissociative seizures is made, then the chances of becoming seizure-free immediately lessens. This may be because the original misdiagnosis delayed the true diagnosis, and we know that the longer people live with dissociative seizures the less likely they are to be cured. Or it may be a product of what a patient has come to believe. If somebody has been told they have epilepsy and has been allowed to believe that they have a serious, potentially life-threatening brain disease, then this belief alone may be so enmeshed in their mind that it affects their ability to recover. If you believe that you could never run a marathon, then you'll probably never try.

The prognosis for any stress-induced symptom also worsens as soon as the symptom has been attributed to an organic cause. Say, for instance, that somebody with neck pain is found to have wear and tear in their spine on an X-ray. Any middle-aged adult might have this same finding on an X-ray just as part of ageing, but if the patient attributes their pain to it, rather than due to muscle tension or stress, they are much less likely ever to be completely free of pain.

And an incorrect diagnosis of organic disease has other implications. It might lead to toxic unnecessary treatment. It might lead a person to make unnecessary life changes to accommodate the disease. But most importantly, the wrong diagnosis will deny the person the correct treatment.

The reluctance to offer a psychosomatic diagnosis is not always so noble as a fear of missing a disease or a reluctance to upset the patient. There are still a lot of medical professionals who believe that psychogenic paralysis is faked paralysis, and that the patient could walk if they wanted to. Or that psychogenic convulsions are deliberate and within the patient's conscious control. In previous centuries, when people were less likely to censor their thoughts and actions, patients suffered the harshest treatment as a result of this attitude. In the nineteenth century one doctor was fond of subjecting patients with psychogenic convulsions to treatment with enemas. He was certain that a patient could not concentrate on both retaining an enema and deliberately convulsing at the same time. Another doctor locked patients in his office and refused to release them until they stood and walked.

These days doctors who hold those views largely do so behind their patients' backs. Largely but not entirely. I have encountered patients who have been confronted with accusations of faking. It is difficult to evaluate their accounts, however, because how a diagnosis of a psychosomatic illness is received is not always how it was meant. I am sure that some patients have been told to 'snap out of it' just as they report. This damning judgement does far more harm than just the superficial hurt it causes. It alienates the patient and feeds the attitudes that are at the heart of the stigma this diagnosis carries.

If the reality is that doctors struggle with the concept of psychogenesis every bit as much as the patients do, and psychosomatic disorders are a mere footnote in a doctor's training, it's hardly surprising it's such a mess. And this isn't helped by cases that feed the uncertainties surrounding these disorders.

Judith had been referred to me with epilepsy. Her doctor's referral letter told me that she had recovered from leukaemia and he wondered if her epilepsy was a late complication of that disease. Judith told me about her medical history.

She was born in England but in her early teen years her whole family had moved to live in Miami for her father's work. She had lived there for six months when she fell ill. It began with unexplained bruises. The first doctor she saw dismissed her. Children fall over and bruise, it's just what they do. But when a chest infection simply would not go away, a series of blood tests revealed the worst. Judith's blood counts were dangerously abnormal. A bone-marrow biopsy revealed that she had acute leukaemia. Judith underwent a series of unpleasant tests that led to a course of chemotherapy. Her hair fell out. Her brain was irradiated and chemotherapy was injected into her spinal fluid to ensure that the cancer had not spread to her nervous system. Her immune system was so suppressed by her treatment that she developed recurrent infections. She became dangerously underweight. She required isolation in hospital for long periods of time. After the treatment Judith went into remission but within three months the cancer had returned. Her only hope was to undergo a bone-marrow transplant. Finally Judith had some luck, as it turned out her older sister was a perfect match.

Judith told me how her parents had taken her and her sister to Disney World as their treat before she went to hospital for the final chemotherapy that would prepare her for her transplant. That whole day she moved between the feeling that this was both the best and the worst day of her life. She was doing something normal for once and yet it did not feel normal at all.

'I wasn't well enough to be there,' she said, 'it felt sort of cruel.'

'It was really great that your sister could be your donor.'

'That didn't feel right either. It felt like I owed her something. But I was a child with cancer and I didn't feel like being grateful.' Judith's voice was monotone, deadpan even.

She spent much of the following weeks in the complete isolation required during a bone-marrow transplant. On the rare occasions that her family could sit in the same room with her they were covered head to toe in the gowns and masks that protected Judith from the outside world.

But it did not last for ever. Eventually Judith's blood cell counts began to recover. First she was allowed out of her isolation room and in time she could go home. She still lived with restrictions. She could not go to crowded places in case she contracted an infection. Her mother cooked all her food, ensuring that her meals were prepared in the most hygienic environment possible. Judith stared from her bedroom window at the children playing basketball and eating pizza in their neighbour's yard and longed for an imperfect day at Disney World.

All of this happened twelve years before Judith and I first met. A lot had changed since then. Judith's family had moved back to England. Judith sat her A levels and eventually left home to go to college. She moved to London and got a job in childcare. Then one day, as she was playing with a toddler under her care, she abruptly collapsed. An ambulance was called and when Judith awoke she was in hospital.

'Hospitals are so familiar to me that it almost felt like I had woken up at home,' Judith told me.

Both Judith and her new doctors felt sure that the seizure must have been a consequence of the brain irradiation that she had undergone to treat her leukaemia. She was started on epilepsy drugs and discharged home. The seizures continued unrelentingly and she was referred to my epilepsy clinic.

As a junior doctor I spent six months working with a haematology team. I saw many patients suffer in just the way that Judith had described. So often the patients were young; several have stuck in my mind. Why, then, did Judith's account of her cancer ordeal fail to move me? I knew why. It was because I did not believe her. All the facts were there but something was missing. What was it? Was the recital just that, a prepared performance? I could not pin down my suspicions. There were certainly some things that did not make sense, but was there enough for me to consider my patient a fantasist, or worse, a liar? Why didn't Judith bring any old medical notes with her? People with complicated medical problems often bring copies of previous doctors' letters and tests and prescriptions but Judith had come empty-handed. And where were her parents? Judith was a twenty-six-year-old adult so there was no reason for her to be accompanied, but parents who have seen their child through a life-threatening illness like leukaemia are usually not far away.

I found myself testing the details of what she had told me.

What antibiotics did you take after your transplant? Correct answer.

Where was the site of your bone-marrow biopsies? Correct again.

Do you remember the type of transplant you had? Autologous? Allogeneic? Right answer.

I felt shame as I quizzed her but I needed to know. If the story of the leukaemia was not true, then why tell it?

What was the name of the hospital where you had your transplant?

'Miami General Hospital.'

It did not sound right. I would check it later.

'What was your doctor's name in case I need to contact him or her?'

'Dr Marrow.'

Dr Marrow!

That was impossibly ridiculous, surely? But then again, maybe not. There was a very famous neurologist called Lord Brain, so why not? Perhaps Dr Marrow had a sense of humour when it came to career choices.

With only this strangely named doctor to go on I admonished myself. Perhaps if you meet enough people who have suffered, your heart hardens, and a girl who tells her story frankly and without sufficient emotion becomes a liar. I shrugged off my remaining questions as cynical and unnecessary and asked Judith to sit on the couch so that I could examine her. Her neurological examination was entirely normal but that is often the case even in people who suffer with the severest epilepsy.

Just before Judith hopped down from the couch I checked one more thing.

'Where was your Hickman catheter sited, Judith?' asking about the central line implanted in every leukaemia sufferer to allow chemotherapy and drugs to be administered.

Judith did not skip a beat, she pulled up her T-shirt and pointed to a small freckle just below her right breast. Not a scar, just a freckle, and not even close to the spot where a central line should be placed. This was the first question that she had not answered completely correctly. But she was only a child when she was sick and it was a long time ago.

Next I asked Judith to sit forward so that I could look at the skin on her back. It was a perfect English alabaster and in the place where I would have expected her repeated bone-marrow biopsies to have taken place it was smooth and white and entirely lacking in scars. How does someone come through such an illness without a blemish? Is that even possible?

When I was finished I told Judith I would admit her to hospital to witness her seizures. I had no proof that anything I suspected was right. I could not even justify my doubts if pressed. But I owed her a fair and open-minded hearing. Even so as soon as she left the clinic I found myself tapping 'Miami General Hospital' into the computer and there it was, just as she had said.

A few weeks later Judith was admitted to the neurology ward for tests. I had not managed to get all of Judith's previous medical history. I had confirmed that Miami General had a haematology department, but when I rang there was no Dr Marrow. I thought I heard the girl on the other end of the phone giggle when I asked. Maybe he or she has moved on, she said politely. But when I pressed, I discovered that the hospital did not look after cancer patients, and nor did it carry out bone-marrow transplants. And there was no record of any patient by Judith's name.

'Judith, I have contacted Miami General Hospital and they do not have any records for you. Do you have any of your old hospital letters?'

'No.'

'When I rang the hospital they said they don't carry out bone-marrow transplants. Do you think you could be mistaken about the name of the hospital?'

'Maybe.'

'Do you think your parents might be able to help?'

'I suppose they could.'

'Could I ring your mum or dad to get more details?'

'No, they are both at work. They can't take phone calls.'

'Can you ask them for us?'

'Okay but they might not remember.'

'That's okay, anything at all would help.'

Judith was admitted to the video-telemetry unit for monitoring overnight. Whatever the truth of her past medical history, her seizures required explanation. The following morning the ward staff told me that they had found Judith lying on the ground the previous evening. The nurse was with another patient at the time and nobody knew exactly what had happened. Judith had injured her hand and had needed to be taken to the X-ray department to look for evidence of a fracture. Thankfully there was none.

I scrolled through the video to find the point of the collapse. The nurses had found Judith on the floor at a quarter past nine. For most of the evening Judith had sat on her bed, flicking through a magazine, watching television. Shortly after nine I watched as she stood up and walked towards the door. The electrodes that were attached with glue to her head allowed her to go just to the threshold of her room but no further. She stood there for a while, looking about, and then gently closed the door. From there, Judith turned and crossed the room again until she was on the far side of her bed. I was horrified to watch what she did next. Judith shook her right hand loosely for a moment at the level of her shoulder and then she struck it roughly against the wall. She winced in pain. I shared her pain for a moment, feeling the need to comfort my own hand. Then Judith did it three more times, and winced again. Then she placed herself gently down on the floor, pulling a plate from her table so that it landed with a loud clatter beside her. A few seconds later a nurse threw open the door and came in. Judith could not be roused.

Suddenly all of the compassion and sympathy that Judith had failed to evoke in me with the story of leukaemia came flooding in. I was touched by the colossal innocence of the act. It was no secret that she was there to be watched. The video camera was set clearly in the wall, not hidden. How could she expect that we wouldn't see? But, then again, perhaps that was the point. Some part of her wanted to be seen. What had Judith suffered that this was the only means she had to ask for help?

Every psychosomatic sufferer fears they will be accused of doing just what Judith had done, lying and deliberately injuring themselves just for the attention that it will bring. They are hurt by the comparison. But for a patient to consciously fake illness is rare. There are always rumours, the woman who put blood in her own urine to convince people that she had a serious kidney disease, the man who rubbed dirt into his wound to cause a deliberate infection. But most doctors will see such behaviour only once or twice in their careers, if at all. And yet somehow the shadow of those who deceive hangs over every person who is deemed to have a physical illness that does not have an organic cause.

Perhaps the longest shadow of them all belonged to Karl Friedrich von Munchausen, the 'Baron of Lies' who gave his name to the syndrome. Munchausen's syndrome is now more correctly called factitious disorder. It refers to those who manufacture or imitate illness for medical attention. It is not done for financial gain, disability payments or compensation, it is done for the care and attention that illness brings. The behaviour of the patients can attract judgement very easily. Or mirth. The seriousness of it is often underestimated. Munchausen's sufferers can expose themselves to life-threatening operations, amputations, unnecessary medications and toxic treatments. And in the background their ordinary lives are destroyed by their pursuit of a certain sort of attention. And most will flee as soon as they are detected so they will never get help. Even those who make it to the psychiatrist are rarely able to recover fully. It is the worst sort of life-destroying medical problem.

Fortunately it is rare. I work with a large number of people who suffer with conversion disorders, which means I might be expected to happen upon Munchausen's more often than most, and yet I have only seen this condition three times of which I am aware. Judith was the third.

My first I encountered as a very junior doctor. She was a woman who had presented to hospital with a headache and a dilated pupil. On a neurology ward a patient with a single fixed dilated pupil can cause great concern. And it did. When scans were normal we were initially flummoxed. Until, that is, a nurse walked into an unlocked bathroom to find the patient self-administering dilating eye drops into the offending eye.

Five years later I met number two. There was nothing especially unusual about Joan at first. She had unexplained collapses. They could be epileptic seizures but nobody was quite sure. The usual range of investigations were normal so she was admitted for observation. Her first blackout in the unit occurred as she sat in bed watching television. The second occurred as she sat in a chair. On each occasion she became deathly pale and slipped limply into a lying position, either in her bed or on the floor. Watching the video and seeing the brain tracing, it looked as if Joan had simply fainted. There were no signs of epilepsy. But healthy young women don't just faint while sitting relaxed in bed, so what on earth was wrong?

The technician I work with saw it before I did.

'What is she doing with that handkerchief?' he said.

We zoomed the picture in on Joan's face and replayed the video. Once we saw it we could not believe that we had not noticed it before. You don't notice what you don't expect to see. Joan took the hanky out of her pocket and appeared to wipe her nose, or so we had thought. But magnified on the screen we could clearly see the small vial that the handkerchief contained. With one hand Joan unscrewed a cap and took a deep sniff. She returned the handkerchief-wrapped vial to her pocket and sat back. Within seconds she became pale and lost consciousness.

Joan absconded from the hospital as soon as we raised our suspicions with her. It was not possible to confirm what was in the vial but it was easy to guess. Vials of just this size are commonly used for amyl nitrite. This is a drug which, when used recreationally in inhaled form, causes a brief high. It has the unfortunate side effect that it lowers blood pressure and can cause the user to faint.

It is tempting to metaphorically point and laugh when one is faced with a factitious disorder – until one realises that those who suffer in this way can do themselves and others such great harm, and they rarely recover. I never knew what motivated Judith. Like Joan, she fled the hospital as soon as I confronted her. She was never seen by the psychiatrist and I never heard from her again. I always wondered where she got the story of leukaemia. It had been so full of accurate detail, more than could be learned from a book. I wondered if parts of what she had told me were true. Some factitious-disorder sufferers have been exposed to illness in childhood. I thought of the trip to Disney World that Judith had told me about in such specific detail. It was the most unnecessary part of her story. I thought of the sister who featured so heavily in that tale and for whom Judith carried such strong resentment. Was it possible that Judith's story was in fact almost entirely true, except that it was not her own?

People lie to or mislead their doctor for different reasons. Scott had something in common with Judith but what he hoped to gain through illness was distinctly different.

Scott worked in a warehouse until his medical problems began. Much of his work was manual, heavy lifting, fixing light machinery. For this reason when he developed pain in his back his life very quickly fell apart. He was the main support for his family. He gave money to his ex-wife to contribute to the care of their three children. He lived with his girlfriend, Debbie, and her two children. Debbie worked in a school canteen but neither Scott nor Debbie earned a lot of money, so if either couldn't work, they quickly felt the pinch.

Scott began to notice the pain after a particularly gruelling few days at work. He took a few days off and stayed in bed waiting to get better. When he returned to work the pain didn't seem quite so bad but Scott felt that the days in bed had left him weaker than before. Heavy lifting seemed twice the burden it had been. Over the following month the pain came and went. Scott began to complain of difficulty climbing ladders. He took a further week off work and saw his doctor who prescribed painkillers and sent him to a physiotherapist. When Scott returned to work again he found heavy lifting almost impossible. He told me he could lift with his arms, but not his legs. His supervisor changed his work so that Scott drove the forklift truck and only needed to carry small loads. For six months this continued. Scott got better but always briefly and always followed by a significant decline. He took erratic weeks off work until his boss began to lose patience with him. A tribunal at work threatened Scott with the sack if his sickness record did not improve. The threat didn't matter much to Scott because within two weeks he developed rapidly increasing weakness in his legs which left him with no choice but to leave work completely.

Over the course of one year Scott lost all power in his legs. He was completely paralysed below the waist, confined to a wheelchair and entirely dependent on the people around him. Debbie had to stop work. They had to give up the home they had lived in for ten years and were rehoused in a ground-floor flat in an area they didn't know. The children had to move school.

I met Scott after he had taken the usual journey from doctor to doctor with some saying that they could find no explanation for his paralysis and some saying they felt it had a psychological cause. Scott navigated his way into the clinic room in an electric wheelchair, his legs covered by a blanket. Debbie was at his side. He did not seem happy to be there. He let me know from the outset that he would not tolerate a doctor who simply told him all the same things he had been told before. As he recounted his story and as I looked through his test results I feared I would be just such a doctor.

When it came to examining Scott I found that his legs were so entirely paralysed that there was no question of moving him from his chair to the examining couch. So instead, Debbie helped me to remove Scott's shoes and socks and roll up his trouser legs so that I could examine him in his chair.

'How do you manage all of this at home?' I asked.

'We manage,' Scott replied.

I stood back and looked at Scott's legs. That is what you are taught in medical school, always look first. Scott's muscles were of normal bulk and I could see nothing out of place. But there should have been, I thought. I bent to move Scott's legs. He had no pain but no feeling either. His legs moved freely and were a heavy weight in my hands.

'Do you have physiotherapy?' I asked.

'I do that for him,' Debbie answered. Debbie was now Scott's full-time carer.

When I asked Scott to move his legs, even if only very slightly, he could not produce any movement at all. When I tested the feeling in Scott's legs he could feel nothing. I applied pressure to his toenail, looking for a pain response or withdrawal of some kind, but he didn't move. When I had completed the examination Debbie and I began to roll down his trouser legs again.

'Debbie will do that,' Scott said.

'Thanks,' I said and turned back to my desk. As I sat down Debbie was awkwardly pulling Scott's right sock on to his dangling foot. Had I imagined something? Had Scott lifted his leg slightly or had Debbie lifted it for him? I put my head down again to write my notes but during another upwards glance I became more certain that Scott had moved his leg, more than once.

All of Scott's clinical findings and tests spoke of only one thing: functional leg weakness. If Scott had moved his leg it did not alter the seriousness of his disability. Perhaps his weakness was not as impenetrable as he thought but that should not detract from the disability he was experiencing.

I told Scott that if he wished I would repeat some of his tests but that I thought it likely that I would come to the same conclusion as the other doctors.

'Do you belicve I'm paralysed?' Scott asked me.

'Yes, I do.'

'Well, what's the point in repeating the tests? Why don't you bloody doctors just admit you don't know what's wrong with me?'

Scott left the consultation that day dissatisfied and with a parting promise that he would never return. I told him that if he changed his mind I would be happy to meet with him again. He spoke as if he meant it, and it was entirely likely that Scott and I would never have laid eyes on one another again had I not been in a rush to get home that day.

Almost as soon as the clinic was finished I gathered my belongings to leave. My car was in a car park ten minutes away from the main hospital building. I walked quickly and soon I was convinced I could see Scott and Debbie in front of me. Scott was propelling himself in his chair and Debbie was walking beside him. I had almost caught up with them when Scott stopped beside a large black people carrier. Debbie walked around to the passenger side and climbed into the front seat. The electric rear door slid open on the driver's side. I was nearly at the car when Scott stood up. He picked up his wheelchair, lifted it into the back of the car and climbed into the driver's seat. As I drew level with the car Scott turned his head and looked at me. Through the closed window he mouthed an expletive and I walked away.

Scott is one of the ones who are not so innocent. They are the smallest in number but somehow they colour every other person in the group. That is the shame of it. Scott is the only one of my patients that I could ever confidently refer to as a malingerer and yet many conversion-disorder sufferers will find themselves lightly, or heavily, tarred with this suspicion.

Conversion disorders, factitious disorders and malingering are three distinct groups. The first two constitute disabling illness, the last does not. Conversion disorders are subconsciously generated, and the patient is mystified to discover that no organic disease has been found. In a factitious disorder the affected person has an awareness of the lies they are telling but they do so out of a need for a certain kind of support and attention. Often they are unaware of their own motivation and cannot control their own behaviour. Malingering, however, is quite different. It is a deliberate feigning of illness for financial gain, to win a court case, to avoid conscription. Malingering is illegal and often requires prosecution rather than medical intervention.

And yet is it quite as simple as that? The *Diagnostic and Statistical Manual* (*DSM*) does not consider malingering to be a medical diagnosis. Sufferers are not referred for medical help once they are discovered. But are all sufferers the same?

Imagine a woman who has fled a war-torn country where she has known every sort of assault and has lost her family. She flees to England and seeks asylum. Facing possible deportation she fakes an illness so that she cannot be sent home.

Imagine a man who slips on a wet floor in a supermarket. He pretends to be paralysed so that he can sue a rich corporation for a large amount of money.

Imagine a man who grew up with a single neglectful parent, a parent who didn't work but lived off allowances and taught their child nothing about how to make their own way in life. When the child grows up he uses illness to avoid work, just as his parent had.

Are all of these people exactly alike and do they all deserve our contempt and equally so?

I am often asked how I spot the malingerers and I answer that I don't even try. I always make the assumption that my patient's suffering is genuine and do not make any attempt to prove otherwise. For some people that stance is difficult. They imagine that comedy sketch where the paralysed man jumps up and dances a jig every time their carer's back is turned. It is possible that some of my patients have had the satisfaction of feeling they have fooled the system, but it is better to miss those rare few than to alienate and demean the rest. I have seen enough patients with conversion disorders to know how damaging an accusation of faking can be and to know which mistake I do not want to make.

I wrote to Scott's doctor and told him what I had seen. He wrote back to say that Scott was in the process of suing his employer, claiming an injury sustained at work had caused his paralysis. In time I received a request from a group of solicitors asking for Scott's medical notes. I sent the notes which included the letter telling Scott's GP that I had seen him not only walk, but do so easily and lift a heavy wheelchair and drive. I received no information about the outcome of the case but it is unlikely that Scott fared well. And yet I still hesitate over Scott. He and I did not see eye to eye when we met and I have a low opinion of his behaviour, but was there more to know? Scott had worked hard for many years. He had not had many opportunities in life. He supported two families. Scott had chosen the wrong way out of his situation but perhaps he had a reason. Perhaps if we knew what motivated him we could learn to understand why he did what he did. Perhaps we would condemn him anyway, but perhaps not.

Malingering and factitious disorders are rare. And the truth is that, even without trying, they are usually easy to spot. The behaviour of those patients is often different to conversion-disorder patients. Innocent or not, if a patient is aware of their own deceit it makes them evasive. Their stories do not ring so true. They fail to turn up for tests, they cancel hospital admissions. They are not on the relentless pursuit for truth that Yvonne was on.

I had wondered if I would see Yvonne again. If a patient is going to resist the diagnosis of a conversion disorder they do not always come back to clinic either. They might go to see another doctor in the hope of getting a different diagnosis. Or some choose to live with their disability. Or some get slowly better and put the illness behind them and call it unexplained. I hoped Yvonne would come back. Her disability was so complete, her life so torn apart, that I could not see that she could continue as she was.

A few weeks after her discharge from hospital Yvonne came to the outpatient clinic. Her daughter brought her in a wheelchair. At home she walked around unaided and her children helped her when they could, but in unfamiliar places she needed more than this. Her daughter told me that Yvonne refused to learn to use a stick for the blind.

'I think she feels that if she uses aids for the blind it means admitting she won't get better,' she said.

'Maybe that's not a bad thing,' I said. 'It means she has hope.'

We had found no physical reason for Yvonne's blindness so there was hope, and I was glad that Yvonne had not given up.

'She has agreed to see the psychiatrist although she has reservations . . . my father has reservations,' her daughter said.

I noticed not for the first time that people seemed to feel the need to speak for Yvonne.

I told them I would arrange the psychiatry assessment and asked if she had anything to ask or say. Yvonne said no and the consultation was over. As her daughter propelled her out of the office Yvonne held her hand out in my direction and I took it in mine.

'If I don't get better I'm no use. Please do whatever you can.'

'I believe you will get better,' was all I could think to say.

I thought our meeting was over and the door was open for them to leave. But as so often happens, the thing that somebody really came to say is left till last and even then only offered reluctantly. On this day it came from Yvonne's daughter. Just as they crossed the threshold she turned back and her words came in a hurry.

'If she tells the psychiatrist that everything is alright at home she's lying.'

I was shocked, not so much by the news, but by the manner of its delivery.

'Maire—' Yvonne said, grabbing her daughter's hand.

'That's all I'm saying,' her daughter said and pulled away from her mother's grasp. And then they were gone.

I did not see Yvonne again after that, but her daughter's words stayed with me. What little I would learn later would come in correspondence from the psychiatrist. These letters were factual, plainly written but always slightly cagey, as they have to be. You cannot put the most intimate details of a person's life into a letter. If a thought that has never been spoken comes out for the first time it is not right to make it permanent by recording it in black and white for anyone to see.

The first letter began with the details of Yvonne's medical

history and a summary of investigations before discussing more personal details of her life:

> Yvonne married at the age of twenty. She stated that she was very happy to be married although it did come with some sacrifices for her, first her job and later her home town. Her husband Gerald, who has very traditional values, had been strongly opposed to her continuing to work and keen to start a family straight away. Yvonne had reservations about having children at such a young age but when her first child, Maire, was born they bonded well. The rapidity of the subsequent pregnancies were dictated by Gerald. Yvonne stated that she 'had difficulty saying no to Gerald'.
>
> Since her husband worked long hours Yvonne brought the children up largely alone but felt great self-worth in doing so and describes herself as having an excellent relationship with each of her children. Gerald was a good supporter of the family and Yvonne regards herself as comfortably off. She is very proud of each of the children but saddened at the partial estrangement of Maire, who has fallen out with her father.
>
> Yvonne states that she has a happy marriage although other statements suggest that this is dependent on her giving way to Gerald's opinion. Yvonne's supermarket job was a great source of tension in the home and partially responsible for Maire's fractured relationship with her father. Gerald felt the job was demeaning and unnecessary whilst Maire encouraged Yvonne to take the position.

Yvonne's accident at work had resulted in an argument at home. Gerald had been called away from work to come to the hospital to collect his wife. When he learned what happened he had insisted that she resign from her job instantly. Yvonne, whose vision was not affected in the immediate aftermath of the incident, tried to plead otherwise. Gerald had phoned Yvonne's employer and offered her resignation on his wife's behalf. Later that evening the argument had become moot when Yvonne discovered she had lost her vision.

The letter went on to state that Yvonne had great difficulty accepting the functional basis for her blindness but was willing to do anything possible if there was any hope of recovery. She was struggling at home, unable to do any of her usual work. Gerald had hired a housekeeper who did all the housework and helped with the children but would not take responsibility for Yvonne. This left Yvonne feeling both superfluous and frightened in her own home.

At the end of the consultation with the psychiatrist Yvonne agreed to an admission to the psychiatric ward for intensive rehabilitation and talking therapy.

The second letter came months later:

Yvonne has now been discharged after a four-week in-patient stay. There was some controversy as to where she would stay after discharge. In the first instance she planned to return to her family home but it was ultimately decided that she would be best placed with her daughter,

Maire, until her recovery is more complete. She seems to have benefited from both occupational and cognitive behavioural therapy. Her vision is partially restored and she plans to continue therapy as an outpatient. We will continue to meet with her and let you know the outcome.

And then the third and last.

I am happy to let you know that Yvonne's vision has returned to normal. She has engaged well with treatment although both she and her husband still struggle a little to accept the diagnosis in full. She has recently moved back to the family home and reports that things are going well and she is getting great pleasure from being with the younger children again. So much so that she has decided it would not be right to return to work.

Yvonne has crossed my mind several times since then and when I think of her it is often with the thought that I did her a disservice. I liked Yvonne. I felt sorry for her. But I did not believe that she was blind. Over the many years since I have watched patients just like Yvonne set out on a desperate search for an explanation for their physical symptoms, having every test twice in the certainty that one would finally give the answer. It took meeting those people for me to realise that I had been wrong about Yvonne.

I remember the first time I saw the invisible-gorilla experiment shown at a conference. I did not see the gorilla. My mind had simply discarded it. What amazed me was that I had not

174

blocked out something meaningless and trivial, only paying attention to the thing that interested me. I had seen the trivial and instead discarded something so flagrant and incongruous that it was a struggle for me to believe it had ever really been there.

I was a fool to question Yvonne's motives and insight because she had, suspecting or unsuspecting, answered my question on the day she was discharged from hospital. Yvonne had told me how things were when she handed me the card she had made. A woman who wishes to lie and fake and fool wears dark glasses and carries a cane and stumbles about. That woman certainly does not draw a picture. Yvonne's drawing was not evidence of guilt but of innocence and, at the moment that she handed it to me, it was I who could not see.

6

ALICE

The colours of the chameleon are not more numerous and inconstant than the varieties of the hypochondriac and hysteric disease.

Robert Whytt, *On Nervous, Hypochondriac, or Hysteric Diseases* (1764)

Most diseases politely restrict themselves to a finite number of symptoms. Heart disease largely appears as just what it is: chest pain or palpitations. People recognise the symptoms and seek the help of a cardiologist. Of course, occasionally it is sneaky and only causes fluid overload and ankle swelling with no chest-related symptoms at all. But for the most part many cardio-logical, respiratory, neurological and other organ diseases obey quite strict criteria of rules, with the greatest variation being not in the type of the symptoms, but in the severity.

There are diseases, however, whose pattern is so varied that they are easy to underestimate when you first encounter them. Autoimmune disorders, such as lupus, can manifest in myriad ways, maybe as a skin rash, or a joint pain, or just fatigue. Lupus affects multiple organs so it may produce a mixture of confusing signs that make it difficult to diagnose. As a result some patients may see a variety of specialists before their medical diagnosis is discovered.

But even compared to the most aggressive multi-system disease, psychosomatic disorders are noteworthy for how little respect they have for any single part of the body. No bodily function is spared or ignored. And how easily and quickly these disorders flit from one place to another, like little rodents evading capture. Just as one psychosomatic symptom is discovered it disappears and, watch out, there is another emerging somewhere else.

As we have seen, the ancient Greeks thought that the uterus wandered about the body causing symptoms. The wandering womb was called 'an animal within an animal'. It was imagined that the womb might leave the pelvis and lodge itself in the throat causing an inability to swallow. The next day it might move to the stomach and cause pain and vomiting. And, however wrong this view might have been, there are elements of the description that are recognisable. But it is not an animal or an organ that wanders, it is sadness. And it is looking for a way out.

Alice's story began with cancer.

At the age of twenty-four Alice had found a lump. She felt it just in the upper edge of her left breast next to her armpit. She first noticed it when she was in the shower before work and, as soon as her hand happened upon it, her heart immediately filled with terrible memories and feelings of dread. She did not go to work that day and instead made an appointment to see her doctor. Her doctor respected her fears and made an urgent referral to the breast-cancer clinic.

One week later Alice was sitting in the outpatient waiting room an hour early for her appointment. She was alone. She did not want to worry her family until she was sure that there was something to worry about. The consultant who saw her was kind and listened to Alice carefully. When the consultant examined Alice she said she could not feel any definite lump and it was possible that there was nothing there at all. Alice was both relieved and worried by what had been said. If there was no lump this was very good news. On the other hand Alice was sure she had felt something and didn't want to be dismissed. She felt better when the consultant arranged for her to have a mammogram and an ultrasound. That way they could both be certain.

On the day of her tests Alice once again turned up an hour early. When Alice was called in for her tests, the middle-aged radiographer remarked, 'Oh, you're a bit younger than my usual customers.' The radiographer chatted about weather and transport strikes as she placed Alice's breast in the machine for screening. A radiologist joined them as the ultrasound was done and the room became quiet. When the tests were completed Alice was asked to wait outside. Had she imagined a change in the radiographer's tone?

Twenty minutes later Alice was called into the consultant's office.

'We have found a lump, Alice, and I think we should act quickly to find out exactly what it is, so I would like to biopsy it here and now.'

'It's cancer isn't it?'

'Let's not jump the gun.'

The result of Alice's needle biopsy came back one week later and her certainty that she had breast cancer was confirmed. The consultant told her that she would need both an operation and chemotherapy but that first she would need a series of tests to assess the extent of the cancer.

After leaving the hospital Alice telephoned work and said she would not be in that day and it was possible she may need to take some time off in the future. She then went to a ticket office in London and bought a ticket to see the stage musical *A Chorus Line*.

'I can't quite explain why I did that,' she would tell me later. 'I got this idea in my head that I could die at any moment and that I would hate to die not having seen a proper musical on the stage. There were two middle-aged women in the seats in front of me and before the play started I could hear them talking about their holidays and their husbands and what they'd had for lunch. I had an urge to scream at them, to tell them to keep quiet but then the show started and for a couple of hours I pushed the diagnosis to the back of my mind. I keep thinking what an odd thing it was to do, to go see a musical at just that moment.'

Alice told her family and close friends about her diagnosis in a series of telephone calls over the course of a week. Her only sister, who lived in Australia, wanted to fly to England as soon as she heard the news. Alice said she would need her more in the future when she was recovering from her operation so she should not come until then. Alice's father insisted that Alice move home immediately from her bedsit in central London, so that she would not be alone. She loved her independence but knew she would need help so she packed a bag and moved to her family home that evening, more for her family than for herself. Then she had only to wait.

Over the next week Alice went to work as usual, only telling her immediate manager what was wrong. She saw no value in sitting at home thinking about her diagnosis. Over the course of the week appointment letters arrived informing her of the dates and times of her tests. The next seven days were spent travelling to and from the hospital, her father always by her side.

Approximately two weeks after she had learned of the cancer, before she had received any treatment, Alice developed severe headaches. For a day or two she tried to ignore them, attributing them to stress. But soon the pain had become so bad that she could barely go to work. She went to see her GP who contacted Alice's breast-cancer doctor at the hospital. When they heard her story she was admitted to hospital as a matter of urgency. There was great concern that the cancer might have spread to Alice's brain. As soon as she arrived at the hospital she had a brain scan. To everybody's great relief the first scan was normal. Alice was reassured by that but it did not help her headache, which was every bit as severe. She was scheduled for a second, more sensitive type of scan. Thankfully that too was clear. Next she underwent a lumbar puncture to look at her spinal fluid for more covert signs of cancer spread. No cancer cells were found. The headache got no better. For the next week Alice could barely get out of her hospital bed. Nobody could explain her headache and painkillers were of little use. A decision was made to expedite the rest of Alice's tests and proceed directly to surgery.

A week later Alice underwent the operation to remove her left breast. Her sister, who could not be held off any longer, was there to watch her being wheeled off to the operating theatre. She was also there when Alice woke up and discovered that for the first time in a week she had no trace of headache. The surgeon came to visit Alice at the end of the day and let her know that the operation had gone very well and Alice could be hopeful of a speedy recovery.

That night, despite her relief that the operation was behind her and delight that she was headache-free, Alice slept fitfully. Sometime around midnight, when the ward was quiet and all the other patients appeared to be asleep, Alice began to experience a pain in her chest. At first it was an annoying discomfort but soon it became an intense burning, worse than any pain she had ever experienced in her life. It hurt to breathe. Soon she felt as if she might suffocate, as if each breath was so shallow that it could not sustain her. When she could bear it no longer she pressed the button to call the nurse. The nurse took one look at the stricken Alice and called one of the doctors. The first thing he did was send Alice for a chest X-ray. It was clear. A heart tracing and blood tests were also entirely normal. Alice was given morphine to stem the pain. That made her drowsy but also made her breathing feel worse than before. Eventually the nurse removed Alice's bandages to check the wound and found it to be clean and the stitches intact. Nobody could think what else to do and all night the nurse sat by Alice's bed to ensure that she was safe. In the morning the consultant saw Alice but could not find an explanation for the pain. A further volley of investigations followed. Nothing abnormal was found.

In time, despite the lack of explanation, Alice felt a little better and was eventually allowed home.

After two weeks, chemotherapy began. Alice was advised that none of her tests had shown any spread of the cancer but, given her young age, chemotherapy would give her the best chance of a cure. Alice's sister stayed in London for the first two weeks to give support. In time, however, she had to return to Australia where she had a job and family of her own. Approximately one week after that, Alice began to notice a burning sensation in her arm. It was most obvious when she was in bed and trying to fall asleep. The burning became more and more unpleasant. When she tested her fingers she found them numb despite the pain. Soon she wondered if her hand was also clumsy. Then one day she woke to find her left arm was completely paralysed. Alice woke her father who brought her straight back to the hospital.

The oncologist arranged for Alice to have more scans, first of her brain and, finding that normal once again, then of the nerves in her shoulder. They were also clear. A neurologist was called, who examined Alice and arranged electrical studies to check the integrity of her nerves, to see what was happening to the messages that should be passing between Alice's brain and her arm, telling her to move. Alice also had a second lumbar puncture. Nothing was amiss on either test. The arm weakness could not be explained.

The following morning Alice was in the X-ray department having yet another scan when she collapsed to the ground and lost consciousness. Stricken staff struggled to cope as she lay on the floor deeply unconscious and convulsing. It was only later that I would meet Alice, and together with her try to make sense of her range of symptoms.

With such an array of possible ways for psychological distress to show itself, I often find myself wondering why this way in this patient and not another? Sometimes I think I know the answer to that question and sometimes I don't. With Alice, I didn't know but hoped to find out in time. Mary, on the other hand, never accepted her diagnosis and, while I thought the cause was obvious, she did not.

'I'm only telling you because if I don't somebody else will,' Mary said. 'My husband is on remand for abusing a child.'

Mary sat throughout our consultation with her eyes tightly closed. That was why she was being seen. Two weeks previously Mary had noticed that she had an irresistible desire to close her eyes. She found herself blinking repeatedly until she was only comfortable when her eyes were fully closed. Gradually she found that she could barely open them at all. For a while she could pry her eyelids apart with her fingers but always with difficulty. Eventually even that became impossible.

'And do you know what the worst of it is?' she said. 'It was his own sister that called the police. Who does that sort of thing to their own family?'

'Do you think your husband's situation might be important? Is that why you're telling me?' I asked.

'I'm telling you because I can't be like this while John's in prison. There's nobody but me and him to look after the girls.'

'How many children do you have?'

'Two girls. Fourteen and eleven.'

Mary suffered with blepharospasm, a movement disorder which manifests as spasm of the muscles around the eye causing involuntary eye closure. It is a condition for which there is no objective diagnostic test. An electrical study on the affected muscles will show that they are overactive but does not easily distinguish muscle spasm that has a psychogenic or emotional cause from that which is due to a brain disease. In fact, when blepharospasm has an organic cause, tests are often normal, which means that even if you suspect it, it is difficult to make a bold statement that the problem is purely due to stress. However, there may be clues to the diagnosis in how the symptoms behave. For example, when there is an organic cause it is usually possible for the sufferer to open their eyes at least a little. Mary could not open her eyes at all, so even if she had not told me about her life, I would have suspected that her problem was stress-related. I told Mary what I thought and I suggested that she see the psychiatrist. Mary blankly refused. She told me that she did not believe me and, besides, who would look after the children while she was dallying about with a psychiatrist? She needed to be better *today*, she said. A decision was made to treat her with a muscle relaxant so she was given diazepam. And it worked. She began to get better and in two days she was well enough to go home.

But all that diazepam had done was to mask Mary's symptoms. The underlying problem had not been addressed. So the little wandering animal was on the move again and Mary was readmitted to hospital only one month later. A neighbour had brought her in. She was found wandering in the street wearing only a nightgown. Mary did not recall ever meeting me before, as she had lost her memory.

The blepharospasm had disappeared and in its place she had a dense amnesia about all the events of her life. She could not remember her name or how many children she had. She could not remember where she grew up or what jobs she had done. She needed to be told what she liked and what she disliked. All her sense of personal identity had been lost.

'Who is with the children?' I asked her.

Mary looked blankly and her neighbour answered. 'They are with mine at home. Her husband got out of prison last week and he's not allowed to be alone with the girls until the trial is over.'

Mary was confined to hospital once again. Her children visited her and taught her what sort of food she liked. They told her about her life.

'They seem like nice girls,' she said after they left.

I tested her memory. I showed Mary pictures and asked her to name what she saw. When I showed her a picture of a horse she told me she could not remember the word but she wondered if it was 'daffodil'. When I showed her a picture of an apple she said, 'I know that one. The girls told me that I like those. It's an apple,' and she smiled at her triumph. When I asked her about her childhood she could not answer any of my questions.

Next I showed Mary a series of pictures of famous people. I asked her if she knew who they were and then I asked her if she knew if the person in the picture was dead or alive. Mary got every 'dead or alive' question wrong. Of course it is almost impossible to get every question wrong like that. Chance alone would see her be correct fifty per cent of the time.

I was forced to tell Mary that her brain scan and EEG were normal, but also the pattern of her memory loss did not fit with any neurological disease. I told her that I suspected stress was contributing to her problem. For the second time Mary rejected my suggestion out of hand. This time after Mary was discharged she did not come back, but she left me with a feeling that I could not shake. My head was filled with thoughts of the things that Mary could not bear to look upon, and the things that Mary could not tolerate to remember.

Psychosomatic illnesses, like their ancestor hysteria, have been likened to a chameleon: every time medicine tries to pin them down they become something different. Hysterical convulsions have long been the quintessential symptom of hysteria. They have waxed and waned in their prominence but have always been, and still are, a well-described manifestation of psychological distress. But they are far from its only manifestation.

Almost any function of the body can be affected in almost any way. One day a woman loses speech entirely and the next day she speaks in the voice of a child. Or a man cannot remember who he is, how to button his shirt or brush his hair. He greets his wife as he would a stranger. A girl feels a lump in her throat and becomes convinced that she cannot swallow. A limb gains a life of its own and begins to wander erratically as if it does not belong to its body. Eyes close involuntarily and no amount of coaxing or prising will open them. A boy repeatedly drops to the ground; every time he stands, he falls. History has seen every one of these things described.

Even within a single individual the possible clinical presentations are protean, sometimes changing slowly over years but other times over days or hours or even minutes. But why does one patient become paralysed and the next suffer stomach pain? Many have tried to answer that question, the most noteworthy of whom were perhaps Sigmund Freud and Josef Breuer.

Freud was another disciple of Charcot and a contemporary of Janet. Charcot would inspire Freud's interest in hysteria and hypnosis. Janet's concept of dissociation and the subconscious would lead Freud to his own understanding of the disorder.

Freud qualified as a doctor in 1881 in Austria. Most know him as a psychoanalyst, but his early work was as a zoologist, neuro-anatomist and pathologist. Then in late 1885 he moved to Paris for five months to study at the Salpêtrière and this experience would change his future irrevocably. Although his stay in Paris was brief, the effect of what he learned would be lasting. In a letter to his fiancée, Martha, Freud wrote of his experience, 'Charcot, who is one of the greatest physicians and a man whose common sense borders on genius, is simply wrecking all of my aims and opinions. I sometimes come out of his lectures as from Notre Dame, with an entirely new idea of perfection.'

Freud left Charcot's tutelage intent on pursuing an under-standing of hysteria. He had been particularly inspired by Charcot's use of hypnosis and his idea that trauma could act as a trigger for hysteria. He quickly developed a close working relationship with fellow Austrian physician Josef Breuer, who shared a similar interest.

Much of what happened next was inspired by Josef Breuer and his long-term patient Bertha Pappenheim.

Bertha had fallen ill in 1880 when she was twenty-one years old. She was an intelligent girl who grew up in a society that was not stimulating for women. She escaped the banality of her existence through a vivid imaginary life. She was also a kind and caring girl and when her father fell ill in 1880 she became his principal carer. It was soon after that her own medical problems developed.

The first symptoms were innocuous: she became weak and stopped eating, but this was easily attributable to lost sleep and long hours spent looking after her father. But soon her symptoms evolved. She became violently disgusted just by the sight of food. At the same time she acquired an insatiable thirst but could not stand to drink a glass of water. Her next affliction began as a simple cough, but one which became chronic and for which no physical explanation could be found. Her illness was soon following a familiar route: bizarre impossible symptoms flitting from one part of the body to another but never explained. Her right arm became contorted and useless. Her legs followed. She suffered double vision and loss of vision. Her speech was affected – at first she had difficulty speaking, but then she became entirely mute. When she did eventually start to speak again she had lost her native tongue of German and only spoke in English.

Over a period of years Breuer had been employing a novel approach in his care of Bertha. The mainstay of the treatment was an exhaustive combination of hypnosis, and talking. He hypnotised her so that she entered a state of suggestibility during which they talked about her symptoms and in so doing traced them back to their source. Together they discovered that if she could identify the moment that a particular symptom arose and then relive it under hypnosis, that symptom would be relieved.

In one example, under hypnosis Bertha suddenly recalled an unpleasant memory from her past that she seemed to associate with her aversion to water. She had a maidservant who she did not like and who had a dog. One day Bertha found the dog drinking from a glass of water. The sight so disgusted her that, from then on, whenever she saw a glass of water a similar disgust arose within her, even though the memory of the original incident had been suppressed. As soon as this memory was uncovered, Bertha's repulsion for water was cured.

Freud combined the ideas of Charcot, Janet and Breuer. He surmised that trauma, particularly if it occurred when a person was in a hypnoid, daydreaming state, could lead to the repression of feelings and memories. This was at the core of his idea of how hysterical symptoms were generated, and it was a psychological rather than an organic process. He agreed with Janet that there was a splitting of consciousness, a dissociation, but in his opinion the unwanted thought had been forcibly consigned to the unconscious so the patient became entirely unaware of its existence. It was a more dynamic process than the person having passively forgotten. He thought that hysterics had in fact actively rejected the unwanted memory. Then Freud began to apply Breuer's method of conversation under hypnosis in the treatment of his own patients. He surmised that psychological trauma could lead to psychical excitation, and that that very excitation, with no other outlet, could then be converted to a physical complaint. Hysteria had become a *conversion disorder*.

In 1895 Freud's and Breuer's experience with this new form of treatment was published in their shared text, *Studies in Hysteria*. The book contained five case histories of which Bertha's was the first, published under the name Anna O. It was she who suggested that the treatment should be named the 'talking cure'.

In *Studies* Freud and Breuer suggested several mechanisms for the manner in which a specific symptom might take hold of a particular person at a particular time. Amongst their speculative theories was the idea of symbolism. For example, if a woman were to experience an insult as if it were a slap in the face, and the negative emotion was not appropriately purged, that might lead to the symptom of severe facial pain. In the same way a woman who swallows unkind words, or a truth that she is not permitted to say, might find herself unable to speak. Alternatively she might be afflicted with the feeling of something stuck in her throat. Symbolic hysterical symptoms thus bore a direct, but subconscious, relationship to the insult that had caused them.

Sometimes the symptom was not a symbol but rather was linked in some way to a painful memory. So, if a person was eating at the moment that some sadness or trauma struck, food might become associated with negative feelings. The mere sight of food might thus trigger psychosomatic nausea and vomiting or an inability to eat.

What was important in Breuer's and Freud's theory was that the triggering incident or insult had usually been entirely forgotten, having been replaced by the physical symptoms. In *Studies in Hysteria* Breuer wrote 'hysterics suffered for the most part from reminiscences'. To Freud and Breuer hysteria was an unbearable memory or feeling made palatable by its conversion to a somatic complaint. To treat the patient it was necessary to uncover the lost memories. To do this they experimented with hypnosis. They followed their patient's illnesses back to their source and found that once the trigger for the symptoms had re-entered the realm of conscious recollection, catharsis could be found. It was a painstakingly slow process, events were followed chronologically backwards and any missed trauma would mean that the cure would only be transient.

More than one hundred years have passed since *Studies in Hysteria* was written. Those years have seen much criticism of Freudian theory. Freud would abandon both hypnotism and his seduction theory, to be replaced with free association and the Oedipal theory. Freud and Breuer would eventually distance themselves from each other and from some of the ideas put forward in *Studies*. Over time many of the hysteria patients that Freud and Breuer had declared successfully treated would prove to relapse. Bertha Pappenheim's symptoms had resolved at the end of Breuer's account of her treatment in *Studies*, but she later relapsed and spent many years institutionalised. Eventually Freud would abandon hysteria altogether and turn his attention to neurosis.

However, for all the shortcomings in the concepts proposed by Freud and Breuer in *Studies*, the twenty-first century has brought no great advances to a better understanding of the mechanism for this disorder. The terms dissociation and conversion are still widely in use, sometimes interchangeably, sometimes as more of a nod in the direction of the history of these disorders than a real intent to identify a mechanism.

The latest version of the *DSM* uses the term dissociation to describe psychological symptoms in which there is an unaccounted loss of contact with surroundings. This might manifest as a sense of 'derealisation', a feeling of unreality, or as a loss of a feeling of personal identity. This manifestation of a dissociative disorder is usually seen by a psychiatrist. To the neurologist, dissociation may present as dizziness, forgetfulness, memory loss or loss of consciousness. The concept is still considered to be a potential mechanism in the development of psychogenic convulsions, which is why they are often referred to as dissociative seizures. Many neurologists and psychiatrists regard dissociation as specifically implying a history of sexual abuse, although this view is inaccurate. The *DSM* does agree that dissociation is usually triggered by some form of trauma, so the overall use of the term is not greatly different to Janet's or Freud's. But there are some differences. Janet considered dissociation to occur as a split in the consciousness of the weak-minded. Freud thought that unpleasant memories were consigned forcibly for ever into the unconscious. We no longer subscribe entirely to those ideas, but the general principles of modern dissociation are not very different to those of Victorian times.

The term conversion disorder, a label drawn from Freud's concept of distress converted to physical symptoms, remains the standard term for the neurological form of psychosomatic disorders. When used now it is not always the case that the doctor who uses it either believes in, or even knows of, Freud's ideas. More likely it is a convenient label, that is not overly pejorative and whose implication of a non-organic disorder is widely understood by the medical community.

So, in day-to-day practice Janet's and Freud's theories are regularly used, or misused. I employ them when I am trying to understand the complex problems that I encounter and am trying to make sense of this disorder for my patients. Because my own hands shake when I am nervous I can see a certain logic in the sense that an emotion has been converted into a physical symptom.

This is not to say that there have been no changes in thinking. Consciousness is no longer considered to be a single amorphous thing, but instead it is made up of many domains including attention, perception and memory, amongst others. Consciousness is the mechanism by which we choose our mental experience; it is not a limitless resource so it must be selective. Attention is the component of our consciousness that distributes our awareness; it makes the selection for us. Once something has entered our domain of awareness, our perception is the means by which we appreciate it. Perception is subjective, dependent on our personal and cultural experiences. Memory can be divided into explicit memory (things we can consciously recall), and implicit memory (those things that are outside of our conscious awareness). Implicit memory allows us to ride a bike even when we haven't done so for several years. It is also the place where our emotional responses may be conditioned by past experiences even without there being any conscious recollection of those experiences – it is our subconscious memory, in other words. Modern technology can now take these abstract ideas and make them more concrete. Techniques like functional MRI can tell us which parts of the brain mediate different aspects of consciousness. There is much still to be understood but we at least know that parts of the frontal lobe are involved in maintaining attention, the medial temporal lobe is integral to supporting memory, and the brainstem is important to maintaining conscious awareness.

Functional MRI has also been used to show that people can indeed have emotions of which we are only aware at a subliminal level. Subjects in an MRI scanner are shown pictures of unpleasant images. The pictures are shown at a rate slow enough to be perceived by the patient but too fast for them to register what they have seen into their conscious awareness. Test subjects report no change in how they feel during the test but changes in heart rate indicate an emotional change of which the test subject is unaware. At the same time that these changes are detected, functional MRI images demonstrate a change in activity in the area of the brain called the amygdala. The study concludes that feelings may be generated outside of conscious awareness and that that is mediated by the amygdala.

So we are now able to produce pictures of the brain that reflect just a little of the secrets we keep from ourselves, but even with these advances we still struggle to understand how symptoms as dramatic as coma or loss of consciousness can be generated from an apparently healthy brain. There are some aspects of how our bodies respond physically to stress that are understood, however. The impact of stress on the mind is hard to objectively measure but its impact on the nervous system outside the brain is not.

Integral to how our body responds to stress is the autonomic nervous system. The peripheral nervous system connects our brain and spinal cord to the limbs and organs. It can be subdivided into different sorts of nerves. We have motor nerves that allow us to move – when we want to lift an arm they transmit the instruction from the brain to the muscles and make it happen. Sensory nerves carry the signal that allows us to appreciate sensations, both pleasant and unpleasant. But there is an entirely separate system of nerves that controls the functions of our body that are not voluntary, and it is these nerves in particular that reflect our emotional state. The autonomic nervous system is in command of our internal organs, it alters the movement of our bowels, empties our bladders, regulates our sweat glands, changes the size of our pupils, constricts and dilates blood vessels, slows and speeds the heart. In turn, the autonomic nervous system can be subdivided. The sympathetic nerves determine how we will react when faced with threat. They prepare us for fight or flight. Their name is drawn from Galen's concept of sympathy; these nerves allow one organ of the body to cooperate with another. When we are frightened they cause our heart to race, our palms to become sweaty, our mouth to become dry. The parasympathetic nerves do the opposite. They exert unconscious control over our organs when we are relaxed.

The autonomic nervous system helps maintain our blood pressure and heart rate but, like every other function of our body, it doesn't always work just as it should. In the face of sudden stress the sympathetic nerves act quickly, but transiently, until the threat passes. This serves a purpose in an urgent situation. But when we are under chronic stress, the sympathetic nervous system might be activated for prolonged periods at a low level. Our bodies do not adapt well to chronic stress and this is when the autonomic nervous system is capable of harm, causing high blood pressure or palpitations of the heart. For Pauline, such chronic stress might have caused her bladder to stop emptying and provoked stomach pain through the increased movement of the muscles of the bowel. In a strange way Galen's theory was right – Pauline's body was simply reacting in sympathy to the distress that she was in.

Another quantifiable way in which the body responds to stress is through the action of the hypothalamic-pituitary-adrenal (HPA) axis. The HPA axis integrates the neurological and endocrine systems. The hypothalamus in the brain can secrete hormones, some of which bind to the pituitary gland. In response the pituitary gland releases the hormone ACTH which in turn leads to the production of cortisol by the adrenal glands. Cortisol plays an important role in the metabolic, cardiovascular, immune and behavioural responses to stress. Also, importantly, cortisol regulates the magnitude of the response of the HPA axis. Rising levels of cortisol will act on both the hypothalamus and pituitary gland to reduce further ACTH and cortisol release. This negative feedback loop is important in order to prevent an overactive response of the various body systems to stress. Both the failure of an adequate response of the HPA axis in the face of stress, and the failure of the negative feedback loop when stress is chronic, have been implicated in psychosomatic illness.

But while the autonomic nervous system and HPA axis can account for some psychosomatic symptoms, they cannot account for others. Dysfunction of the sympathetic nerves alone cannot explain psychogenic paralysis of the limbs. Voluntary movement begins in the motor cortex of the brain and spreads through the motor pathways to the motor nerves. These nerves communicate directly with the striated muscles of the limbs, resulting in movement. The autonomic nervous system exerts control over the smooth muscle of the bowel and blood vessels but has no role to play in movement of the arms and legs. Nor can sympathetic nerves produce psychogenic seizures. Autonomic nerves can lower blood pressure causing a faint, but there is no mechanism by which they could cause a convulsion accompanied by a normal blood pressure and a normal brainwave pattern.

So while heart palpitations and changes in bowel motility (intestinal contractions) might have a biological explanation, the majority of conversion disorders still do not. In the early twentieth century most attempts to find an answer focused on emotional distress and the subconscious, but more recently doctors have started to think about the illness differently. Some wonder if the mechanism might not necessarily be located in the subconscious, nor be the result of stress or trauma, but may instead be an illness of behaviour or a social illness. Freud's and Janet's theories require a psychosocial conflict to be present to make the diagnosis, but many patients will deny a specific stressor. In the 1970s Issy Pilowsky, professor of psychiatry at the University of Adelaide, emphasised the importance of the sick role or illness behaviour in development of psychosomatic illness. The concept of an illness behaviour disorder does not require a specific event to trigger psychosomatic symptoms, but instead depends on the varying ways that different people evaluate and act on symptoms that they experience. Some people medicalise every physical sensation and that in itself can lead to illness. Linked to this idea is the concept of a social illness, in other words illness as a rationalisation for psychosocial problems or as a coping mechanism. Most people prefer to feel well, but for some, being unwell provides escape or an explanation for failure. Some may say that is not a new idea either.

A related theory is that some psychosomatic disorders are illnesses of perception. People's perceptions of the severity and persistence of their own symptoms can be very inaccurate. Pain and fatigue cannot be measured so we must take their descriptions at face value. However, some symptoms can be quantified and when that is done and the patient's account is compared to the measurements taken, the results can be very surprising. Tremor is a common psychosomatic symptom. Sometimes it is so severe that it can be very disabling. Movement-disorder neurologists use a device called an actigraphic watch to quantify tremor. The patient wears the watch and it records the movement in the arm around the clock, and when the doctor reviews the recording it allows them to assess the persistence of the tremor throughout the day. Simultaneously the patient uses a diary to record when they think tremor is present. It is not unusual for the patient to report almost continuous tremor and yet when the recording is reviewed the tremor has only been present for a fraction of the day. The patient wasn't lying, but their worry about and vigilance of their own symptoms results in the belief that the tremor is more persistent than it is. These sorts of observations raise the possibility that it is not the symptoms themselves but how we think about them that is at the heart of the disability they cause.

The greatest modern advance in thinking about psychosomatic illness has probably been the move away from brain–mind dualism. We are less inclined to think of the brain and mind as separate. It is not the case that the brain is healthy and the mind is sick but instead that the two are interdependent on one another. People with brain diseases like epilepsy and multiple sclerosis often suffer from problems like depression. People with mental illnesses like schizophrenia have been shown to have irregularities on structural brain imaging. Psychosomatic illness may well be an illness of the mind, but there must be something happening physiologically in the brain to produce the disability.

To this end much modern research focuses on an attempt to understand the neurobiology of these conditions. Stress may or may not act as a trigger, but what exactly is happening at a pathological level in the brain at the time of the symptoms? That is what patients really want to know. Functional MRI is also in use in this area of research. Several studies have looked at functional MRI in patients with a variety of psychogenic disabilities including paralysis, sensory loss and dystonia. As we've already seen, biological changes can be observed in the brain in patients affected by these conditions. People with sensory loss have been shown to have reduced activation in the sensory parts of the brain. People with motor weakness have been shown to have increased connectivity between the amygdala, a brain area important in motivating attention, and the supplementary motor area of the frontal lobe, a region that helps control movement. Several studies show increased activation in the right prefrontal cortex in patients with psychogenic conditions.

The problem arises when we ask what these changes on functional imaging actually mean. They could be interpreted to imply that people with conversion disorders have *faulty wiring* in the brain in the first instance. Alternatively the findings could be a manifestation of neuroplasticity – a change or reinforcement in neural pathways secondary to a psychological trauma or even stress – a marker for the illness rather than a cause. Or MRI findings may just be evidence for the increased effort required for affected patients to make any movement – not a sign that there is something wrong in the brain but a sign of the concerted attempt to move.

There is no doubt that functional MRI studies have given us interesting information. They put us on the road to the idea that psychosomatic disorders are not all in the mind. And yet, the functional MRI studies are far from providing us with a full explanation. All the studies have involved small numbers of patients, and results between studies are variable and not always reproducible. Similar functional MRI findings have also been seen in patients with organic dystonia and epilepsy, so they are not exclusive to patients with psychosomatic disorders. Also the way that the results are interpreted is only speculative – scientists are trying to extrapolate from shadows on a scan to an understanding of the complex workings of the brain. While the functional MRI findings tell us that the brains of people with psychosomatic problems are behaving differently to control subjects, that does not necessarily imply a brain disease but does support the view that the symptoms are not imagined.

So we have new ways of thinking about and looking at the brain and the mind. Psychosomatic symptoms are far less likely to be considered symbolic than they were in the past and less likely to be considered 'all in the mind'. But still it often feels to me, and to my patients, that we are as far away from answering any of the mysteries that surround hysteria as we were when Charcot, Freud and Janet were alive. And that was a very long time ago.

Alice's symptoms did not rely on symbolism. Her experience of having cancer was moulded by her knowledge of disease and by all the experiences that she had had in her life. Alice was the youngest of four children. She had two brothers and one sister. When Alice was only twelve she had watched her mother die of cancer.

Alice's mother was forty-six when she discovered a breast lump. Her story began much like Alice's but it had escalated more quickly. Even before the lump had been removed scans suggested that she had enlarged lymph nodes, meaning that the cancer was not confined to her breast. It was suggested that she should have chemotherapy to shrink the cancer in advance of any operation to remove it. Once the chemotherapy was due to start it was impossible for her to shield Alice from what was happening. Quickly Alice saw her mother, who had been so full of life, wither before her. Every day when Alice came home from school she feared what she might find. Her parents wanted to send her to stay with her grandparents until the chemotherapy was finished but Alice would not be parted from her mother. She was old enough to know that chemotherapy did not always work.

Once the chemotherapy had shrunk the tumour Alice's mother underwent surgery to remove her breast and any affected lymph nodes. Next she had extensive radiotherapy in an attempt to kill any remaining cancer cells. After that Alice and her family had a very brief reprieve. Small bristles of new hair appeared on Alice's mother's head and with it Alice felt she might be getting her mother back. Their happiness was short-lived. One day Alice's mother began to complain of severe pains shooting down her arm. Her arm became gradually weaker until it hung down by her side. The less she used it the more swollen it became. The doctors told her that the muscles in her arm had become weakened by the damage that the radiotherapy had done to the nerves in her shoulder. At least it was not the cancer coming back, the family had sighed in relief.

Over the course of the next month Alice's mother appeared to gain weight and recover some of the energy she had lost through the treatment. But before long she began to complain of stomach pain and vomiting and the weight she had gained fell away again. The cancer had spread to her liver. Doctors said there was nothing more that could be done.

Alice and her family cared for her mother in their own home for as long as they could. Then one day the back pain began. She was taken to hospital once again where it was discovered that the cancer was now in her bones. The oncologists said that she would not last long. They could give her steroids to reduce any swelling and allow her home to die with her family. She died before any of this could be achieved. Alice's mother had lived that one painful year before her death and Alice was at her bedside when she died.

Watching her mother's illness had a profound effect on Alice. There was much that was terrible about the experience but not every memory was bad. As awful as that year had been, there was time at least for Alice to be with her mother. It was the sort of intense time that only occurs when you know that you are going to lose someone and you need to make the time you still have count.

Alice had seen how the doctors and nurses at the hospital had cared so expertly for her mother and she found inspiration there too. Before her mother died Alice told her that she wanted to be a doctor when she left school. Six years later Alice entered medical school as she had said she would, and five years after that she qualified. She was glad her mother knew something of her daughter's future before she died. She would not know, however, that in her first year of work Alice herself would be struck down by cancer.

Alice told me that when she discovered that she had cancer she could barely stand to tell her family. It took almost twenty-four hours for her to ring her father. She could not tell him in person, knowing the terrible memories she would see in his eyes. As soon as her family did know they rallied around her, as she knew they would. They insisted that she move home. They would no longer let her go to appointments alone. But with every bit of comfort they offered she also saw them reliving her mother's death through her.

'I think I would have preferred not to tell them, to go through it on my own, but it's not something you can hide.'

Throughout her illness Alice's father insisted on being with her at every hospital appointment. He felt that Alice should not receive any bad news when she was alone. Alice loved her father. He had raised her after her mother died. Many of her most vivid childhood memories involved the care that he had given her. She wanted him by her side, and yet quickly she discovered that having him there stayed her questions. How could she force this widower to relive the illness that took away his wife? How could she ask blunt questions and have him hear the answers? After a while she begged him to let her go to the hospital alone. He reluctantly agreed although he still insisted that he collect her after each appointment. She knew he worried that one day he would be waiting outside the hospital entrance and she would not appear.

Alice told me about the night after her operation.

'I was uncomfortable. I couldn't sleep. It wasn't the pain. It was the whole experience. Because of the bandages I was having to try and sleep on my back, which I never normally do. It was the narrow unfamiliar bed and a cold unfriendly room. In the evening my family had visited and my sister had stayed with me and everything had felt alright. Once it got late I told my sister to go home. I'm a grown-up and I'm a doctor and I'll be fine, I told her. But in the middle of the night it was dark and in the darkness I stopped being a grown-up and a doctor and, when I did, the demons came to visit. I'm a doctor, I know about all the possible complications of surgery, the wound could get infected or could fail to heal and get broken down. About an hour after lights out my mind ran to all the possibilities. Soon I felt the first pain. Suddenly I got a feeling as if bugs were crawling around inside my chest. I had a vivid picture in my head of the infection. With every passing hour things became worse. I knew I was being ridiculous but that didn't stop it. By the early hours of the morning I thought I could feel the wound in my chest tearing if I took a deep breath. I was convinced of it. I tried to peep down the bandage and, when I did, I thought I could see something black that shouldn't have been there. In my mind it was gangrene. And I knew that it didn't make sense. But common sense means nothing at four o'clock in the morning when you are alone. The more I imagined it the worse the pain got. In the end I had to call the nurse. I told her about the pain and when she called the doctor and he started doing tests it just got worse instead of better. I think the tests made my imaginary pain real. I have wondered since if all that was really needed was for one of them to simply say, "There, there, everything will be alright."'

'Like a mother might.'

'Yes, I suppose so.'

'It's hard not to relate what happened to your arm to what happened to your mother.'

'I knew there was nothing wrong with my arm. It's hard to explain. I knew, but the weakness and pain felt so real that I couldn't always hold that conviction. I hadn't had radiotherapy. I hadn't had the lymph nodes removed from under my arm. I knew I had no reason to develop the complication my mother had developed but that gave me no consolation at the time.'

'And when the tests were normal?'

'My arm immediately got better and I just felt stupid that I had let them do the tests in the first place.'

'You should try not to be a doctor here. Let yourself be a patient. Let your doctors care for you as a patient not as a doctor.'

Alice liked the breast surgeon and oncologist and all the nurses and doctors on the team who were responsible for her care. She might have imagined it, she said, but she sometimes thought that they gave her extra time in acknowledgement that she was a colleague of sorts. But she also felt that they did not know quite how to communicate with her. Should they talk to her as they would any other patient, or as a doctor would talk to another doctor? People were considerate, technical terms were used so that Alice would not feel patronised. There was honesty. When Alice asked if normal screening tests were reliable in ruling out cancer spread the doctor had replied, 'Cancer cells can seed in the brain or elsewhere in the body, so, I'm sorry, but no, a normal scan does not provide an absolute guarantee.'

In *Studies* Freud told the story of Fräulein Elizabeth. Amongst her many disabilities she suffered a continuous pain in her leg that had, for a long time, gone unexplained. Through extensive exploration of her psyche, Freud eventually discovered that the pain originated at exactly the point in her leg where Elizabeth had once cradled the leg and foot of her dying father. In the moment of horror at her father's death it was into that pressure point that all her distress had flowed. When the consultant told Alice that cancer cells could seed in the brain, for a moment, Alice became Fräulein Elizabeth – and her doctor's hand was resting firmly on her head.

'The stupidest thing happened one day that I never told anybody about. It was a miserable grey rainy day and I had been walking around the city centre looking in the shop windows. As the day ran on I began to notice a numb feeling in my right foot. Every now and then I'd stop and shake my foot and try to get the feeling back but it wasn't working. Over an hour or so it became so bad that my foot felt painful and

I could barely feel the ground underfoot. I really started to worry. In my head the cancer had invaded my spine and eroded the nerves going to my foot. I began to notice a pain in my back which had never been there before. I decided that I had better go home and in the half-hour that the journey took I had almost written my last will and testament in my head. When I got home I sat on the sofa and took off my shoe so that I could massage my foot. When I did I discovered that my sock was drenched through and ice cold. I looked at the bottom of my shoe and a hole had worn through the sole and was letting the rainwater in. There was nothing wrong with my foot. My anxiety about the cancer had become so heightened that all good judgement was lost, I could no longer tell the difference between the spread of cancer and a hole in my shoe.'

Symbolism attributes a deep meaning to symptoms but, in my experience, psychosomatic disorders rarely follow that pattern. Occasionally, as in the case of Mary, I can fashion some symbolic attribution to explain a specific disability. I always believed that Mary simply could not face up to, or bear to think of, what her husband had done. In my experience, however, the physical manifestations of stress are much more likely to be influenced by the sufferer's past experience of illness, what they know about the body and what lessons their life has taught them. Some factors that shape illness come from our personal lives and others come from the society in which we live.

The term *run amok* is mostly used to describe a sort of chaotic behaviour that is usually frenzied but benign. It might describe a group of children let loose at a party. But the word *amok* refers to a set of symptoms and behaviours attributed to illness and seen particularly in the Malay culture. A man struck down by *amok* flies into a rage that is unprovoked and out of character. In a typical attack he is launched on a violent killing spree often directed against strangers and taking place in crowded open spaces. Very often the victim of *amok* dies either at his own hand or at that of another. In the Malay culture this behaviour is viewed as an illness with the cause attributed to possession by an evil tiger spirit. This belief removes all blame from the sufferer. The sufferer becomes victim and his suffering takes on a cultural acceptability that would not be offered to a person who was violently depressed or who committed suicide in a more traditional way.

The *DSM* considers *amok* to be a psychiatric diagnosis belonging to a group of conditions referred to as the culture-bound syndromes. They are disorders that are familiar to and common within specific cultures and unusual outside those cultures. Other culture-bound syndromes are more easy to see as medical. *Koro* is a condition almost exclusively seen in Asian men. It is a disorder in which a man becomes convinced that his penis is shrinking. He might come to the hospital with his penis held firmly in his hand to prevent further retraction into the body. In another example, the jumping Frenchmen of Maine were a group of lumberjacks who lived in an isolated community and who were struck down by a condition manifesting as an excessive startle reaction in response to noise or fright. *Grisi siknis* is an affliction seen in the Miskito tribe of Central America. It manifests in women as nausea, dizziness and bouts of frenzy leading to loss of consciousness. Society, culture and superstition plant ideas that mould our concerns about our bodies and that help to determine what counts as an acceptable public manifestation of distress.

The media is also important in determining the sorts of symptoms that people will develop. In the 1990s I saw many patients who were convinced that their miscellaneous physical symptoms were due to candidiasis. Popular magazines and newspapers were publicising a candida epidemic at the time. One website described the symptoms of candidiasis as a feeling of being run-down, irritability accompanied by bloating, itchy ears, poor concentration and a craving for sugar. The media had described the symptoms in detail and people came to the hospital with just those symptoms, and a conviction about their own diagnosis. Candida is a fungus that can cause simple medical problems like thrush or serious life-threatening illness in those with immune dysfunction, but in the candidiasis sufferers I am describing here no infection could be found. Patients rarely ask me about candida any longer. In the twenty-first century the exact same symptoms are more likely to be attributed to gluten sensitivity or allergies. I recently went to a dinner party where every person bar two, at a table of ten, reported that they had an intolerance of or allergy to at least one foodstuff. Most had developed the allergy in middle age which is not really how an allergy typically behaves. People look for explanations for changes in their bodies, something to account for every unpleasant feeling. There is an unwillingness to accept behavioural or emotional factors, or the effects of ageing, as an explanation. Society and the media are often available to provide a more agreeable answer and to add to the symptom pool available. People are suggestible. If you ask somebody if they have itchy ears as if it is diagnostic of something important, people will search for that symptom in the reaches of their memory and a surprising number will find it there.

Personal life experience is also a great moulder of psychosomatic illness. A girl faints in a circumstance suited for a faint. A month later she develops convulsions. Her body, inspired by a normal physiological response to heat or stress, has learned a new way to behave. Many people with dissociative seizures have experienced seizures or collapse in some form before. Either they have fainted or they have suffered seizures in childhood. People who work with epilepsy sufferers or who have a family member with epilepsy have a higher risk of developing dissociative seizures. Someone who has a friend who has suffered a brain tumour might find themselves developing headaches. Someone who has worked with motor neurone disease sufferers begins to notice muscle cramps. There are many anecdotal reports of medical and nursing students developing the symptoms of the disease they are treating.

If psychosomatic symptoms arise in the subconscious, their manifestation will depend on what else lives there. Our subconscious is filled with our memories, and that is what we draw on. The health service does not provide an exhaustive psychoanalytical programme for the sufferers of conversion disorders so it is rarely possible to follow every symptom to its source as Freud might have advocated. Often we must be satisfied with making a sound diagnosis and giving the patients what support we can and accepting that not every question has an answer.

I do not exhaust myself with trying to solve every time the puzzle of why this symptom in this patient; my time is taken up with the fickle nature of the symptoms and knowing how difficult they will be to explain. Being aware of that mutating quality, how something new steps in to replace the problem that is just departing, forces me to stay alert.

'Please do NOT start any new medications or arrange any tests or procedures without speaking to me first.'

About six months into my first consultant job this is the instruction I began to leave on the front cover of all my patient notes. I wrote it in red ink, capitalised and underlined – I had learned a trick or two from my patients about how to be heard. But still I was holding back, what I really wanted to write was 'No wheelchairs, no crutches, no morphine, no appendicectomy, no surgical procedures of any sort.' As usual this is something I had learned the hard way.

There are many examples but Lorna is memorable for the night of lost sleep she caused me. A junior doctor telephoned me at home to let me know that Lorna had been taken to theatre to have an exploratory operation and had started convulsing in the anaesthetic room and nobody knew what to do. That afternoon I had left Lorna sitting quietly in her monitoring room and now, from nowhere, somebody was preparing to cut her open.

Lorna had the recognisable history of multiple unexplained medical complaints that by now should be familiar: chronic headache and joint pain, recurrent burning pain passing urine, episodic difficulty swallowing. She had come to me with seizures and I did not doubt the diagnosis of dissociative seizures but, as usual, that was just my opinion until I had found proof. I had seen Lorna less than eight hours before and she had not mentioned any hint of stomach pain. But now I learned that close to midnight a junior doctor had been called because Lorna was suddenly doubled over with pain in her abdomen. That junior doctor had not met Lorna before. Seeing how distressed she was he called a member of the surgical team who examined her and took some blood tests. Lorna's temperature was said to be slightly high and her blood tests showed a minor irregularity, not an unequivocal abnormality but a result on the borderline of normal. Lorna was writhing in distress and was given morphine, and a decision was taken that there was enough evidence that she might have appendicitis. She was disconnected from the monitoring equipment and was taken to the anaesthetic room to be prepared for the operating theatre. I think it is highly unlikely that anybody gave her notes any more than a cursory look during the time it took to reach the decision to operate.

When I took the phone call I imagined Lorna showing her pain in every way possible. The night-time peace of the ward was probably broken apart by it. Other patients would get upset. What was wrong with that poor girl? Why was nobody helping her? Nurses and junior doctors would soon begin to feel out of their depth. Nothing they said or did would seem to be helping and an air of panic would begin to set in. There would be inevitable widespread relief when it was decided to anaesthetise Lorna and take her to surgery.

The morphine she had been given did not put her asleep fully but sedated her sufficiently that she could be prepared for theatre and wheeled to the anaesthetic room. When she arrived there the anaesthetist was told only that Lorna was being investigated for blackouts and was on no medication. He was entirely unprepared therefore when Lorna's whole body abruptly stiffened, her limbs began to thrash wildly, her pelvis thrust forward and her head started to hit itself repeatedly against the cot sides of the bed. He wanted to give her sedation but she had pulled her intravenous catheter out of her arm and she was now flailing so wildly that nobody could resite it. Which is when I was called.

I got straight into the car and went to the hospital. When I arrived at the operating theatres it didn't take long to find the correct room. I could hear the shouting from the end of the corridor. By now Lorna was lying on the floor. One doctor was holding down her legs while another and a nurse had taken an arm each. There were two pillows under her head to protect it as it hit against the floor. Under the grasp of her captors Lorna was straining and fighting against three adults who were barely a match for her.

The anaesthetist was standing to the side and he was furious. 'Why has this girl not received treatment for her seizures?' he shouted at me when I walked in the door.

I suppressed the words that were perilously close to the tip of my tongue and instead I turned to the other people in the room and asked them to stand away from Lorna.

'But every time I let go she keeps kicking the wall,' a very young-looking doctor said, and I thought he seemed as if he was just about to cry.

I guaranteed him that letting go was the right thing to do and I asked everybody except the nurse to leave the room. And, of course, as soon as they let go Lorna's thrashing became even wilder than before. The young doctor looked at me worriedly, half bending towards Lorna again, expecting that now I had seen he was right I would tell him to return to holding her legs still. Instead I told him that we needed to remove the pandemonium from the room and that it would be more helpful if everybody gave Lorna the space she needed.

When Lorna and the nurse and I were alone there was a thirty-second period when I crossed my fingers and hoped that I was right. During that time Lorna's body had travelled across the floor and her legs were now beating roughly against a trolley. The nurse and I moved the trolley and throughout I spoke to Lorna, letting her know that everything was fine and that this would all be over in a moment. And then it stopped, as abruptly as it had started, and Lorna was lying with her eyes closed, taking deep gasping breaths. The nurse and I looked at each other. We were both very relieved. Five minutes later Lorna was sitting in a wheelchair, upset, not recalling anything that had happened, but able to communicate normally.

I left her with the nurse and went to speak to the other doctors, thinking that the crisis was over and I could return to my bed. I was disappointed therefore to meet a still-angry anaesthetist and junior surgeon who asked me if they could now put Lorna to sleep and take her to surgery as they had originally planned. Have you learned nothing, I wanted to say, but instead I managed to make a less inflammatory comment and suggested that we wait before planning anything invasive because Lorna had a history of somatising disorders and it was likely the abdominal pain would disappear spontaneously, just as the seizure had.

The junior surgeon was not happy with this and rang his consultant, who was at home.

'This girl has a high temperature, a high white-cell count and severe abdominal pain,' the consultant told me over the phone, 'she needs to go to surgery.'

'Lorna has a borderline high temperature and a borderline increase in her white-cell count, either of which could be normal on retesting and either of which could be caused by the stress of her seizures,' I countered.

After a period of stalemate we agreed to repeat her blood tests and wait for the results and to use that time to see if things would progress or improve. She could be taken to theatre if there was any deterioration in the meantime. By the next morning the abdominal pain had disappeared completely without treatment and no surgery had been necessary. When I went to see Lorna she was not happy to see me, but I was happy to see her. She was no better than when she had been admitted to hospital, but at least she was no worse. That was the best outcome I could have hoped for on that day.

I have seen a lot of Lornas, none of whom have ever undergone unnecessary surgery, but many have found new ways of expressing their distress when a first method has proven inadequate. I have told two patients that they have psychogenic seizures and have come back to the ward a day later to find them sporting crutches. Both patients' seizures went into full remission but neither could walk unaided for several weeks. I have seen many people give up one diagnosis and immediately replace it, and I am forced to realise that nothing has been learned. They come to clinic with knee braces and tales of exploratory operations, new medical problems emerging just as the dissociative seizures melt away.

When relationships break down some get angry, some deny and some quickly try to replace what they have lost. Losing a grasp on the physical illness you thought you had can be every bit as devastating as any other sort of loss and, for some, a quick substitute is necessary. It is a little bit like an addiction. In giving up an addiction some addicts find that they replace one crutch with another, but hopefully one that is less harmful – replacing cigarettes with food, or drugs with cigarettes, for example. When illness behaves as a crutch it too is difficult to relinquish and something is required to take its place. That substitute may be something positive, but that is not always the case.

7

RACHEL

What's in a name? That which we call a rose by any other name would smell as sweet.

William Shakespeare, *Romeo and Juliet* (1597)

Some psychosomatic disorders are extreme and rare. Others are so common that even if you are not personally affected you probably know several people who are, although many of those people will of course hotly contest any suggestion of a stress-related cause. Psychosomatic symptoms are by their very nature evidence of denial. When a symptom cannot be measured, that creates an ideal opportunity for denial to flourish.

We all perceive sensations differently, although the method by which our bodies communicate those messages are the same for all of us. A tiny odour molecule stimulates a receptor in our nose or a vibration strikes our eardrum and a signal is released. An electrical discharge travels upwards through the nerves and to the brain. In just the same way that sensory and motor nerves transmit information by means of an electrical impulse, so too are smell and hearing messages carried to the brain. The speed, integrity and size of this response can be measured and the measurements are very similar between individuals. Each nerve is just a bundle of cells and fluid, and the message it carries just a flow of ions. A nerve is like a living piece of electrical wire. Remove the nerve from the body and preserve it and it will transmit its message as if it still existed in the living human being. It doesn't need the brain to function. A nerve's response is standardised but how we react to the message it transmits is not. Somewhere inside our heads the message is interpreted, and it is in that interpretation that we become individuals again.

Our experience of each sensation is our own. We like the smell of a perfume or we don't. We love to have our feet massaged or we cannot bear for our feet to be touched. We each have individual thresholds for sensation, differing pain tolerance, a fondness for cold or for heat, varying experiences of taste and smell. And just as we all feel pain differently, fatigue too is an experience that is uniquely ours.

In medicine fatigue is a particularly enigmatic problem. There is something in its nature that makes it difficult to pin down. We all experience it from time to time but we can only know how it feels to us. It is absolutely subjective and absolutely normal – until it becomes not normal, that is, and when that happens it is not always easy to say why it has. Trying to understand why a patient is suffering with excessive fatigue can point a doctor both nowhere and everywhere. If there are no other clues the cause might lie in the brain, or the heart, in the blood, almost anywhere. An endless number of medical conditions are associated with excessive tiredness: multiple sclerosis, lupus, diabetes, cancer, HIV, thyroid disease, anaemia, heart disease, coeliac disease and many more. Excessive fatigue does not necessarily imply illness. It is part of all of our lives from time to time, when we are not looking after ourselves or we're working too hard or are missing out on sleep for whatever reason.

Another feature of fatigue is how little sympathy we have for it at times. If your workmate rang you up and said they could not work today because they felt too tired, how would it make you feel? When a loved one has had a bad day at work and is complaining about their exhaustion, sometimes we sympathise but other times we can only counter that person's description of their tiredness with our own. Perhaps it is precisely because we have all regularly experienced fatigue – and it was not so bad for us and we were able to keep going – that we cannot quite get the measure of why others complain so bitterly about it. After all, a good night's sleep will cure it, won't it?

Part of the problem is that fatigue can be described but never objectively quantified. I describe my tiredness today by comparing myself to other days because it is the only measure I have. So if I am the only frame of reference I have, how can I really know how others experience it?

One way that *normal* fatigue might be distinguished from that which indicates illness is in how it responds to rest. If I am tired because I am overdoing it and then I rest, I usually feel better. But where the tiredness has reached the point of a disability, rest often fails to give relief. That is how it is for sufferers of chronic fatigue syndrome.

People in the waiting room moved back as Rachel wheeled herself slowly past them to get to the door of the room where I stood waiting for her. Chairs faced one another in rows and the space between them was narrow. Seated people turned their legs to the side and pulled their children up on to their laps as the wheelchair travelled forward. A man and a woman who I took to be Rachel's parents were walking behind her. I moved to help but the woman stopped me.

'She has to do things for herself.'

I could only stand and watch, then, as Rachel laboured forward. Once settled in the room, her parents seated on either side, Rachel asked for a moment to compose herself. Even before a word had been exchanged I felt that a point had been made.

Rachel had been unwell for three years. When her problem began she was a dance student, hoping and expecting to follow a career in modern dance performance. Rachel's love of dance began when she was six years old after her mother had enrolled her in a ballet class. Soon she also studied modern dance and jazz. At the age of twelve she enrolled in an acting class. One day a casting director came to her class looking for a child to take the lead role in a television advert. Rachel got the job. It made her a minor celebrity at her school for a term. At the age of fourteen she left mainstream education and transferred to an academy for the performing arts. By the time she was sixteen she had decided that her strength was as a dancer and she planned to make that her future career.

Even outside of her interest in performance Rachel was a very active girl. She went for a run every morning, in her spare time she enjoyed swimming and playing tennis. That Rachel was a girl who never sat still only added to her distress when she fell ill.

Rachel was in the first year of a degree course in dance when she suspected there might be a problem. She had recently returned from a holiday in America and expected to feel refreshed as she got back down to work. Instead she felt quite the opposite. The first sign was that she found it increasingly difficult to stay awake during lectures. She would regularly drift off and then wake with a start. No matter how soundly she had slept the previous night she could not concentrate for any significant length of time. She soon fell behind in her academic classes. While this was the least important segment of her course it still caused Rachel great concern. The course was competitive and Rachel knew that only a small number of students would successfully make a career out of performance alone. She clung to the knowledge that she was one of the best in her practical dance classes, which made it even worse when she began to suffer problems there too.

All the students in her class experienced minor injuries from time to time. The college provided a sport physiotherapist to monitor the students' physical well-being and to provide treatment when injuries occurred. Rachel began to notice that after her more strenuous classes she felt that her joints were swollen and that her hips and lower back ached. She consulted the physiotherapist who advised her on her posture and gave her exercises to strengthen her back and legs. Despite closely following the advice given, Rachel did not improve. Soon she found that when she was asked to carry out more energetic dance steps she did not have the power that the other dancers her age seemed to. Several times she had wavered and had almost fallen. She began to suspect that there was more going on than the usual dance-related injuries.

When Rachel went home for the holidays and described her

problem to her parents they became very concerned. Rachel's mother took her to the family doctor and he wondered if her symptoms indicated that she might have multiple sclerosis or a muscle problem. He referred her to a neurologist who examined her and told her that he could not find anything amiss – there were no signs to indicate a neurological disease and he did not think that tests were necessary.

The next term at college Rachel's problems worsened. Aches and pains moved around her body. Dance practice, which could last two hours or more, became impossible for her. Lectures were worse. Rachel was unable to concentrate. When she reviewed her notes at the end of a class she found that what she had written was sometimes close to nonsense.

When it was obvious that Rachel was falling behind, her teachers suggested that she take the rest of the term off. They told her to go home and try to figure out the source of the problem before returning. Rachel's parents were very upset to find a tear-stained Rachel on their doorstep one evening.

When Rachel saw her doctor she told him that she was over-whelmed with fatigue. Every day felt like the day after a major dance recital. Her whole body was consumed with aches and pains that moved around and became worse with every activity she attempted. She had stopped dancing and she could no longer take her morning run.

Rachel saw another neurologist. This time some blood tests were taken and Rachel was referred for an electrical test to check the integrity of her nerves and muscles. The tests were normal. With Rachel deteriorating fast and at risk of losing her career, the neurologist arranged for her to have a muscle biopsy, concerned that she might have a muscle disease. Again the results came back normal. The neurologist discharged Rachel and her worried mother took her back to see her doctor again. This time he referred her to a rheumatologist. The rheumatologist repeated much of what the neurologist had done and came to the same conclusion – he could find no explanation for Rachel's symptoms.

For the next two months Rachel's parents watched their athletic energetic daughter fade in front of them. Unrefreshed by sleep Rachel spent most of the day lying on the sofa, in and out of a half-sleep. Soon the energy required even for simple tasks like reading was no longer available to her. She was unable to eat and became pale and thin. When her mother asked her how she felt, all she could talk about was the pain.

Rachel's mother researched her daughter's symptoms on the Internet. She came across several accounts of young people who had suffered in a very similar way to Rachel. She had heard of myalgic encephalomyelitis before but she had not realised until that moment that the symptoms fitted so perfectly with those of her daughter. Rachel had ME, she was certain of it. A website for ME sufferers gave a list of recommended doctors and Rachel's mother rang one of those listed and arranged for Rachel to see him.

This new doctor listened very intensely as Rachel described what she felt. As soon as she had finished her story he asked her about her recent trip to the States. Just before she had fallen ill Rachel had spent two weeks in Washington state, staying with cousins. When he heard this the doctor was certain that he had the answer: Rachel suffered from Lyme disease, contracted while on holiday. Lyme disease is an infectious agent transmitted through insect bites and is common in parts of the US. The doctor suggested that he take some blood and look for evidence of infection. Since the result of the test could take weeks, he also suggested starting Rachel on antibiotics in the meantime.

One week after starting the antibiotics Rachel could not believe the improvement. Her energy levels doubled and she felt well enough to take a daily walk. She began to eat normally and put on weight. Suddenly she could foresee a return to her beloved dancing.

When Rachel went back to see the doctor for her results she was shocked to discover that the test for Lyme disease had come back negative.

'Not to worry,' the doctor said, 'the test is not positive in everybody and the improvement with antibiotics is proof enough that the diagnosis is right.'

Rachel completed the course of antibiotics and negotiated with her college to allow her to re-enter the class she had left. Her good records from the time before she fell ill stood her in good stead. However, as soon as Rachel tried to return to class her pains and tiredness returned. She thought she must have tried to do too much too soon. She saw her specialist again and he suggested a second course of antibiotics, and then a third. This time there was no improvement. Once again, she had to leave college and move back to her parents' home.

Next the doctor told her that while the infectious organism causing Lyme disease had probably been cleared from her body, she was now suffering from a complication of the disease in the form of chronic fatigue syndrome. He suggested a variety of painkillers and a meeting with a physiotherapist. Nothing worked. Rachel deteriorated and became housebound. Her poor concentration made it impossible for her to enjoy even normal pursuits. She could not follow the plot of a television programme. When the principal of her college rang to ask if they could expect her to return that year, Rachel and her family finally admitted to themselves that it would not happen. It was agreed that if she improved she could resit the same class the following year. Rachel now had four months to get better.

Her parents took her to another rheumatologist. He did not agree with the diagnosis of Lyme disease and told her that he thought she was depressed.

'Of course I'm depressed, I told him, I haven't been able to do anything but lie on the sofa for months. That shut him up.'

He suggested that Rachel take an antidepressant and see a psychologist, but she refused.

Over the next three months Rachel suffered setback after setback. Every good day filled with hope was followed by a day full of despair. Soon she was sleeping for sixteen hours a day. Her parents converted the dining room into a bedroom for her so that she did not have to take the stairs. They bought a wheelchair so that they could take her out of the house occasionally.

'We had to do everything for ourselves. If we didn't buy that wheelchair that poor girl would have been stuck indoors for months,' her father said.

Two weeks before the new academic year was due to begin Rachel's father phoned her college and told them that Rachel would not be coming back.

Unable to continue paying for private treatment they asked their doctor to refer her to another rheumatologist on the NHS. Over the next six months Rachel saw two rheumatologists, an immunologist and another neurologist. She was again told by one that she was depressed. Another said she had fibromyalgia and prescribed painkillers and an antidepressant.

'Is that the only treatment you doctors have heard of?' her father asked rhetorically as the family recounted the story.

When Rachel finally agreed to an assessment by a psychologist the report came back saying that, if the test result was to be believed, she had the mental capacity of a six-year-old.

'They mean you didn't even try,' the doctor who had ordered the test told her.

'If you think that's bad,' Rachel said, 'one doctor told me all I needed was a holiday. Or a boyfriend!'

Her parents turned to the Internet again for help and found the name of another doctor who ran a specialist clinic for ME sufferers. Her GP agreed to make the referral and when Rachel turned up to the appointment she was heartened to find herself sitting in a waiting room alongside a group of other people who she could tell felt as she did. She fell into conversation with a girl sitting beside her and when she heard the girl's story it was the same as hers.

'One doctor told me to go for a jog and I'd feel much better,' the girl said and Rachel laughed for the first time in months.

Meeting the specialist Rachel felt that she might finally be making some progress. He listened carefully to everything she said. He had read through all her old notes and seemed to grasp what she was telling him.

'He seemed to believe me. I was finally believed.'

The doctor suggested that she be admitted to hospital. He would review all her test results and repeat anything that was necessary and together they would consider her treatment options.

'Leaving that clinic that day I felt better than I'd felt all year. He really meant to help me, I could feel it,' Rachel said. 'He fooled me.'

'He fooled us all, sweetheart,' said Rachel's mother as she took Rachel's hand in her own.

Rachel's admission date soon came around. Her first inkling that something was not right came before she had even reached the ward. Her mother was with her and when they arrived at the main entrance of the hospital they stopped at the reception to get directions. The man behind the desk told her to follow the orange line on the floor and to look out for signs for the psychiatric hospital. Seeing the expression on Rachel's face her mother said, 'Don't panic. He just means that ward is beside the psychiatric hospital.' Even as she said it she prayed that she was right.

Five minutes later Rachel and her mother found themselves outside a locked door leading into a psychiatric unit. Both women were furious. Rachel would have turned and left immediately but her mother insisted that they go in and find somebody who could tell them 'what the bloody hell was going on'. After pressing the buzzer and being admitted to the ward Rachel's mother asked to speak to somebody in charge. An exchange followed in which both women made it quite clear how they felt about being 'tricked'. An experienced senior staff nurse assured them that while this ward was 'technically' part of the psychiatric hospital, the section of the ward where Rachel would be based was solely occupied by those suffering from chronic fatigue syndrome and related disorders. Rachel was not in the least pleased with the explanation, but with so few options available to her she agreed to stay for one night.

The first night in hospital was not as bad as Rachel had feared. She was sharing a room with three others, all girls her age and all of whom had been diagnosed with ME. Meeting people who understood how she felt helped Rachel, although it was a mixed blessing in some ways. One girl was so severely disabled that she had not walked for five years. Another seemed almost unaffected to Rachel's eyes. She watched that girl leap from her bed and run to the bathroom without any clear evidence of difficulty. Rachel could not quite decide which upset her more.

The following day she had a meeting with her doctor and her first question was why she was on a psychiatry ward.

'This is a psychiatry-led service, Rachel. I thought you knew that.'

'Are you a psychiatrist?'

'Yes, I am.'

'You should have told me.'

'I'm sorry, I assumed you were aware of that when we met. Maybe it would help if I told you that this is a specialist service for people who have ME. It is not intended as a primarily psychiatric intervention. It is a programme to treat the physical disabilities caused by ME.'

'I'm not insane.'

'Nobody here thinks you are.'

Rachel was just about persuaded to stay.

The next day Rachel tried her hardest to engage in the treatment that was scheduled for her. She saw the physiotherapist who did a detailed assessment and gave her a programme of graded exercise. She was also seen by an occupational therapist who asked her about her plans for the future.

'If we could put this illness behind you what would you do?'

'I'd be me again. Rachel the dancer, not Rachel the wheelchair-bound cripple.'

'And if it takes a while to get there and we can only hope to meet small goals, one at a time, building upwards – what then?'

'I'd like to be able to walk from my bedroom to the bathroom without feeling drained.'

'Okay, let's start there.'

Rachel also had a reluctant meeting with a psychologist. She had not fully recovered from the results of the last psychologist report. She was relieved to find that this psychologist was different. She didn't bombard her with questions but listened while Rachel talked.

When Rachel's mother phoned her that evening she felt relieved to hear her daughter sounding optimistic. The next night's phone call was not so positive. On the first day of her exercise programme Rachel had fallen out with the physiotherapist. Having agreed to at least try the exercises, Rachel found she just couldn't do it.

'She kept saying, you can do it, don't give up, keep going, as if I wasn't doing the exercise by choice. I just didn't have the strength and she just wouldn't listen.'

Rachel managed four days in the unit. On the fifth day she

was sitting in the shared lounge when another patient became acutely distressed. She crouched in the corner and started screaming following a disagreement with a member of staff. Rachel rang her mother that evening and asked to be collected. The consultant was called to see her before she went home.

'He thought he could talk me into staying. What's the policy of this unit anyway, I said to him, bully people better? I should never have been admitted to that ward.'

It was now one year later and as I listened to Rachel's story I felt sympathy for how difficult her life had been and how little progress she had made, but at the same time I wondered what she hoped I would do differently. With this thought in my mind I asked Rachel if she could transfer from her wheelchair to the couch to be examined.

Almost as soon as I had made the request I could see that Rachel would not be able to do what I had asked. Even with the support of both me and her father she could not bear enough of her own weight to get up on the couch. This was not an unusual situation in a general neurology clinic where many people are immobile for different reasons. Usually I examine people on the couch if they can make it there, otherwise I examine people sitting in their chair. But in Rachel's case she simply would not be dissuaded from trying. It was a vivid display. Every sinew of her body strained with the effort. All of us in the room tensed in preparation to catch her if she fell. I wondered if it was possible that Rachel needed me to share her experience of the impossible task I had set her. Perhaps she felt she had not convinced me yet. I reminded myself that exaggerating to convince is not the same as exaggerating to fool.

Some cries for help are louder than others if they have previously gone unheard.

Eventually Rachel relented. As I examined her in her chair I asked, 'Do you agree with the diagnosis of chronic fatigue syndrome?' Doctors are just like their patients. It is in the casual gaps between formal questions that the truth of what we want to know can be found. I was looking for a way in, but I was about to learn that I had got it wrong.

'No,' she said firmly. 'Have you even been listening? I don't have chronic fatigue syndrome, I have ME. Fatigue is something that everybody gets. The word is an insult. Fatigue happens if you go to bed late or exercise too much. You rest and then you feel better. I'm not tired. What I feel is nothing like fatigue. I feel like somebody has literally drained all the life out of me. Death would be an improvement compared to how I feel. I do not have chronic fatigue syndrome, I have ME!'

'ME, you're right, I'm sorry.'

'Can't you see how bad things are for me?' she said.

For everything she had told me and all she had done to convince me, I had left Rachel feeling that she had not done enough.

'I guarantee you, Rachel, that I am in no doubt about how bad things are for you. What I'm not certain about is how I can help you. I have looked through your test results and listened to what has happened to you and I agree with the diagnosis of ME. I'm not convinced that any more tests will make a difference.'

'I don't want any more tests. I want treatment. I have heard that interferons used to treat people with multiple sclerosis can help people with ME. I want you to prescribe them for me.'

'I'm really sorry, Rachel, but the treatment you are talking about is very dangerous and it isn't licensed for use in ME. There is no way that I can put you forward for it.'

'It doesn't matter how dangerous you think it is. I'm the one who is taking the risk, not you.' Rachel was pulling a newspaper and a number of magazines from her bag, a new vigour to her movement.

'You've seen how disabled Rachel is. You say you believe her. If you do then you know she has nothing to lose,' her father added. Her mother sat to one side, a handkerchief held to her face.

'I'm sorry. I have no say in this at all.'

'You mean the health service won't pay the money for the drug,' her father said angrily.

'I could just go to America and pay for it,' Rachel said, 'but I shouldn't have to do that. I should be able to get treatment here.'

'Interferons are not licensed for use in ME in any country. I'm sorry.'

Rachel thinks I have access to a treatment but I am withholding it. Or that she is a victim of a health service that is short of funds. But it is not a question of money or what the NHS can or cannot provide. A quarter of a million people in the UK and at least 2 million people in the States have ME (or chronic fatigue syndrome, as it is also known). To a certain degree each of those people will be at the mercy of the doctor they see; some will be dismissed, some will undergo inappropriate investigations, some will be prescribed antidepressant drugs and others will be referred for alternative therapies. It is possible that those seen by private doctors or alternative medical practitioners, in any country, might find themselves more likely to be offered unnecessary tests and unproven therapies. On his website one private doctor makes the uninterpretable claim that he treats ME by altering the patient's 'biological terrain', others offer magnesium injections or vitamin supplements. These are placebos at best, or evidence of profiteering at worst. But beyond the variations in practice of individual doctors there is no difference in the treatment of ME between developed countries, and Rachel will not be prescribed immune-modulating therapies no matter where she goes.

Having said that, sometimes patients persuade doctors to do things that are against their best judgement. I may not be able to make Rachel better, but I could possibly protect her from the danger of other inappropriate treatments and investigations. But Rachel had strong views about her illness and about how she wanted to proceed and they were hard to counter.

'Do you even believe that there are serious immune problems in people who suffer with ME?' she asked.

'I believe that ME is a serious disabling illness that nobody has yet fully explained.'

'That's a no,' Rachel's father said and turned to her. 'We're wasting our time once again.'

Rachel's mother let out a gasping sob that spoke for everybody in the room. We all felt the despair of a difficult road with nothing worthwhile to reward us at the end. Rachel was climbing a hill and every time she thought she had made it to the top she discovered she had not. I worried that Rachel would never reach her destination because that place does not exist. People have searched for it for centuries.

Chronic fatigue syndrome (CFS) has been subject to many explanations and has been given many different names. Its nineteenth-century ancestor was called neurasthenia. Neurasthenia was a syndrome with a long list of symptoms, many of which are very familiar; chronic fatigue, nerve pain, joint pain, depression, difficulty sleeping, anxiety, impotence, headache. A very particular feature was that the sufferers were not refreshed by sleep although many slept for most of every day. Patients exhibited a very extreme form of exhaustion although no physical weakness could be found in the limbs to explain it. The fullest early descriptions of the condition were given in 1869 by George Beard, a prominent American physician. Beard championed neurasthenia as an organic disease, imagining some depletion of resources in the peripheral nerves or brain as a result of overuse. Neurasthenia struck down the successful and the intellectual almost as if they had quite literally exhausted the nervous system through excessive use of their higher faculties. It was a modern illness attributable to the fast pace of life in the latter half of the nineteenth century. Here was an illness that victimised the elite.

Neurasthenia had much in common with hysteria. Both were defined by medically unexplained symptoms that led to disability but not to death. They came with no objective evidence for disease. But neurasthenia also had one feature all its own. Whereas hysteria was viewed, rightly or wrongly, as an illness mostly of women, neurasthenia was an illness that predominantly, although not exclusively, affected men. And nerve exhaustion would prove more robust than its sister hysteria. When the doctors in Europe who had championed hysteria began to disappear, neurasthenia grasped the opportunity to take over the world. By the early twentieth century neurasthenia had become the '*maladie à la mode*' in Paris, while in Harley Street it became one of the most frequently offered diagnoses.

With this new diagnosis came the possibility of new treatments. The most famous, or infamous, treatment was the Weir Mitchell rest cure. Developed by a neurologist based in Philadelphia, it subjected the neurasthenia sufferer to an unnatural sort of rest, in which they could not move, read, have a conversation, nor be subjected to stimulation of any kind. Patients were not allowed to stand and had to use the bedpan lying down. Extreme rest was combined with force-feeding with fatty foods and took place continuously over months. Many doctors made their fortune from this sort of 'cure'.

In time, however, neurasthenia would follow the trajectory of Charcot's hysteria. As more became understood about the physiology of the nervous system the idea of a finite energy source depleted by overuse was no longer viable. It also became obvious that the Weir Mitchell rest cure was as ineffective as it was costly. But the thing that cast neurasthenia most fervently in a new light was the dawning realisation that members of the lower orders, and even women, were just as likely to be affected as were rich and successful men. This flew in the face of all that was understood about nerve exhaustion reportedly brought on by excessive use of a superior intellect. The neurologists who had fought so hard for possession of the illness soon abandoned it with just as much fervour. Once the label had been rejected by the rich and successful, it was rejected by all society.

Neurasthenia became less prominent as a diagnosis although it did not disappear completely until at least the second half of the twentieth century. It still lurked in neurologists' offices, sometimes offered as an organic disease and other times as a polite alternative to depression. Fatigue did not disappear, of course, it was just reclassified. Some neurasthenic patients gained the label of melancholics, others had their symptoms attributed to infections or use of chemicals or one of a host of different physical complaints.

By the mid twentieth century the concept of a syndrome defined by fatigue had faded from doctors' arsenal of diagnoses. It would take a series of seemingly unrelated events occurring in different parts of the world to see chronic fatigue re-emerge with all the old controversies intact.

In 1955 in north London a mystery illness swept through the patients at the Royal Free Hospital. Soon the illness spread to the nurses and doctors. Over 200 people were struck down and the hospital was forced to close for two months. Patients presented with a flu-like illness followed by muscle aches, tiredness, headaches and memory lapses. The clinical features of the illness suggested to doctors that their patients were suffering from some unexplained inflammation of the brain and nerves. The term myalgic encephalomyelitis was applied. No cause was identified and no one died. This outbreak was the origin of the label ME.

Following on from this epidemic similar cases began to appear individually or in smaller numbers elsewhere. Scientists investigated a variety of different viruses and other organisms in an attempt to find an explanation. Every now and then, over many years, in an explosion of excitement, a new *cause* was found. Each was quickly disproved.

Then, in Incline Village, Nevada, in 1984, the Centre for Disease Control was called as 120 people out of a population of 6,000 fell ill with a mystery disease. No two patients were identical. Each had their own mix of symptoms, many included dizziness, numbness, aching joints, tiredness. At first there was no explanation, but then, after exhaustive tests, it was discovered that a large percentage had antibodies in their blood that suggested exposure to Epstein–Barr virus (EBV). A link had been created between chronic fatigue and EBV that would last to the present day. The fact that the majority of most adult populations do not suffer chronic fatigue but will have been exposed to EBV at some point in their lives, and therefore will also carry an antibody to the virus, did not deflate the enthu-siastic investigators in the least.

The 1980s was the era in which chronic fatigue became chronic fatigue syndrome. A veritable outbreak occurred. Newspapers and television shows blossomed with evocative stories about the disease that doctors didn't understand. People who had suffered for years found an explanation, if not a solu-tion. And the old neurasthenia debate began in earnest once again: was it even a real illness?

Chronic fatigue syndrome is defined in the simplest terms as an overwhelming fatigue that has been present for at least six months, is disabling, and where there is no psychiatric illness or other physical disease to explain it. ME is synonymous with chronic fatigue syndrome, and is the term favoured by some sufferers, particularly in the UK. To include ME/CFS in a book primarily concerned with the description of those suffering with psychosomatic illness is foolhardy to say the least. A fierce argument has raged for decades between those who consider this to be a purely organic disorder and those who view it as psychologically driven.

It is tempting to be obtuse at this point, to hide my opinion on the matter amongst the opinions of others. This is a very contentious issue whatever stance one takes. One of the foremost experts in CFS in the UK is reported to have received regular death threats for his position on the disorder. He is responsible for the largest number of scientific studies into CFS and yet he is accused of discouraging research in the area. He devised the most effective treatment programme for sufferers and at the same time he has been vilified for encouraging neglect of patients and leaving them to die. He is the person in the UK who has taken this illness the most seriously and who has devoted much of his career to solving the riddle, and yet he is accused of quite the opposite. His sin is that he is a psychiatrist and that he has emphasised the importance of the psychological mechanisms in the development and perpetuation of the chronic fatigue symptoms.

I will not be obtuse. I believe that psychological factors and behavioural issues, if they are not the entire cause, at the very least contribute in a significant way to prolonging the disability that occurs in chronic fatigue syndrome. Do I know that for sure? No, nobody does; but I am influenced by the lack of evidence for an organic disease. ME/CFS sufferers do not usually have any objective physical findings to explain their fatigue. They have been likened to those who had multiple sclerosis before that disease was properly understood. Their plight has also been likened to those victims of AIDS who died before the virus causing it was discovered. But even before the plaques of inflammation that are responsible for damaging the nerve cells were found in the brain to explain MS there was objective evidence of neurological deterioration to confirm the physical nature of the disease. Even before HIV was discovered as the cause of AIDS there were multiple blood test and other abnormalities that left no doubt as to the physical basis for the disease.

There is always much concern amongst ME/CFS sufferers that their condition simply hasn't been found yet. Doctors have the same worry, that they have missed something. In fact long-term follow-up studies of ME/CFS patients show that if the original diagnosis was made in a sound manner in the first instance, it would be exceptionally unusual for an organic diagnosis to emerge at a later date. The same studies also show that full recovery from the syndrome is very rare. The illness usually continues unabated but no evidence for an organic illness is ever found.

The World Health Organization classifies ME/CFS as a neurological disorder. To a neurologist this is more of a practical classification than an indication that ME/CFS is a neurological disease. In truth the term myalgic encephalomyelitis has been alienating to neurologists. Encephalomyelitis in its literal interpretation means inflammation of the brain and spinal cord. It is a condition seen by neurologists regularly, either caused by viral infections or autoimmune disease. Affected patients are often morbidly ill and confined to intensive care units. Absolute evidence for the presence of that inflammation is seen on scans, in the spinal fluid and on blood tests. It is often a fatal disease. There is no evidence for inflammation of either the brain or spinal cord in ME/CFS sufferers and the misnomer creates a barrier between neurologists and those with ME/CFS. Nor has there been any convincing evidence for a muscle or nerve disease as a cause. Most neurologists therefore do not see ME/CFS sufferers. It is not that they do not believe in the validity of the patient's suffering, but rather that they do not believe that they can help. In my early years training in neurology I encountered many patients with CFS, but more recently neurologists have distanced themselves from this disorder and patients are more likely to seek help from immunologists or endocrinologists. I do not currently see patients for the purpose of diagnosing or treating ME/CFS, but many of my patients with dissociative seizures have a history of ME/CFS and there is something very interesting in that fact alone.

Many ME/CFS sufferers cite evidence from scientific publications that they believe supports an organic cause for the illness. Indeed a variety of scientific studies have demonstrated reproducible anomalies in a range of different investigations carried out in CFS. Several viral infections have been implicated in the cause. There is certainly evidence that ME/CFS can be precipitated by exposure to an infecting agent, but once the infection has cleared there is no way of explaining how the syndrome of chronic fatigue develops, except perhaps to consider the psychological vulnerability of those affected and their behavioural response to the original illness.

A number of studies have shown irregularities in the immune system of those with ME. But the research is contradictory and the findings are not consistent amongst sufferers and therefore do not provide a coherent explanation for the symptoms they are said to produce. More recently scientists have become interested in the hypothalamic-pituitary-adrenal (HPA) axis which, as we've seen, helps control our response to stress. In ME/CFS sufferers it has been shown that there is dysfunction in this pathway, so perhaps sufferers cannot mount a sufficient hormonal response to stress when it is required of them. This might explain why stressful events, either psychological or physical, can trigger the illness and why those affected cannot recover when faced with stress. But again there is controversy, not all studies agree, and not every patient shows a hormonal abnormality.

No single scientific study provides either an absolute explanation or a diagnostic test for ME/CFS, but what they all do is confirm the physical reality of the illness, that systems of the body are not functioning as they should. They are evidence that even if the cause is psychological, the symptoms are not imagined.

So is it a somatisation disorder? ME/CFS is an illness in its own right that has not traditionally been referred to as a somatisation disorder, but that is not to say that it does not share common ground with psychosomatic disorders. It manifests as multiple medically unexplained symptoms. Sufferers of both disorders carry similar behaviours and illness beliefs and neither leads to evidence of organic disease however long you wait. ME sufferers also have many characteristics belonging to the diagnostic features of depression. Depression can manifest as tiredness and difficulty sleeping, for example.

And of course ME/CFS and psychosomatic disorders are linked by the same overarching question: are they real? Ask the 250,000 ME/CFS sufferers in the UK that question. Their lives are devastated by this illness. The reality of how life-destroying this problem is cannot be argued with. The question that we, the unaffected, must answer for ourselves is, can we give a disability that has its roots in behavioural or psychological factors the same respect that we offer to a physical disease? If the answer is yes, then none of the other controversies matter any longer.

It is important to recognise that ME/CFS sufferers have good reason to be defensive of their diagnosis. Many medical staff and lay people do not see this illness as either psychological or organic. Many people consider ME to be a non-illness, more a personality flaw than a medical complaint. Although CFS is not common many of us will have encountered someone in our lives who is affected and in those encounters I suspect some of us have had moments of cynicism.

So Rachel rails against the attitudes of others, and why shouldn't she when there is so much judgement about? But at the same time the strength of the defence that people mount against a psychological paradigm for this illness can be a problem. Sometimes, the more strongly something human and ordinary like sadness or stress are denied, the doctor becomes suspicious of subterfuge or of something being hidden. I have heard it often from my own patients: 'I had the most wonderful life until I fell ill, I hardly ever had a reason to feel stress.' And I think, how could that be? I have not had a day in my life with no stress at all. And my patients who have a diagnosis of an organic disease, such as epilepsy, are very open in their admission about how stress affects their illness. Stress makes everything worse – epilepsy, diabetes, asthma, migraine, and psoriasis are all exacerbated by it. So why would that not be the case for somatising disorders or CFS? In the absolute rejection of stress in these sufferers is there something for us to learn? It's possible that many patients worry that if they admit to any hardship in their lives then the doctor will latch on to that as the culprit for their illness and lose the ability to keep an open mind. Or perhaps it is not that simple. People with conversion disorders are often recognised to be alexithymic, which is a loss of the ability to interpret your own emotional state. Ask somebody with dissociative seizures how they feel, and you may get the answer 'tired' or 'cold' – neither answer contains anything of their emotional state. Perhaps those who deny stress do so because they do not feel stress, having converted it to something else.

Fortunately ME/CFS is not a common illness. Somatic symptom disorder by its strictest definition is also rare. The motor manifestations of a conversion disorder such as paralysis and convulsions will only ever affect a modest number of us. Those illnesses are the dramatic and sometimes bizarre end of a spectrum, but at the other end of that spectrum lies a more pedestrian set of somatic symptoms that many of us will experience many times in our lives. Somatic symptom disorder affects one in a hundred, but transient somatic symptoms resulting in illness without long-term disability affects one in four of the population.

A large percentage of people attending gastroenterology clinics have recurrent abdominal pain where no bowel disease is found. Irritable bowel syndrome (IBS) is a common explanation. Like CFS it is poorly understood and a psychological mechanism for it is not always easily accepted by the sufferers. But there is a close relationship between the presence of psychological distress and IBS, even if it is not the absolute cause. IBS sufferers often have a range of other somatic symptoms. They have a higher incidence of ME/CFS, they have a higher rate of illness in childhood, and a higher rate of attendances at their doctor's surgery. Many of the patients that I see with conversion disorders, particularly those with dissociative seizures, have a previous diagnosis of IBS, and that association once again gives me pause to think. And like ME/CFS patients, those with IBS have a very high rate of depression and anxiety.

Fatigue may be common, but pain is the commonest psychosomatic symptom and it is represented in every sort of hospital clinic. In the rheumatology clinic, joint and muscle pain that cannot be explained are seen frequently. Fibromyalgia is one disorder fairly often seen there. It presents as widespread muscle pain and is diagnosed when there is evidence of pain in eleven out of eighteen potential tender points. Fatigue is also a ubiquitous feature. Fibromyalgia has so much in common with ME/CFS that many doctors now consider the two disorders to be manifestations of the same illness.

Pain comes to the neurologist as headache. Chronic headaches are increasingly called chronic migraine, with old names like tension headache falling out of favour. And yet antidepressants, psychological intervention and relaxation exercises remain standard in the treatment – which is telling in itself. Chronic headache comes with mood disturbance and with all of the common features of ME/CFS and IBS.

Every sort of clinic is equally represented with potential somatic disorders presenting as pain. In the cardiology clinic there is non-cardiac chest pain. In the gynaecology clinic there is pelvic and abdominal pain. In the urology clinic there is pain passing urine. But while pain is the commonest somatic symptom it is far from the only one. Respiratory physicians see patients with unexplained shortness of breath. Dermatologists see itching and rashes that quickly come and go. Ophthalmologists see people with blurring of vision, ENT doctors see people with hearing loss. ME/CFS by its fullest definition is not very common, but chronic fatigue not fulfilling the criteria for CFS accounts for one in ten consultations with a family doctor. Dissociative seizures are rare in the wider community but one in five people who go to an epilepsy clinic transpire to have dissociative seizures rather than epilepsy. Thirty per cent who go to a rheumatology clinic suffer with pain for which medicine cannot account. Fifty per cent of those who go to a general medical clinic have symptoms that cannot be explained. Sixty per cent of women who go to see a gynaecologist have symptoms for which no cause is found. The impact of our emotional well-being on our health is not a trifling problem. I only wish I could convince Rachel of this.

Samuel Johnson said that the chains of habit are too weak to be felt until they are too strong to be broken. There are ways to help Rachel but she must be willing to give something up and to change some patterns of behaviour. So I tell her that although we differ on some points, there is one thing about which we are both in absolute agreement: that she is getting worse instead of better.

She says, yes.

'If we agree on that, then can we agree that your current way of managing your fatigue is not helping?'

'Yes.'

'And if that is the case then what is there to lose by trying a different way?'

'It depends what it is.'

I could not persuade Rachel to consider anything but medication to treat her fatigue. The only treatment proven to offer at least some benefit to those with ME/CFS is a graded exercise programme and cognitive behavioural therapy (CBT). And Rachel was quite right, CBT is no magic bullet, it is hard work, it doesn't help everybody and she had tried it before. I reminded her that if somebody with diabetes doesn't get better with their first tablet, they don't abandon the treatment, they try a higher dose. If someone with asthma does not get better with one inhaler, they try a second. ME/CFS is no different to that, some people get better with one course of treatment and some people need a second. Rachel would not be moved. As we talked I was aware that she didn't really want a better treatment, she wanted a better diagnosis. And why shouldn't she? ME/CFS is a disabling illness, the treatment is laborious and slow, the outcome is often poor and for all of that, outside her family, she would get very little understanding or sympathy.

The diagnostic label that a doctor offers the patient has many implications. With a diagnosis comes treatment and prognosis.

'You have gastroenteritis. Take this tablet and you should be better within one week. Most people recover and the problem is not usually recurrent.' Once you know what's wrong you can convey it to friends and colleagues. You know what to expect next and when you might recover. A label validates our suffering, both to ourselves and others. If I have a cough and a runny nose and I tell people I'm suffering with a cold, I am saying I don't feel great but neither is it all that bad. But, with no evidence except how I feel, I might instead choose to tell people I have the flu. I have elevated my suffering. But what if I take the word 'flu' and add a prefix, 'man-flu'? The entire illness has been transformed again.

Neurasthenia, hysteria, melancholia, depression, chronic fatigue syndrome, chronic fatigue immune dysfunction syndrome, myalgic encephalomyelitis, yuppie flu: all these labels impact upon how a patient receives their diagnosis, how they move forward and also how they are received by the world. If you have been housebound for a year, have lost your job and your relationship has broken down, it's not hard to understand that the label 'yuppie flu' does not encapsulate the experience. I see this in my clinic regularly when I tell a patient that their seizures are not due to epilepsy. In my early years as a consultant I often called dissociative seizures by another common name, psychogenic non-epileptic attacks. Using that label I had many conversations that went something like this:

'The seizures you have are called psychogenic non-epileptic seizures.'

'So now I'm a psycho, am I?'

'You know that's not what I mean.'

'What do I tell my employer?'

'Tell them you have seizures. You don't have to go into the specifics.'

'They'll want a medical report.'

'I will word the report carefully and anything you want to keep confidential, you can.'

Then the patient would meet the psychiatrist before we met again.

'He told me the proper name for the seizures is dissociative seizures. Why didn't you just tell me that?'

The naming of dissociative seizures has changed several times in the years since I qualified as a doctor. For a very long time they were referred to as 'pseudoseizures'. 'Pseudo': something that is pretending to be something it is not. How do you give that diagnosis to your loved one or your boss? Now 'non-epileptic attacks' is commonly used. In my experience that label says a lot about what is *not* wrong and so little about what *is* that patients walk away feeling that they have been given no diagnosis at all.

For many years I had a preference for the term 'psychogenic non-epileptic seizures'. It acknowledges the seizures and the psychological factors that might act as a trigger. If a patient can accept the psychogenic component of the illness they are far more likely to recover fully. But more recently I have come to see that sometimes the use of the word 'psychogenic' is presumptive and exposing. So now I do say, you have dissociative seizures. It is a diagnostic label that is descriptive rather than demeaning or judgemental. And yet, when I use this term I have a lingering concern. The name shields patients from the judgement of others but does it also allow a person to hide something from themselves? While psychiatrists and neurologists understand the term dissociative, most people do not and it could inadvertently strengthen the conviction that a disease is physical in origin. That can preserve dignity in the face of suffering, but the more completely somebody has denied the psychiatric diagnosis and imagined a particular physical paradigm to explain an illness, the more prolonged that illness becomes.

Maybe it is time to stop changing the labels and start changing the attitudes to psychological illness instead.

Hypochondriac is another common label applied to people whose symptoms are medically unexplained.

Daniel was twenty-three years old. He was generally fit and well. He had never had any significant illness. He came to see me because he had headaches. He described them as a small twinge of pain in the back of his head, 'like something burrowing under my skull'. The headache was not severe enough to require painkillers, nor severe enough to stop him doing normal things, but it was worrying him. An acquaintance had died suddenly of a brain haemorrhage.

I had listened to all of Daniel's story and the headache he described did not have any of the features of a brain haemorrhage.

'If it's not a haemorrhage, could it be a brain tumour?'

Again, very unlikely.

'I think this is a very benign sort of headache, Daniel. Why don't you try waiting a couple of weeks, look after yourself, drink water, avoid alcohol, do some exercise and it will probably be gone before you know it.'

'I do believe it's nothing serious but I would believe it more if you did a brain scan.'

'I don't think you need a scan, Daniel.'

'It will make me feel better.'

What Daniel didn't know was that it could well make him feel worse. There is a terribly delicate balance in the investigation of benign-sounding symptoms. One must investigate to rule out a physical cause if it seems necessary, but the line where investigations should be stopped is drawn very faintly. *Primum non nocere.* First, do no harm. If you investigate and find something incidental, what do you do? And when do you say no more tests?

Whenever I am faced with these dilemmas I think of a patient I once had called Eleanor. She had a diagnosis of epilepsy but epilepsy was not the illness she started with. Since her teen years Eleanor had suffered many unexplained medical complaints. She had numerous tests, none of which had ever shown an abnormality. Then, after years of chronic pain in her back and in her joints, Eleanor began to complain of headaches. Her GP referred her to a neurologist and she was told that her headaches were nothing serious. Her GP advised some lifestyle changes. But Eleanor just could not shake the idea that her headaches had a sinister cause. The neurologist agreed to arrange a scan to give Eleanor some peace of mind. It was not successful. The scan did not show a brain tumour, but it did show a five-millimetre aneurysm, an area of weakness in the wall of a blood vessel which was like a small balloon. Eleanor's anxiety levels were higher than ever.

The type of headache that Eleanor described could not be

caused by the aneurysm so this was an incidental finding. It was likely that the aneurysm had been present for many years and Eleanor could have lived happily for a lifetime without ever knowing that she had it. But now she did know.

If an aneurysm bursts it causes a brain haemorrhage, but not every aneurysm will burst. In up to five per cent of autopsies of people who have died for other reasons, an incidental unruptured asymptomatic aneurysm is found. There was no reason to believe that Eleanor's aneurysm had ever bled, so treatment was not automatically recommended. But Eleanor could not live with the sense of this time bomb in her head, waiting to explode. Therefore she chose to have treatment.

Eleanor was taken to the X-ray department and given an anaesthetic. Once she was asleep, the radiologist passed a catheter into Eleanor's groin and threaded it up through the blood vessels of her abdomen and into the blood vessels of her brain. The radiologist could follow the progress of the catheter on an X-ray projection. He placed the tip of the tubing into the mouth of the aneurysm. He began to inject. He was going to fill the aneurysm with a platinum coil so that it was rendered harmless. The procedure did not go well. It caused the aneurysm to burst. Eleanor had a serious haemorrhagic stroke from which she never fully recovered. She was paralysed down one side and suffered with epileptic seizures from then on.

No one will ever know if, without the treatment, the aneurysm would have ruptured anyway at some point in the future. Or if, without the scan, Eleanor would have lived all her life happily without ever knowing it was there.

MRI scans are such sophisticated and sensitive ways of imaging the body that it is not unusual for them to pick up incidental findings that do not necessarily cause illness. We are as different on the inside as we are on the outside. Sometimes, for example, scans detect small cysts that have been present since birth and are entirely harmless. But if you have a brain scan for reassurance and such a cyst is found, will you feel better or worse?

Many investigation results are misinterpreted by doctors. Lyme disease, one of Rachel's diagnoses, is another very good example of this. Lyme disease is potentially a very serious disorder but a lot of doctors are very bad at interpreting the test results for it. In the United States, where this tick-borne disease is endemic in certain areas, it is a commonly over-diagnosed disorder. One study looking at patients attending a Lyme disease clinic showed that sixty per cent had been given the diagnosis in error. Each was exposed to unnecessary treatment, were led to believe they had a serious disease, and deprived of their true diagnosis and correct treatment. Lyme disease can cause many vague symptoms including pain and fatigue. In people with psychosomatic illness it can provide a more palatable explanation for their symptoms than a psychogenic explanation will.

Blood tests, X-rays, every test, comes with the same risk. Some tests are particularly difficult to interpret and therefore open to errors. To carry out a test is not a benign procedure, so I made a deal with Daniel.

'Why don't you give this headache time to go away naturally first. Drink more water, eat healthily, get more sleep and wait a month. If you don't get better we can re-discuss the scan.'

As Daniel left I knew that the consultation had not gone well because he looked like a small child who had not got his way.

I wondered if he would see another doctor and ask them for the scan instead. Two days later my secretary took a call. Daniel could not wait to have the scan. Could you arrange it now please? I was reluctant but, because I thought Daniel could not find peace of mind without it, I made the appointment for him. Even as I did it I wondered if I was making a mistake. The day after the scan Daniel rang to ask for the result. The scan was normal. I was as relieved as Daniel, but for different reasons.

A month later Daniel and I met again to see how he was doing. He was happy that the scan was normal but now he was wondering if there was a more sensitive type of scan he could have. The headache was no worse but he was worried that something had been missed. He pointed out a single point on the back of his head where he located the pain. He told me again that he felt something burrowing or bursting through that point of his skull. 'I feel something pressing against my brain.' He asked me to feel the point on his skull and I told him again that I could not feel anything out of the ordinary. As we talked, his hand reached unconsciously to the back of his head every few seconds. I assured him that the scan he had had was very sensitive and showed nothing at all to cause concern. With his agreement I referred him to the physiotherapist for relaxation exercises. As he walked out the door he was a little boy lost once again. I felt as if my words of reassurance had bounced off him. I wondered what it would have taken to make him believe me, but if I knew that I would have done it.

We met again. The pain was a little better, but still there.

Daniel had done some research. He knew that high blood pressure could cause headaches so he had bought a blood pressure monitor from a local pharmacy. He had brought a detailed list of the blood pressure readings he had taken over the past week. Each day he had recorded at least thirty measurements. Some of them seemed a little high. I had to explain to Daniel that the readings were not nearly high enough to account for his headache and, besides, the sort of headache he had was very different to the sort caused by high blood pressure. Daniel accepted that his head pain was not due to hypertension but now he would like to meet a cardiologist to discuss his blood pressure.

We all do it a little – worry about the thing that might never happen – but some make a sort of habit of it and, when they do, the anticipation of illness can be so life-destroying that when the illness happens it is almost a relief. It is quite normal to be worried about your health from time to time. As a doctor I am often asked by family and friends and acquaintances to give my opinion on some ailment.

'How long does it normally take to recover from a viral infection? Is two weeks too long?'

'My daughter slipped and banged her head. Her head hit the floor really hard. How do I know if she's okay?'

'Look at this lump, what do you think it is?'

Although it is normal to seek reassurance, some people can find themselves pursuing every symptom until it is the pursuit itself rather than the symptoms that lead to an inability to function fully in the world. That is the plight of the worried well.

People who suffer with hypochondriasis, the modern term for

which is health anxiety, can find themselves obsessed with their health and the anticipation of ill health so that their lives are almost taken over by it. In conversion disorders or somatic symptom disorders the disability is caused by real physical symptoms such a paralysing fatigue, weakness, convulsions and so on. Health anxiety is very different from this. There is no physical disability. The symptoms themselves may be innocuous. It is not the symptom that disables but the anxiety about the symptoms.

Unlike conversion disorders, where the patient may feel emotionally well, in hypochondriasis that is not the case, and the sufferer's life is taken over by anxiety. Every small ache and moment of dizziness is imagined into something bigger. A habit of self-checking can develop. Does that red mark on my arm look different than it did yesterday? How many times did I go to the toilet today? Every symptom that is monitored is kept in the mind, and in doing so it is perpetuated. And every test that is ordered brings the thought of ill health to the fore.

I tried to explain to Daniel that I feared his anxiety about his health was his real problem. We had a long discussion and Daniel recognised that he was anxious. His family and friends told him he was obsessing over nothing so he had heard this view before. Daniel had already spent over six months believing in a serious cause for his headache. Nothing had been uncovered but his every waking moment had been taken up with it. I told him I was worried that he could stay trapped in this vicious cycle for years if his anxiety was not addressed and that I would like him to see a psychologist and to consider cognitive behavioural therapy. Daniel could learn to respond differently to changes that he notices in his body. He agreed to see a therapist.

Could Daniel learn to do things differently?

Consider Daniel's usual pattern: he feels a pain in his back that he immediately suspects – no, he *knows* – is something very serious. He researches back pain on the Internet and is shocked by the list of possibilities. He can imagine cancer spreading through his bones. When he is in the shower he searches his body for the source of the cancer. He can't find anything amiss but he wonders if that's worse. Perhaps he wouldn't be able to have chemotherapy if they don't know where it began? He makes an urgent appointment to see his doctor. The doctor says that the back pain is nothing and that Daniel should just forget about it. Daniel does not go to football practice that evening for fear of exacerbating the problem. He tries to rest but that night he cannot sleep. Daniel waits seventy-two hours before calling his doctor again. This time the doctor agrees to arrange for an X-ray to be done. Daniel takes the X-ray request to his local hospital. On the way there he noticed that the pain had spread to a place between his shoulder blades. After he has had the X-ray he asks the radiographer if it shows anything abnormal. She said the result would be sent to his doctor. As he leaves the room he watches the radiographer looking at the picture on the computer. She is pointing at the screen; what is she pointing at? Every day for the next week Daniel phones his doctor's office for the result. They say they don't have it. Are they afraid to give him the news? It can't take one week to report a normal X-ray, he thinks. While he is waiting for the result he keeps a diary of how severe the pain has become. It began as a three out of ten and now it is a six. One week later he sees his doctor again and is told that the

X-ray is completely normal. 'But that's impossible,' Daniel says. His GP sends him home and tells him to stop worrying. Daniel does not stop worrying. He has not yet been given a satisfactory explanation for his pain and he wants to see another doctor and to have more tests.

If Daniel learned to react differently to his symptoms the pattern might look more like this: Daniel feels a pain in his back. For a moment he is very worried but then he reminds himself that most people get aches and pains from time to time and in young people they are rarely serious, and most just disappear. He observes the pain for a moment. It's not severe, and he reminds himself that he is otherwise well. He decides to carry on his day as normal as he has practised with the psychologist. He doesn't search the Internet or tell his colleagues about the pain. When at work he notices the pain again and feels the familiar wave of panic, but Daniel replaces the thought with something relaxing and pleasant that he has practised with his therapist so that he can carry on with his day. When he finds himself thinking of telephoning his GP he flicks the elastic band on his wrist and it acts as a reminder that most symptoms are transient and due to nothing serious at all. Daniel has a busy day at work and for almost an hour he forgets the pain completely, but that evening it comes back. He spends half an hour meditating and feels better. His inclination is not to but he does go to football that evening as usual. He maintains his normal routine for one week and somewhere in that time the back pain has disappeared. He is not quite sure when it happened. He never knew exactly what caused the pain, but now it is gone that doesn't seem to matter.

But of course it would not be quite as easy as that. Daniel had borne his worries about his health for many years. Before any recovery would happen more reassurance would be needed. Less than twenty-four hours after our last conversation I got another phone call. Daniel would like one more scan before he goes to see the psychologist. In a way I understood what had happened. In the cold light of day, sitting with me in my office, his normal scan pictured on the computer screen, Daniel could believe, for the moment at least, that everything was okay. But alone at night in the dark it would be a long time before he could learn to keep his anxiety at bay.

8

CAMILLA

The most remarkable example of the way in which the two states were entangled yet unaware of each other.

Sigmund Freud, *Studies in Hysteria* (1895)

When I met Camilla for the first time she was sitting on her bed in the video-telemetry unit. She was a slight creature; I towered over her. Accompanied by a team of junior doctors and nurses, we surrounded her and could so easily have made her appear diminished. We were in our work clothes, she in her night clothes, we were rifling through paperwork, she was half reclined on the bed. But, somehow, Camilla maintained a rare sort of dignity. In the future I would wonder if it was not just that forbearance that had been Camilla's weakness all along.

Camilla's life had been full of opportunity from the start. There was no way to anticipate how a single event would change everything for her. She referred to her family as 'comfortably off'. Her father worked as a banker. Her mother, an air hostess, had given up her job to start a family. Camilla's upbringing was a happy one, she was allowed to be a child when that was appropriate and then an independent teenager, but her parents were always there waiting to give her support when needed.

The result was that Camilla grew up to be well balanced and confident. But a little sheltered, she would add. At the age of eighteen Camilla had gone to university to study law. She told me that when she was interviewed for her university place she had told her interviewers tales of all the good she wanted to do, how she would help the defenceless and punish the guilty.

'I think I was lying when I told them that,' she said, 'I had barely been out in the world. I didn't know hardship then so I had to make something up that I thought they'd like.'

It may have been true that when Camilla was eighteen she had never met the defenceless she spoke of, but eventually her prediction for her future would prove correct.

Camilla had had an insular and protected upbringing, but that did not mean she did not have the ability to look outside herself. She was interested in the world around her. She enjoyed politics and world affairs. They had felt remote to her when she lived at home but university life helped transform the wider world into something real.

'I wish I could go back to that time,' she said, 'when everything seemed possible and I thought I could solve any problem I encountered. Life really knocks that out of you, doesn't it?'

After leaving university Camilla took a job in a big City firm in London, fancying that she would pursue a career in business law or follow her father into banking.

'I think I always doubted how suited I was to that sort of work,' she told me, 'but I went along with it for a while.'

Over the next few years Camilla's life followed the course mapped out for her. Hard work saw her well respected in her workplace. Her personal life was also fulfilling. At the age of twenty-four she had fallen in love with an old college friend, Hugh. They were both twenty-seven when they married.

'Hugh and I married at the exact same age that my parents had,' she told me.

A year later they moved from their small flat in central London to a modestly large home suitable for a family. The fifteen years that followed brought many changes in Camilla's life. The couple became a family with the arrival of their two small children. In a decision that she would never have predicted when her career was just beginning she took six years off while her children were young.

'I'm not old-fashioned,' she said, 'I just wanted my children to have the childhood I had: hot summer days and paddling pools. That's how I remember it at least.'

Once the children were at school Camilla decided to return to work. That was when she noticed the change in herself.

'I couldn't even contemplate going back to a corporate environment,' she said. 'As soon as I tried to imagine myself in a meeting, defending my client's position, poring over heaps of documents, I realised my heart wasn't in it. I knew it was the wrong career for me.'

Hugh was partner in a large law firm by then so, with no pressure to return to paid work, Camilla initially took a job volunteering at a free legal advice clinic. She would later say that this was the most rewarding job she had ever done. She had found a fight that she could invest in. Most compelling for her were the family cases; cases of neglect, abuse, deprivation – she was helping people survive the most harrowing experiences. After a year of volunteer work she began the process of retraining in family law. Camilla brought the compassion of motherhood and the negotiating skills of her training in business to her new role and rose quickly through the ranks. Before long she was fully qualified and working almost as hard as she had done before the children were born. Her new job required her to work long hours, sometimes travelling throughout the UK. She had felt a little guilty about this at first. Lengthy conversations with Hugh eventually convinced her that she could be a mother and have a demanding career at the same time. The children were now nine and eleven years old, Hugh also worked long hours but could work from home when needed and they had plenty of extended family to help out if required.

'The first time I had to stay away from home overnight I couldn't sleep, I felt like such a bad mother. But when I got home the children had had a great time without me, all treats and games with their grandmother. That made it a lot easier the next time.'

It was on one such trip that Camilla fell ill. She had been working in Cumbria for two days and was due to return home. She had just come out of a meeting when her head felt light and a wave of nausea struck and she thought she might faint.

'The meeting had been a huge success,' she said, 'it was a jubilant moment. There was no reason for it to happen just then.'

Camilla sat down in a corridor after telling a colleague that she felt strange. The building was overheated and people brushed past her as she tried to bend forward to rest her head in her hands. A local colleague was with her and he said that he would get her a glass of water. As he disappeared she noticed that her right hand began to tremble. Within one minute the trembling moved to her left hand. She sat back and laid her head against a wall as she felt the shaking become more violent. She felt the intensity of how alone she was. Strangers filed past, creating an arc around her, as if she had suddenly become contagious. Some stopped to stare. By the time her colleague had returned the shaking had spread to her legs so that she was half slipping from her chair with all four limbs flapping. Her heart was pounding in her chest. She tried to ask for help but found that no words would come.

An ambulance was called. When it arrived Camilla was lying on the ground, her eyes fixed open, her breath held, her limbs still moving out of her control. Her colleague had attempted to lay his jacket under her head but she was moving so much that it did not help and her head repeatedly hit the floor. By now several strangers had come to her assistance; one gripped her shoulders as if he could stop the shaking just by force.

Camilla vividly recalled the moment when the paramedic stooped down to her. She was awake and aware of the shaking but powerless to let people know that she could see and hear them. He spoke to her in a thick accent and she could not understand what was being said.

'He was a huge man,' she said, 'he got down on his knees and was so close to me that I could feel his breath on my face. I could hear kindness in his voice but I was terrified. When I didn't answer he stood up again and placed a stretcher on the floor beside me. Another paramedic helped him lift me on to it. I remember being acutely aware of the feeling that my skirt was riding up my thighs and of everybody looking at me.'

Camilla had a terrifying ten-minute journey to a local hospital. For the whole trip her arms and legs flapped wildly, her back arched and her breathing alternated between nothing at all and huge gasps. She was certain that she would never see her children or husband again. Once in the casualty department she was wheeled into a dark room where a doctor and nurse were waiting.

'They looked panicked,' she said, 'as if they didn't know what to do. The nurse grabbed my arm and the doctor took blood. After a while more people came running into the room. It was chaos. Eventually three nurses were holding me. They rolled me over and gave me an injection in my bottom. It made exactly no difference. It didn't help.'

Camilla was given three injections before the movement in her limbs quietened, after which she slowly drifted out of consciousness. When she awoke she was lying in a different room with a drip attached to her arm. Another patient lay in a bed beside her, an old woman with rasping breath. An old man sat by the woman's bed gripping her hand.

'I felt utterly disorientated. Like going to bed in your own house and waking up in Narnia. I tried to sit up but felt so dizzy I had to lie back again. I looked around for my handbag so I could get my phone to call Hugh but it wasn't there. The old man saw how upset I was and said he would go and get the nurse.'

The nurse arrived a few minutes later and told Camilla that she had suffered a seizure. They had stabilised her with drugs and the doctor would see her later. Camilla's colleague, who had seen her collapse, appeared soon after. He had followed the ambulance to the hospital and had waited there for Camilla to wake up. He had also phoned the London office and had been given Hugh's mobile number, but had been unable to get hold of him. The colleague had kept hold of Camilla's handbag and returned it to her. As soon as she could Camilla rang Hugh's office and was told that Hugh was at a meeting but they would track him down as a matter of urgency and have him phone her back.

Half an hour later Camilla was alone and still had not spoken to Hugh when the doctor came to see her.

'They told me that I had suffered a seizure and that they thought I might have a brain tumour. They said I needed a brain scan but that they couldn't do it. I would have to go somewhere else for that. They were trying to arrange for me to go to another hospital but they didn't know how long that would take.'

Shortly after, Camilla's phone rang. A panicked Hugh was on the other end of the line. He told Camilla that he was getting straight into the car and would be with her in a few hours. He arranged for his mother to care for the children. Another colleague came to sit with Camilla while she was waiting for Hugh to arrive. The colleague had gone to her hotel and collected her overnight things and brought them to the hospital.

'For the second time, all I could think was that these relative strangers had seen my underwear. The whole experience was so degrading.'

In the hours that followed Camilla had three more convulsions until eventually her colleague was asked to leave and she was alone with the nurses again. Hugh arrived later the same day and, after he had seen Camilla, he asked to speak to the doctor in charge. He was also told that they thought it very likely that Camilla had a brain tumour. They were in the process of arranging for a transfer to a hospital that had scanning facilities but it could take several days for a bed to become available. Hugh did not hesitate. He contacted his medical insurer and arranged for Camilla to be admitted to a private hospital in London. A private ambulance was booked and cancelled four times over the course of the next few days. Every time Camilla was scheduled for transfer she had another seizure and the doctors did not think she would survive the journey. Eventually, heavily sedated and accompanied by an anaesthetist, Camilla was allowed to travel.

'For six days I believed absolutely that I had a brain tumour. I was so relieved when we got the scan result. And now . . . I wish it had been a tumour.'

Camilla spent ten days in hospital in London. She underwent a series of tests. None were conclusive but eventually the doctors were sufficiently convinced that she had epilepsy and started her on treatment. Her seizures slowly disappeared. When Camilla was finally discharged her children were waiting excitedly at the front door of their house to welcome her home. They had decked the house with banners and balloons that said how glad they were to have their mother back.

Camilla spent the next two weeks recuperating. The seizures settled down in time and Camilla was happy to return to the normality of work.

The following eighteen months were full of hopes raised and dashed for Camilla. The seizures which seemed so well controlled at first kept recurring. And they changed. In the beginning she was helpless but awake for the duration of the convulsion but over time the seizures brought a deep loss of consciousness that she found particularly distressing. Her doctor increased her medication and then changed it and changed it again. Each new drug brought a brief reprieve, a few weeks seizure-free, but the improvement was never sustained.

'If I hated one thing more than anything else about the seizures it was the unpredictability. They teased me. *Camilla . . . go back to work . . . everything will be alright*, they said. But they were lying. Every time I thought I could get on with my life, there they were.'

In fact Camilla did continue to work. She was never far from the computer at home and during the lulls in her illness she continued to travel.

'It teased me and I defied it,' she said, 'but it won in the end.'

When the seizures continued unabated, Camilla's neurologist became concerned and referred her for video telemetry. During that admission she had suffered several seizures that led to the revision of her diagnosis.

'I'm sorry, but I think the original diagnosis was wrong. The attacks we have seen are not due to epilepsy; they are non-epileptic attacks, they have an emotional cause,' she was told.

Two weeks later I received a letter from her doctor:

This very nice woman has been told that she has pseudo-seizures. She is having great difficulty accepting this. I have known Camilla for many years, she is a very intelligent, sensible, successful woman and I share her doubt about the diagnosis. I would appreciate if you could admit her for further tests.

And a while later, following a further week of video telemetry, Camilla and Hugh and I had sat together so that I could tell her that I agreed that she had dissociative seizures.

'I still don't believe it. I'm not that sort of person.'

What sort of person, I think, but do not say.

'I'm happily married with two beautiful children; my life has never been so full or so rewarding. I've had times in my life way harder than now, why didn't it happen then?'

'I'm not sure I can answer that. But that can be explored and understood and you can get better.'

Camilla had fixed me with an emotionless gaze throughout our conversation. She challenged me to back down, to change my mind.

'Do you understand how humiliated this makes me feel?'

This is the saddest of truths. For Camilla this diagnosis was more like an insult than an explanation of what was wrong.

'This could happen to anybody. It's an illness, it needs attention and treatment.'

In fact the humiliation meted out to Camilla by her illness extended far beyond just the implications of the diagnosis. She had suffered many seizures in strange places surrounded by people she did not know. During a period when she believed the seizures were in remission she had gone on holiday with Hugh and the children to Morocco.

'I collapsed in a public square when I was there. Hugh was

in a shop with the girls and I was on my own for the only time during the whole holiday. I was surrounded by a throng of people when it began. I didn't have time to get somewhere less public, I collapsed right where I was in the most frightening place I could imagine. A man called a group of women to help me so I suppose I was lucky. They did look after me, but it was awful. Two sat on me. I was flapping about the place and they were straddling me. The others broke into some sort of prayer, a high-pitched wailing. They were waving their arms and shouting up to the heavens. They meant well, I suppose. All around them men and children craned to see the spectacle.'

'That must have been awful. Did it stop you travelling?'

'Why not travel?' she was incensed now. 'Do you think having a seizure in England is any less degrading?'

Camilla helped remind me what it feels like to find yourself helpless in an unsympathetic, voyeuristic world.

'I have collapsed in the street lots of times. I chose to get on with my life. I didn't want to hide indoors. Lots of people are compassionate and helpful. They might try to pin me to the ground but those people mean no harm, I know that. I've had a couple try to stick their fingers in my mouth in some sort of attempt to stop me choking. It's disgusting but, again, they are trying to help. But do you know what happens all the time? People video me on their mobile phones and walk away laughing.'

It did not stop there.

'I was standing outside a shop one day, talking to Hugh on my phone. I felt it coming on. Sometimes it starts in my arms and I have time to sit down but this time it started in my legs and I just dropped to the floor. The shaking was moving from limb to limb but I was still awake. A man got down on his knees beside me and asked me if I was okay. I couldn't answer. And do you know what he did? He picked my mobile phone up off the ground and ran away.'

I imagined how the powerlessness of it must have left her feeling.

'I was on a train about half an hour outside London when I had one once. I have a note which I carry in my wallet and if I have time I get it out to show people. I can't talk so it tells people not to panic and to leave me be. My whole body was shaking as I showed the note to the people sitting beside me. It says, I have epilepsy but I'm fine, the seizure will wear off in its own time, there's no need to call an ambulance. A bunch of do-gooders decided my best interests would be served by removing me from the train. They manhandled me to a standing position and half walked, half carried me to the exit. They then put me on the platform with my bag and told the stationmaster that I needed a doctor. I was desperate to tell them to let me stay on the train. I just wanted to go home. The words wouldn't come out. What will my note say now? I'm mad, stay clear it might be catching?'

But it was not only the reaction of strangers that proved a problem.

'Even before I was told that these attacks were in my head people at work said terrible things to me. I had several convulsions at work and one day I was lying on the ground with a really nice girl from the office fussing over me when a colleague came up to her and I heard him say, leave her alone, there's nothing wrong with her. I couldn't believe it but once he'd said it I started to see that attitude everywhere. Some people were nice but some people decided I was going mad even before I knew they were right. One day there was a meeting scheduled and I was told not to attend. My seizures might detract from the important discussions of the day.'

'You know the Disability Discrimination Act applies to this illness?'

'Don't you see? I was embarrassed. I didn't want to do anything that would draw even more attention to me. I wanted to crawl into a hole.'

'But you didn't.'

'Now I have to. I can't tell them this.'

The revision of Camilla's diagnosis added another dimension to her struggle. When a patient receives a diagnosis of dissociative seizures within days or even weeks of their onset they often disappear almost the instant the diagnosis is delivered. I did not think that Camilla would be so lucky. Her pattern was set. She had lived with the belief of a diagnosis of epilepsy for nearly two years and now that diagnosis was being taken away. Her distress was exacerbated by the protracted nature of her journey.

'Can she have a second opinion?' Hugh asked.

I was Camilla's second opinion.

'Of course, you need to be happy that the diagnosis is correct. I do need to keep you in hospital while I withdraw your epilepsy drugs. Can I ask that you do one thing while you're still here? Will you see the psychiatrist, just to explore all the avenues?'

'But there's nothing on my mind. Nothing is bothering me. Any problems I've had in my life I've dealt with.'

'You may be right but there is very little to lose by having one meeting.'

Camilla agreed and, for a moment after, we sat looking at each other in silence.

'Okay?' I asked as I left.

'Okay,' she said, and just as I crossed the threshold, 'I do believe that things like this can happen to people through stress, you know. I've seen terrible things in my work and I've seen the catastrophic reactions that people have in the face of them. I just don't believe that something like that could affect me.'

'It could happen to anyone.'

'Have you had anything like this?'

'Not to the point that it caused illness, no. But, like most people, my body reacts to stress all the time. I've often felt dizzy and light-headed when I'm worried about something. But because I recognise it, it doesn't bother me. I think of it as my friend, my early-warning system.'

'You would like me to make friends with my seizures?'

'As ridiculous as it might sound they may be there to protect you from something else. They may already be your friend.'

Sometimes people appear to behave in a way that brings them unhappiness or harm. People create arguments where none are necessary. They stay in abusive relationships when they could escape. They give up their ambitions for seemingly little reason. Behaviour that seems irrational might make more sense if you could appreciate the purpose it serves. Sometimes we create conflict with others because the intensity of feeling it leads to makes us feel less lonely. To feel hated can be less distressing than to feel forgotten. Sometimes being with anybody is better than being with nobody. Sometimes giving up feels better than failing. Sometimes failing through illness feels better than just failing. The unconscious substitutions we make to protect ourselves do not make sense when we do not understand them fully. I didn't understand Camilla's seizures yet, but that didn't mean I never would.

Where it is possible to identify why an individual has developed a psychosomatic illness, it is far easier for the doctor to make the diagnosis and for the patient to accept it and in turn to recover. The most frequently asked questions – Why me? Why now? – are the most difficult to answer. Patients like Camilla face a diagnosis that doctors cannot fully explain in terms of its mechanism or its causes. Their desire for certainty is matched only by the lack of it.

Charcot, Janet and Freud all agreed on one thing in their work on hysteria: those who developed the condition were vulnerable for some reason. Charcot firmly believed that hysteria was an inherited disease, the onset of which could be triggered by trauma. This theory did not prove to be correct, but neither did it entirely lack merit. While there is no current evidence to support the likelihood of a genetically inherited cause, numerous reports agree that people with somatic symptom disorders are more likely than others to have a family member who is also affected by them.

Pierre Janet believed that hysteria occurred as a result of a dissociation between the conscious and the subconscious mind. The split was caused by trauma and it occurred in people who were mentally weak or defective and therefore vulnerable to the fracture. So the person was flawed even before the fracture occurred.

Freud agreed with Janet's concept of dissociation but did not agree that the sufferers were mentally inferior from the outset. In contrast to Janet's view he observed that many patients under his care were of superior intelligence. In *Studies in Hysteria* he said 'hysteria of the severest type can exist in conjunction with gifts of the richest and most original kind'. He noted that his female patients were restricted by society and wondered if it was, in fact, lack of intellectual stimulation that led them to hysteria. So, quite the opposite to the opinion held by Janet.

But for Freud it was not only the restrictive social circumstance that created vulnerability. He believed that the vast majority of hysteria occurred as a result of a repressed memory of a childhood sexual abuse. He based this belief on the memories of abuse that he elicited from his patients, usually under hypnosis. He later changed that belief when, just like in the later sodium amytal experiments, hypnosis was said to produce the perfect conditions in which to elicit false memories. Despite his detractors Freud published a number of papers expounding the 'seduction theory' before revising his theory to say that the memories that he had at first taken to be real were in fact fantasies. He believed that these fantasies provided evidence for infantile sexuality and this belief led him to replace the seduction theory with the Oedipal complex theory.

The vulnerability that they described might be inherited or due to a mental weakness or a history of repression or abuse. It is still the case that doctors consider some people to be more susceptible to psychosomatic symptoms than others. The factors that can create susceptibility are varied and numerous but in the case of conversion disorders, and in the most disabling cases of somatic symptom disorder, the role of childhood abuse is still thought to be of great importance.

Many neurologists believe that almost every conversion disorder sufferer they see, particularly those with dissociative seizures, has been the victim of serious sexual or physical abuse. That view is only partly right. A history of sexual abuse is far more common in people with a conversion disorder than in the general population, so it is always worth considering. However, it is not true to say that it is found in the majority of sufferers. Studies vary but it is believed that up to thirty per cent of people with non-epileptic attacks have suffered sexual abuse. This means that at least seventy per cent have not. If a doctor approaches a patient with a conversion disorder with the belief that every individual has been the victim of such abuse, then they will be wrong at least seven out of ten times.

Sometimes the sort of childhood experience that creates vulnerability is subtle. Not all abuse is tangible or can be easily detected on direct questioning. An ignored or neglected child is more likely to develop somatic symptoms as they get older than a child who feels loved and secure. Having a father who is remote and uninvolved has been particularly associated with the later development of somatic disorders. But the impact of a distant, unloving father is not easily measured, nor is it easy to detect just through questioning the child who has now become an adult.

Many doctors think that sufferers of conversion disorders and somatic disorders have a particular sort of personality. This too can be a sticking point in making the diagnosis. If we believe that only a certain type of person tends to somatise in response to stress, then this makes the diagnosis a statement about personality as much as about medical illness. Those perceived to have the *right* sort of personality for psychosomatic disorders will be offered the diagnosis too often, and those deemed *the wrong sort* will have their diagnosis missed.

The concept of a somatising personality is not entirely wrong, though. There is evidence to suggest that people who have anxious or neurotic personalities, those with a tendency to worry or feel anger, guilt and depression, are more likely to develop somatic complaints. The same can be said for those with a tendency to be overly dependent on others, and people who see others as powerful and successful and themselves as helpless. Also a history of psychiatric illness is seen in fifty per cent of sufferers; but that means it is also absent in fifty per cent. So, having a particular personality or a history of psychiatric complaints increases your chances of developing a somatic disorder, but it does not mean that somatisation is the exclusive domain of any particular sort of person.

To a degree we are all vulnerable, we all have a threshold and if we are pushed beyond that point any one of us could develop a psychosomatic disorder. Our early lives help to determine both where our threshold will lie and what it might take to cause us to respond to stress through illness or psychiatric symptoms.

When psychosomatic illness does occur there is often a trigger that sets events in motion. Charcot, Janet and Freud were also in agreement on this point. They recognised that a specific precipitant could be identified before the onset of symptoms. But what counts as a trigger event? Some things are considered stressful by any standard. The loss of a loved one is not an uncommon starting point for psychosomatic illness, particularly where the loss was tragic in some way or guilt-ridden. A serious physical or sexual assault has also commonly been described as a precursor for illness.

Yet many life events are not so easily categorised as purely good news or bad, so it may not be easy for the patient to acknowledge or recognise the stressor. Having a baby may be unqualified joyous news to the couple who have longed for just that, but might be a more complicated event for the twenty-four-year-old who is just starting out in her career. To a twenty-five-year-old banker living in London, redundancy is something he or she will face at some point in their career and they will usually find a replacement job in due course. Redundancy to a fifty-year-old factory worker in a small town is quite another experience. What's more, the trauma can be hard to quantify if the person does not recognise it as stress at the time. Moving to a beautiful new home, emigrating or getting a promotion can all be a positive change in our lives, while at the same time being a great source of stress.

The denial of stress seems to be inherent in conversion disorders. If unpleasant emotions have indeed been converted to a physical symptom, the patient is not always aware that they ever existed in the first place. That makes it difficult for scientists to study the association between stress and the onset of symptoms. In order to try and establish the type of triggers that might lead to psychosomatic illness, a group of scientists compared people with a recent diagnosis of conversion disorder with those recently diagnosed with an organic disease. They did not ask the patients to identify a stressor but instead showed them a list of life changes or possible traumas and recorded every event that they had encountered in the previous year, irrespective of whether or not the patient considered it relevant, or stressful. The respondents with functional illness were twice as likely as the others to have experienced a significant life event in the year before they fell ill. Examples of triggers were a birth, a death, a change in employment, moving home, being the victim of a crime, meeting a previous abuser, the break-up of a relationship, financial problems and so on.

In clinical practice I am constantly looking for these triggers. Sometimes there is an unequivocal stressor on which everybody can agree. When that is the case it makes the diagnosis far easier to accept and it offers a focus for treatment. But too often there is no discrete event at which to point the finger. The cause may be nebulous and therefore hard to pin down, perhaps the chronic low-level stress of poor housing or long-standing marital dishar-mony rather than one big stressful episode. Situations that make people feel trapped appear particularly likely to lead to somatic illness. Or there could be a series of small stressors that feel cumulative. Mild unhappiness in a relationship coincides with chronic dissatisfaction in the workplace; worry about financial stability adds to concern about how the children are doing at school. Out of several *small* worries a major anxiety is born.

To think of psychosomatic illness as a single illness with a single cause is a mistake. It has more in common with a medical condition like epilepsy. Epilepsy is not a single disease, it is a group of disorders, all of which result in seizures, and in each case the cause, treatment and prognosis are different. A child who has genetically determined epilepsy cannot be compared to an old man who develops epilepsy as a result of head injury. The same rules do not apply, and that is also how it is for psychosomatic illness. It is not a single condition, there are many distinct causes and two people cannot easily be directly compared. The end point may be similar but how people get there can be very different.

While it does seem to be true that for many of the patients who develop sudden onset seizures – or the more flagrant and dramatic of the conversion disorders – a clear psychogenic cause or trigger is present, not every somatic disorder can be explained in this way. Some arise as a result of dysfunctional attitudes to illness and a tendency to seek attention and help for every medical complaint. In these cases, somatic illness comes about because of particular behaviour rather than a trigger event or trauma.

The tendency to somatise often begins in childhood. Recurrent abdominal pain is common in children but an organic cause is found in fewer than ten per cent of those affected. It causes great disruption to families and to schooling. The mechanism for it is poorly understood. It does not lead to the development of disease and it is linked to anxiety and depression. Children who suffer recurrent abdominal pain are more likely than others to have a family member with a history of chronic ill health. Its incidence is higher where a parent suffers with multiple medically unexplained symptoms. A history of parental anxiety in the first year of life is associated with it, as is a history of a parent who suffers with obsessive traits or neuroticism.

Not all the childhood experiences that make us vulnerable to somatic disorders fall into the category of abuse. Some are almost the opposite. Over-attentiveness, particularly when a child is sick, can also serve as a risk factor for unexplained medical illness later in life. Attitudes to illness and health can be in part learned through experience. Chronic illness, either in a child or in a member of their family, can modulate how they manage illness and respond to stress in the future. Early exposure to chronic ill health can inadvertently encourage illness behaviour and, as we have seen, shape how psychosomatic illness presents, with patients often suffering from symptoms they have come across before in others.

Behavioural factors may also be important in the development of chronic pain and chronic fatigue syndromes. Disorders like ME and irritable bowel syndrome may not have their origins primarily in stress but instead in mistaken beliefs about how best to respond to changes in your body and illness. The tendency to respond to every bodily sensation, rather than ignore most of them as the majority of us do, may be learned at a very young age.

In irritable bowel syndrome, one explanation is that the sufferers have abnormal gut motility and an oversensitivity to foodstuffs and stimulants that leads to their symptoms. Another argument says IBS is in fact a disorder of perception, that those affected are overly observant of every internal sensation and change in their bowel motions. They are reacting to symptoms that others might dismiss, and those reactions serve to heighten the symptoms and awareness of them.

There is one further risk factor for psychosomatic illness that I have been withholding, a single personal characteristic that is

seen in the majority of those who develop a medically unexplained chronic illness: they are female.

More than seventy per cent of patients with dissociative
seizures and chronic fatigue syndrome are women. Somatic
symptom disorders may be up to ten times more common in
women. This imbalance has been recognised since records began.
As doctors we have been very good at making this observation
but not quite so successful when it comes to explaining it. In
this, I too will fail.

Of course we must start with the name, hysteria, from *hystera*,
the Greek for womb. The womb provided a compelling explanation and source of hysteria until the early twentieth century.
The ovaries were also vibrant at communicating their distress
to the rest of the body; and the clitoris, if not used appropriately,
was also highly suspect. A woman's attempt at self-gratification
might lead to excessive stimulation of the nerves, and that might
lead anywhere . . . But underuse might also do the same. Only
in the twentieth century, as the organic hypotheses for hysteria
slowly receded, did the interest in the female organs begin to
wane.

Although the large majority of cases continued to be women,
men were also seen to be affected: Charcot had pointed out
quite clearly that he diagnosed many men with hysteria. He
noted that pressure on the testes could produce the same bene-
ficial effects in men that pressure on the ovary produced in
women, he opened a ward for male hysterics at the Salpêtrière,
and stated that he did not consider hysteria to be a female
disease. Yet all his most famous patients, such as those paraded
at the Tuesday lessons, were women.

Freud also had male patients who were hysterics. He did not propose that hysteria exclusively affected women, but he did feel that women might have traits that put them at risk. Women had more time on their hands and were therefore more prone to daydreaming, and such daydreaming could lead to pathological associations. He did not think, as Janet did, that their vulnerability was due to weakness. But once again, even though Freud did not consider this to be an exclusively female problem, he did not help to dispel that impression because every patient detailed in *Studies in Hysteria* is female.

More than a hundred years has passed since Charcot's and Freud's hysterics. Men have had hysterical epidemics, but they were given labels of their own. Neurasthenia was the first, but British men returning from the First World War also exhibited many of the signs of Charcot's hysteria. A new diagnosis was created for them: shell shock. Even allowing for these outbreaks of male hysteria, the perception that it is a female illness has not changed very much at all to this day.

I will always remember a day in my early training as a neurologist when this was brought sharply into focus for me. The team I worked with had just seen a young man with bizarre muscle spasms in one foot. The problem had followed a minor injury to his leg that had occurred at work. He had not worked since. Gradually, his foot had contorted into a position that made it difficult for him to walk. He had been extensively investigated. Tests were always normal. When we reached the point where there was nothing more we could do I wondered if the problem might be psychosomatic. In response, the middle-aged male consultant I worked for had turned glibly to me, and to the group of female medical students with me, and announced that the problem could not possibly be psychogenic since the patient was male and psychogenic disorders were disorders of young women.

Even now, years later, as an experienced consultant, this view comes up time and again. I once made a firm diagnosis of dissociative seizures in a middle-aged man and, in reply, the male consultant who had asked for my opinion in the first instance made it clear that I could not possibly be correct.

'Men don't get psychogenic seizures,' he stated, reflecting almost exactly, I thought, the words of the French physician Jean-Baptiste Louyer-Villermay in 1819: 'A man cannot be hysterical; he has no uterus.'

Perhaps Louyer-Villermay was simply being literal about the meaning of 'hysteria' but perhaps he was demonstrating an attitude that has also been suggested as a contributing factor when it comes to the apparently female nature of psychosomatic disorders: male doctors are reluctant to make the diagnosis in men. Certainly in the eighteenth and nineteenth centuries, when doctors were almost exclusively men, and women were considered to be the inferior sex, it seems likely that this sort of prejudice had an effect. Although such attitudes are less frequent and less overt now, they do live on in the twenty-first century. Some clinical studies have shown that doctors are likely to pursue the cause of difficult to explain physical symptoms less aggressively in women than they are in men; and labels such as emotionally disturbed or histrionic are more likely to be applied to a woman than a man.

I do believe that male dominance in medicine has played its

part in moulding hysterical illness, but I realise I am also being disingenuous. The majority of patients that I diagnose with conversion disorders are also women. Even when one removes the male doctor one is still left with mostly female patients. The reason is very difficult to determine.

One important factor is that women are more vulnerable to some of the traumatic events that are thought to trigger these disorders. In 2012 in England and Wales, of the 6,634 reported sexual offences committed against children, 5,156 were against girls. Similarly, adult women are more likely to be the victims of physical abuse than men. They are more likely to find themselves threatened or trapped or victimised – just the sorts of inescapable stresses that are understood to promote psychogenic illness.

An alternative theory involves differences in what is deemed to be socially acceptable in the behaviour of men and women. Women are permitted to display emotion while men must be strong. It is more socially acceptable for a woman to appear weak and to seek help. Men must simply carry on. This may result in the development of a culture where women are more likely to report their symptoms and to seek help, while men are more likely to ignore them.

Psychiatric disorders such as anxiety and depression also affect women significantly more often than men. But men do not have less stress in their lives, so on the surface the higher incidence of depression, somatic and conversion disorders in women might seem to suggest that men cope more effectively with life than women do. But perhaps that view might be changed if we also look at other gender differences. Women drink less alcohol and have fewer alcohol-related problems than men. Men are more likely to self-medicate stress with alcohol. Men are more prone to aggressive outbursts or high-risk behaviour, and are more likely to be arrested, harm their children, and have affairs. So perhaps it is not a matter of one sex coping better or complaining less, but rather a case of each suffering but differently. On the face of it, women turn their distress inward and men turn it outward.

The complexities of chronic medically unexplained illness never end. But whatever it is that makes us ill, there may be a whole other set of reasons why we don't get better.

Peter lost his job at the age of fifty. He had worked for the same company since leaving school. He had started out driving a van and graduated to a job in sales. Peter had expected to work there until he was sixty-five and then he and Liz would retire and do the things they had been waiting to do. Peter calculated that the mortgage would be fully paid off by then, leaving them with the freedom to take their caravan around every county of the United Kingdom, something Peter had always dreamed of. Liz had her own ambitions. She had never been to America and wanted to take her grandchildren to New York.

Suddenly Peter, who had never known an idle day in his life, lost his job. He was unemployed and unemployable. He had no education and no formal training. He lived in a moderately sized town where more men were losing their jobs than finding new ones. Liz was a hard worker like her husband. She was a supervisor in a supermarket. She did not like her job much but it served its purpose. Once Peter stopped working her salary was just enough to cover the mortgage payments but left little for anything else. She increased her hours at work. She hoped it would be a temporary measure. Even then, money was short. Peter and Liz began to dip into their savings. Liz watched the New York money slip away.

Three years went by. Peter could not find another job. He had always been a proud man and now he was demoralised, sitting at home, his wife at work, his life savings depleted. Liz was still working long hours and coming home each night to a different sort of husband to the one she had married. A depressed man with all his thirst for life gone. Their relationship, which had always been strong, began to fracture. Liz was exhausted and began to feel depressed and suffer debilitating headaches. Then, at the end of a particularly gruelling day, she collapsed at work. Peter received a phone call to say that she had been rushed to her local hospital in a coma. When Liz woke an hour later Peter was by her side, her hand in his. The doctor told them that they believed that Liz had suffered a seizure.

Peter and Liz were devastated. How could their lives become even more difficult? What had they done to deserve this? They prayed for a quick recovery.

'We'll lose the house if I can't work,' Liz said.

Over the course of the next week Liz suffered several seizures and had to stay in hospital. Peter sat by her bed, he could barely be persuaded to leave her side. In time Liz was ultimately diagnosed with epilepsy and started on treatment. When she was discharged from hospital she was advised to stay off work for a further week until she felt better. With her diagnosis a lot of things began to make sense to Liz. Epilepsy was the reason that she had such difficulty coping. Epilepsy was the reason she had felt depressed.

Liz's seizures did not come under control immediately. The doctor told her that this was to be expected. He would adjust the drugs until things improved but it could take several months. Liz was signed off from work but continued to receive full pay. Peter, who had had so little to do for so long, found a purpose in looking after his wife. After six months Liz still had not fully recovered. She was let go from work and began to receive disability payments. A social worker and occupational therapist helped Peter and Liz with modifications to their home to accommodate her epilepsy. Peter was afraid to leave Liz alone. Since he still could not find work he became his wife's paid carer. He stopped looking for a new job.

A year and a half later when Liz was still not responding to epilepsy medication she was referred for video telemetry, and that was when I told Liz that she did not have epilepsy.

In that moment I turned Peter's and Liz's life on its head. The diagnosis of dissociative seizures threatened all the security that the diagnosis of epilepsy had inadvertently offered. The presence of Liz's seizures had strengthened Peter's and Liz's relationship, it had allowed Liz to avoid a job that exhausted her, it had provided the family with the social and psychological support that they had desperately needed. Were I to take Liz's seizures away I would consign her back to working long hours in an underpaid job, returning home every evening to a depressed despondent husband who resented her. Liz did not choose her diagnosis, it was given to her; relinquishing it meant relinquishing a lot.

Of course, I had changed Liz's diagnosis but I had not cured her, and the seizures continued. That's what I tried to tell her.

'I'm not saying there's nothing wrong, Liz. It's just not what we originally thought. The seizures are still a serious problem.'

But Liz suspected that dissociative seizures would not come with the same rewards as an organic illness, and she was right. The world would care less about Liz's suffering now that its nature was known. Her seizures were as distressing and life-destroying as they had always been for her, but others wouldn't see them in the same way. Her disability would be downgraded. Liz was no longer sick, she was just weak. She would find her benefits under threat. Family and friends would see her differently. *Snap out of it, Liz.* In an ideal world Liz and Peter would get the psychological and social support that they needed and Liz might learn to find things easier and get better in time. But in the real world where only *real* illness counts, Liz would not necessarily get any help and might not get better.

Gain from illness might take the form of sympathy or loving care or financial reward or avoiding a problem. Most often gain is not sought, but there are gains that can hold a person unconsciously to disability. Perhaps you are not coping at work. You have a major presentation coming up and you are not prepared. Coincidentally you develop low back pain and find you have to take a few days off work. Your boss does your presentation for you. Inadvertently your illness has been rewarded. What happens the next time there is something at work that you just cannot face?

Your husband rarely stays home on a Sunday. Against all your protestations he usually spends the whole day playing golf and you are left on your own with the children. One weekend you don't feel well and have to stay in bed. Unusually he stays home to help. Illness has achieved what nothing else could.

Such rewards, whilst not consciously planned, can reinforce illness. Sometimes, for everything that is lost through illness, there is also something that is gained. Even disability can be difficult to relinquish if the gain is sufficient. But this too is an unconscious process.

For a long time after I first started to see patients with conversion disorders I believed that if I could understand the three factors of vulnerability, trigger and gain, I'd have the key to the patient's recovery. In many cases this has proven to be true. Where it has been possible to understand the cause and the maintenance factors it has been far easier for the patient to accept the diagnosis, to move forward to treatment and to recover. Like Jo.

So many of my patients are young women that when a mother stopped me in the corridor of the hospital and asked me if I remembered her daughter I couldn't bring her to mind.

'Her name is Jo,' she told me.

I felt discomfort creep over me, announcing itself in the form of a red rash starting at my neck and spreading up my face. I just couldn't remember.

'You saw her about six years ago.'

'I'm sorry . . .'

'I'm here with my other daughter today,' she said. 'She's in the epilepsy clinic. I came to find you to tell you about Jo. You saw her in the video-telemetry unit and diagnosed her with non-epileptic attacks.'

Now I had a tightness in my chest, an undeniable feeling that my day was taking a downward turn.

'I just wanted to tell you that you changed Jo's life. You really helped her. I wanted to thank you.'

My chest released a sudden breath, I felt my muscles relax and there was a real chance that a tear would escape there and then. I had been sure that something awful was going to happen but it was the opposite. The relief combined with how pleased I felt took over for a moment, and I didn't take in everything she said next.

'She gave up her job once she realised it was making her sick. She decided to become a physiotherapist. She's just qualified. She's so much happier. She lives in Edinburgh now. She really wanted me to let you know how well she was doing.'

'I'm so pleased. Thank you so much for taking the trouble to tell me.'

After she had gone I walked back to my office with a feeling of my heart fluttering, a secret smile on my face. But I still didn't remember Jo. Sitting in my chair I tapped her name into the computer. I only needed a small reminder for it all to come back to me.

Jo had come to the casualty department with a prolonged convulsion. The casualty officer had given her diazepam. Jo had been diagnosed with epilepsy six months before. Since then she had suffered ten seizures. Her sister had a diagnosis of epilepsy and since it can be genetic it was assumed that that was the cause of Jo's seizures. All her tests had been normal but that is frequently the case in somebody with epilepsy in between their seizures. Jo had been prescribed an epilepsy drug. That didn't seem to have helped because the seizures began to occur more frequently, leading to this presentation to the casualty department. A neurology registrar was called. After seeing Jo he concluded that she needed a second epilepsy drug and he provided her with a prescription and prepared to send her home. Had Jo been allowed home her story might have ended very differently, in years of drugs in escalating quantities before somebody perhaps would question the original diagnosis. Jo's mother would credit me with making her better but what happened next was probably much more important. It was the policy of the hospital to ask the epilepsy specialist nurse to meet with patients like Jo before they went home. The nurse would discuss the diagnosis and treatment in more detail and counsel Jo, if it was needed. But after her discussion she did not let Jo go home, she rang me instead.

'I know the registrar said this girl has epilepsy, but I don't think so.'

'Why not?'

'I can't put my finger on it, it just sounded wrong for epilepsy. Can we bring her in?'

This is medicine as an art once again. There is more to a story than the facts. There is the manner in which it is told. A scientific study published in the journal *Epilepsy & Behavior* in 2009 examined the linguistics of how people describe their seizures, and it found a distinct difference in the way people phrase their description between those with epilepsy and those with dissociative seizures. A specialist linguist can thus listen to a tape of a consultation and help predict the diagnosis without knowing anything about epilepsy. Or a specialist nurse, experienced and empathetic, can talk to the patient in the casualty department and do the same. I trusted her judgement.

'Okay, we'll admit her for some video telemetry.'

Three days later we had seen two of Jo's seizures and the diagnosis of dissociative seizures was made. The next stage in the process was not mine either, although I would be given the credit six years later. Jo agreed to meet the psychiatrist. In the casual in-between bits of conversation I had already gleaned some of what might be upsetting Jo but the psychiatrist would help us to see the full story.

Jo was twenty-five, a beautiful and engaging girl. She was a photojournalist working for a major newspaper, a huge achievement for a person of her age. She lived with a group of friends in London. She had grown up in London and so her family lived nearby. Jo's sister, Martha, had developed epilepsy at the age of thirteen. Throughout Martha's teens and into her early twenties she had suffered frequent seizures. Jo was three years younger and her sister's illness had occupied a prominent place in her childhood. Eventually Martha's epilepsy had come under control but she was still closely monitored.

Jo was *the lucky one* in the family. She did not have epilepsy. She was both creative and clever. She did not disappoint her parents. Throughout her school years she had loved photography, teaching herself and setting up her own darkroom in part of the family's garage. After leaving school she trained formally in media photography before spending a year travelling. She returned with a huge portfolio. She immediately created her own website and began to bombard local and national newspaper editors with her CV. She had many rejections before she received a letter from a major newspaper asking to meet her. Ultimately they offered her an internship with a view to more permanent employment if she did well.

The warning signs were there on day one, but Jo had underestimated them. She had just been introduced to her department when she heard one man whisper to another, 'She has the skirt for the job.'

For the first three months Jo hid the feeling of discomfort that she felt while at work. She had never had any difficulty getting on with people so she assumed that things would improve once people got to know her. Her colleagues spoke to her warmly so, when her unease did not lift, she convinced herself that she was imagining it. As time progressed, however, it became impossible to ignore the fact that something was not right. Her photographs were constantly criticised. As a very junior member of the team she did not expect that she should always be praised for her work, but it seemed that she could do nothing right. A male intern who had started work at the same time as Jo had several of his photographs used in the newspaper. Jo didn't feel she could complain. Perhaps her work was simply not as good as that of her fellow intern and she did not have the judgement to see it.

One day when Jo felt certain that she had produced publishable work that had been overlooked once again, she asked the editor about it. She had not meant to be derogatory but in the course of a long conversation she found herself pointing out a published photo taken by her male colleague and asking how it was superior to her own.

'No need to be catty, young lady. Jealousy is not an attractive quality.'

Jo did not like what this sentence suggested to her and she answered strongly.

'I'm not being catty, you are comparing my work to the others in the department and I am doing the same. I'm not behaving any differently to you. I am just asking you to help me by pointing out what makes one photograph better than another.'

He didn't listen. The conversation ended with a firm suggestion from her editor that she adjust her attitude. There was a distinct deterioration in the situation after that. Colleagues began to exclude her from meetings. The more challenging or interesting assignments were offered to others and she felt herself slowly drift into the background. But this was the career that Jo had dreamed of for years, so she would not give up that easily. She began to work twice as hard. It didn't help.

One morning she came to work at seven to attend a weekly meeting held at that time, but found the office empty. When people began coming in later, she discovered that the majority of the department, interns included, had spent the previous evening together at a local restaurant, a bonding exercise that had been a tradition for many years. They had postponed the morning meeting as a result. As soon as Jo realised that she had been excluded she knew she was going to cry. She had gone to the bathroom, berating herself for caring. A secretary who bumped into her in the bathroom let her boss know that she was upset. He called her to his office later that day.

'Outbursts of emotion in the workplace are really not appropriate.'

After that Jo felt she was drowning. Everything she did or said seemed to be wrong. And yet even though she knew that, logically, she would not be kept on when her internship came to an end, she could not give up the hope that fairness would win out and hard work would eventually be noticed. She feared that if she didn't turn the situation around she would get a bad reference and her career would be over before it had started. Her family had been so proud of her achievements that she could not bear the thought of telling them how badly things were going. She could not stand to think that the people at work, who were not giving her a fair chance, might win. She had an overwhelming feeling of being trapped. One day, getting ready to go to work, she had her first seizure.

It was a credit to Jo that once we told her about her diagnosis of dissociative seizures, it did not take long for her to understand that her feeling of entrapment was like something boiling over inside her, something that had to be released. She had been unable to admit what she perceived as failure to her friends and family so when the situation came to a head her body called for help on her behalf, using an expression of distress with which it had long been familiar. The psychiatrist had referred Jo for therapy and she had re-evaluated her life and made the changes she wanted to make without regard to how they would be perceived by others. My meeting with her mother told me that Jo had made the right decisions for her.

I should have remembered Jo when I met her mother because she was an example of how well things can go when the system works as it should. Not every diagnosis of epilepsy will be right – it is a diagnosis dependent on a clinical history, the evaluation of which is open to error. When it became clear that Jo wasn't getting better on the treatment for epilepsy the diagnosis was reviewed, the correct diagnosis was made, and the correct treatment started. Seventy per cent of those with dissociative seizures continue to have seizures, particularly those who don't get the diagnosis quickly enough or in whom no underlying cause is found or where there is no appropriate psychiatrist to provide care.

Medicine is a career that is full of highs and lows. When working with people with dissociative seizures, success stories can feel hard to come by at times. Too many patients never see a psychiatrist and too often I never find out where their story ends. Jo had recovered completely once she understood her seizures. I felt greatly heartened to hear how well she had done.

In time Camilla would also make me feel that way, but not until she came to a very difficult realisation.

Camilla remained in hospital for a further two weeks after her diagnosis had been confirmed. During that time I monitored her progress as I withdrew her epilepsy medication. She continued to struggle to believe that her seizures were not due to epilepsy but she carried her doubt calmly and with dignity. Her evenness unsettled me. It spoke of denial. I wanted her to shout at me, to give me a display of emotion that I could understand and to which I could react. But if there was something hidden Camilla could not reach it, and nor could I. If I had upset her with the diagnosis she could not feel it – or could not show it. Soon I began to worry I was wrong. And every time we met Camilla would tell me that she believed that emotions could make you ill, but it was not happening to her. It was something that happened to others.

Some somatic disorders happen insidiously with no great trauma to explain them. Some happen for a reason that is obvious and some because of something secret. Dissociation involves a separation: one part of the mind is not aware of the other, memories from the past are kept away from the present. My last meeting with Camilla would let me know how absolute that separation of consciousness can be.

Camilla had stopped all her epilepsy drugs with no ill effect. Her seizures were ongoing but there was still no evidence to suggest that any of them were due to epilepsy. On the day she was due to go home I met her and her husband for one final conversation. They sat facing me on the edge of Camilla's bed.

'Is there anything more you'd like to ask before you leave?' I asked.

'Just what I always ask,' Camilla laughed. 'If this is true, why is it happening to me?'

'You know I don't know the answer to that. It might take time to figure it out.'

'They happen anywhere, watching the television, reading. There is no pattern.'

'Sometimes I think it is useful to think of the very first attack. Sometimes that is the one that tells us the most. The first attack might have been triggered by something and then all of the others may have been spontaneous, not following any pattern and therefore confusing us. Your first seizure happened in

Cumbria, didn't it? Can you think of anything that happened there, even something small?'

'I had a very successful meeting. There was nothing.'

Camilla's husband sat by her side, her hand in his. He now seemed to wrinkle up his face and look at his wife as if he were confused.

'Darling?' he said.

It was not an endearment, it was a question.

'What?' Camilla turned to him.

'You know that wasn't the very *first* collapse?'

'What?' Camilla said again.

The beginning of Hugh's and Camilla's relationship was touching. Hugh claimed that he had known he would marry her the very first day they met. Camilla claimed that he had worn her down. They had been in the same social group throughout college and their friendship survived the dispersal of their college friends. They both took jobs in London and began to spend time together. They fell in love as Hugh had said they would. Hugh claimed that he had wanted to propose almost as soon as the relationship had begun but he had waited nearly two years out of a sense of decorum. One year after that they married.

Both Camilla and Hugh worked long hours and they decided to wait before starting a family, although both agreed that they wanted as many children as possible. However, two years into their marriage their best-laid plans were interrupted by the arrival of their unplanned first son, Henry. Camilla took maternity leave for one year and then returned to work. She loved spending time with Henry, marvelling at all the little changes. Her return to work had been reluctant.

One Saturday, when Henry was eighteen months old, Camilla had arranged to meet another mother in the park. It was a play date for Henry and a chance for Camilla to catch up with an old friend. The walk to the park had taken fifteen minutes. Sitting in his buggy Henry had chatted animatedly to himself for the whole journey.

Just at the entrance to the park Camilla had met another friend that she knew from the area. She stopped to say hello and they fell into the usual conversation about schools and day care and nannies. As she talked, Camilla could see the mother she had come to meet pushing her daughter on the swings just on the other side of the fence that bordered the park. Henry must have seen them too because he started to scream loudly and strained to be released from his buggy. Camilla told him to shush, that they would not go on the swings if he was naughty. She turned the buggy to face away from the park. Henry screamed again and arched his back and kicked his legs.

'Better go,' Camilla smiled at her friend and bent down to say goodbye to her friend's child, who was by now looking precariously close to joining Henry in his tantrum.

What Camilla had not realised was that, as she turned the buggy around, she had released the brake but had not engaged it again. Henry was still wrestling to get out of his straps and as he did so the buggy began to move forward. The narrow pavement was gently sloped and it did not take long for the buggy to reach the road. At this point, if Camilla had noticed, she could still have reached the handle and pulled it back. But she didn't notice and as the buggy rolled over the high kerb it fell forward so that Henry lay beneath it in the middle of the road. Camilla's friend, who was facing the road, looked first. She let out a scream and lurched towards Henry. Camilla turned just in time to see the car round the bend, brake but fail to stop before her son's buggy disappeared beneath its wheel.

'Everything felt unreal. They say that you see disasters like this in slow motion, but it wasn't like that. It was fast, as if the buggy had just vanished . . . puff.'

The driver of the car came to a quick halt. Camilla ran into the road and lay on the ground, trying to get to her child. The buggy was wedged against the undercarriage of the car. It was folded in such a way that she could not even see Henry.

'There was so much screaming, me, my friend, the driver, that it took me minutes to realise that I couldn't hear any sound coming from Henry.'

It took the fire brigade twenty minutes to free Henry from beneath the car. By that time Hugh had arrived, so they were both there to see the fireman's expression as he handed the lifeless body of their child to the paramedics. Camilla and Hugh were not allowed to travel with their son in the ambulance, they followed immediately behind in a police car. Camilla was standing at the door of the emergency room watching as paramedics failed to resuscitate her son. A nurse turned to look at her and ushered her and Hugh back out to the waiting room. Half an hour later they were told that there was nothing that could be done. The doctors believed that Henry had probably died as soon as the car had hit. That night Camilla collapsed and had a seizure for the first time.

When I had asked Camilla how many children she had she had not told me about Henry. She had not mentioned him to any of the doctors or nurses she had met during any of her hospital admissions and my questions had not been direct enough to seek out the hidden things.

Camilla had not forgotten Henry, nor the day he died. Her life had moved forward, she had had two more children, but he was never forgotten. His picture was up in nearly every room of the house. She would have told us about him had we asked, but in the absence of that direct question she believed that she had dealt with her loss and so didn't offer it. Had we asked she would have told us that she was lucky to have had Henry in her life, even if only briefly, and she was lucky to have gone on to give birth to two more healthy children when other people had none. She had not forgotten Henry but her loss was behind her. That's what she would have said.

Until, that is, she found herself standing in a meeting and Henry had popped into her mind. The meeting had gone well. She had negotiated successfully on behalf of a mother and child whose home life was not safe. She was feeling happy until she thought of Henry.

'I helped save that child but I couldn't save my own.' She pushed the thought quickly from her mind.

Five minutes later she had her second seizure.

Camilla had consigned her pain to a place in her brain that she could not fully access. She knew that she had lost a son but she had forgotten the pain of it. Her pain was locked in a box in her head. The seizures were the monster that protected that box. They were her monster and they served a purpose, and only when their secret was revealed did the seizures disappear.

9

LAUGHTER

> Your vision will become clear only when you can look into your
> own heart.
>
> Carl Jung, *Memories, Dreams, Reflections* (1961)

I cannot imagine the person who would meet Maria and fail
to like her. She is fifty years old but she has a childlike quality
that endears her to everybody. She has been in hospital under
my care three times now. Each time she brings George with
her. George is her stuffed bear. He is almost as old as Maria
herself. She would not dream of leaving him alone at home.
Nor is she ever without a picture that shows her beaming broadly
beside her favourite football player. Maria does voluntary work
greeting people at the entrance to a stately home. That was
where she met David and shook his hand, and where he had
kindly paused so they could have a photograph taken together.
Maria tells me the story of their meeting almost every time I
see her. If asked, Maria would mark this as the best moment
in her life.

'What about the times that Manchester won the league?' I
asked once.

They were good times, but meeting David was better.

'All the girls will be jealous when they see that picture,' I teased Maria and she laughed.

Maria was a healthy child until the day that she had her first epileptic seizure. She was five years old when they began. They continued until she was fourteen. During the time when Maria's brain should have been maturing it had been disrupted by frequent convulsions. As a result Maria's intelligence lies just in the region that means she has been categorised as mildly learning disabled.

Maria's parents had provided her with a loving home but they had an old-fashioned sense of self-sufficiency that did not allow them to take advantage of all the services that might have been available to Maria as she grew up. As a consequence she spent much of her life at home with her mother, isolated from people her own age. Maria's learning was interrupted in every way by her frequent hospital admissions. When she should have been finding out about life she lay in hospital or at home. She spent very little time at school and left with no qualifications and very few life skills. What Maria knew she had learned from her mother. When her mother cooked, Maria watched and stirred the pots. When her mother cleaned the house, Maria followed her carrying the sprays and dusters. When her mother's friends visited, Maria delighted in putting on an apron and acting as waitress. Maria rarely went out and never formed close friendships outside her family. It was her father who had encouraged her love of football. Whenever possible he took her to see a match. The only other regular outing that Maria enjoyed was her weekly trip to church with her mother.

Maria was an only child with few interests. That hadn't

mattered much because, as the centre of her parents' world, Maria was well cared for and never alone. That the situation was unsustainable had not fully dawned on anyone until her mother had her first stroke. She recovered well on this occasion but her mortality had been brought sharply into focus. Plans needed to be made for how Maria would manage if and when her parents were not around. The local learning disability and social works teams arranged for Maria to attend a day centre. They also organised weekly volunteer work. Her parents set up a fund with administrators so that Maria would always be provided for. When Maria was in her late thirties, her mother suffered the second stroke, the one that would take her. Maria and her father muddled on together for a while. When Maria was forty-two years old her father died.

So now Maria lives alone in her family home. Because of the measures her parents had put in place she has a carer who visits briefly every morning and evening. Most days she has activities, either volunteer work or at the day centre. Maria's preferred work is the greeting, which she does at a supermarket as well as the stately home. At the supermarket Maria gets great pleasure from shouting a loud hello as soon as somebody approaches and handing them a shopping basket. She does not always take it so kindly if the hello is not returned. Once she followed a customer into the shop and down an aisle when they failed to acknowledge her. After that she had lost her job for a while until a kindly social worker intervened and asked the shop manager to give her another chance.

'If they don't say hello back, I'm not allowed to say anything,' she told me.

'Not everybody is as friendly and happy as you, Maria, so we have to remember that,' I replied.

'My social worker said that some people are too busy to say hello.'

In fact I suspect that Maria brightens many people's day. For all the people who do not respond there are others who make a point of stopping. Anybody who knows Maria at all knows that she can always be drawn on the subject of football, and I suspect many lively conversations happen at the door of that shop.

At the age of forty-five Maria had her first seizure in thirty years. She had been taking her epilepsy medication since her teenage years. Attempts to withdraw it when she was a child had resulted in seizures so it was felt prudent that she should stay on it all her life. One Monday morning Maria's carer had called to see her as usual only to find her lying on the floor of her sitting room, a carpet burn extending from her elbow to her wrist. She came around when the carer shook her but did not know how long she had been lying there. Maria was taken to hospital where tests were normal. A blood test showed an unusually low level of epilepsy drug in her blood and the doctors feared that, in the absence of supervision at the weekends, Maria might have forgotten to take her tablets.

After that Maria suffered clusters of collapses occurring months apart. Her doctor increased the strength of her epilepsy drugs and a carer was employed to visit at the weekends to supervise Maria as she took her tablets. The seizures continued. As the source of the problem was clearly not missed medication, Maria was eventually admitted for video telemetry to verify what was happening when she collapsed.

On her first visit to the hospital Maria had spent the biggest part of every day standing at the door of her room calling out to the nurses working on the ward. Leads that were attached to her head to record her brainwaves during an attack did not allow her to wander out into the corridor or around the ward. Just through standing at her doorway and calling out she made friends with other patients and soon she had people visiting her room throughout the day.

The day before Maria was due for discharge I was told that she had been found the evening before lying on the floor of her room. I looked at the video to see what had happened. Evening was the quiet time for Maria, there were fewer staff on the ward and other patients were with their visitors. Maria had been pacing her room, sitting down briefly to watch television and then walking to the door and calling out to somebody who didn't come. She had been behaving restlessly in this way for almost an hour when I saw her take some magazines and throw them on the floor. Then she went to the door and I could hear a distant shout, 'Help, help.' She returned to her room and, using her bed for leverage, she lowered herself carefully to the floor. She lay still then, with her eyes closed, but nobody came. After a minute or so of waiting she stood again and did the same, walked to the door and cried for help. This time, when she returned to the room she also pressed the alarm button before she lay down again and closed her eyes. Only when she heard the nurses arrive in the room did she begin to shake. The nurses were very experienced and recognised straight away that Maria's seizure was unlikely to be due to epilepsy. They talked to her and reassured her that she was safe. One got down on her hands and knees beside Maria and stroked her arm and told her that everything would be okay. When they got no response the second nurse began to talk.

'The match is on soon, Maria, you don't want to miss that.'

Maria's eyes were tightly closed but her face broke into a partially suppressed smile.

'Is David playing tonight?' The nurse knew Maria very well. By now Maria's teeth could be seen in the smile.

'I'm not sure they'll win. They have not been playing so well,' the nurse added.

That was far too much for Maria who opened her eyes then. 'They will so win!'

The shaking had stopped, Maria stood up again, and lively debate about the finer points of football ensued.

With the help of a nurse, I sat Maria down to discuss her blackouts. Her innocence stopped the conversation before it had properly begun. A childhood of epilepsy made it impossible for her to consider any alternative explanation and our conversation came to a quick halt when Maria fell to the ground and began to shake. The shaking didn't stop until I had left the room.

The next day the psychologist met with Maria but it was clear that she could not engage in a conversation about non-epileptic attacks in any meaningful way. So we set about finding other ways to help.

I contacted her doctor and her local casualty department to explain her diagnosis. Usually when Maria collapsed she was rushed to hospital by ambulance. Once there she was given drugs and on one occasion she was admitted to the intensive care unit because the seizure failed to stop with medication; often in this highly fraught situation non-epileptic convulsions are mistaken for epilepsy and treatment is started that does more harm than good. In Maria's case this would mean the risk of serious side effects from receiving unnecessary drugs and the potential life-threatening complications of intensive care units and ventilation, including chest infections or blood clots. What was happening to Maria was harmless, but the treatment could put her in danger. By ensuring that the diagnosis was well communicated to all the doctors involved in her care I felt we might at least be able to make sure that they thought carefully before intervening too aggressively when the next attack occurred. She could be treated just with love, attention and reassurance.

And we put Maria in touch with the social worker again. Despite her volunteer work and her hobbies Maria was spending long periods every day on her own. The social workers helped her to find a befriending service, someone who she could ring in the evenings when things were very quiet at home. Maria's childhood had been filled with love but the adult Maria found herself alone without the language to explain how she felt. There was very little intent in what Maria had done in hospital. Her first collapse in adulthood was probably due to epilepsy, caused by a missed tablet just as her doctor suspected, but somehow that seizure had inadvertently acted as a reminder. In her loneliness Maria had reverted to something from her childhood that had been a benefit of sorts to her then. When Maria lay down on the ground her brain was recalling a time when a small girl had a seizure and a mother came running.

I think of Maria when I need to remind myself that there is no single solution to psychosomatic illness. To look for one is akin to looking for the cure for unhappiness. There is no single answer because there is no single cause. Sometimes you just have to figure out what purpose the illness serves, find what is missing and try to replace it. If illness seems to be helping solve the problem of loneliness, then treat the loneliness and the illness will disappear. Or find out where the gain lies and address that. Or if the problem lies in maladaptive responses to the messages the body sends, that can be relearned. Break the patterns of fear and avoidance. Or if there is a specific trauma triggering illness then address it. There is no shame in asking for help. If there is no explanation and nothing else has helped, talk to a psychiatrist. What have you got to lose? We only have one life, why not explore it?

All my patients are individuals with their own story to tell, their own set of problems and their own solution. Even where the symptoms of their distress are very similar, the roads that bring them to me are not. Each of them teaches me something important, just as each new patient I meet reminds me that there is always more to learn. But, for all their differences, there is one thing that every patient shares, and that is the confusion of their journey. But when neurologists know that conversion disorders are so common, why does the news come as such a shock to patients? If psychosomatic symptoms are so ubiquitous why are we so ill-equipped to deal with them?

Consider the statistics once again: in 2011 a German study showed that twenty-two per cent of people attending a primary care centre had a somatising disorder. A UK study looking at medically unexplained symptoms in hospital clinics found them common to every clinic; in some clinics they represented more than fifty per cent of those attending. A Norwegian study asked over 900 consecutive patients at a GP practice if they thought they suffered with any of the following: amalgam poisoning, irritable bowel syndrome, candida syndrome, chronic fatigue syndrome, fibromyalgia, electromagnetic poisoning or food intolerance. Each of these diagnoses is considered either entirely medically unexplained or only partially explained and with a large psychological component. Nearly forty per cent of respondents thought that they might have at least one of these complaints. In the United States, where medical insurance is expensive and the system is very different from the NHS, the prevalence of dissociative seizures in most epilepsy clinics is thirty per cent – much the same as in the average UK epilepsy clinic.

And then consider the impact on the health service: in 2011 three GP practices in London identified 227 patients with the severest form of somatic symptom disorder, those like Pauline. These 227 patients constituted one per cent of the GP practice populations – confirming that it is a rare illness. Those patients attended secondary-care facilities 1,077 times in one year. They each had twenty appointments with their GP and underwent numerous investigations. These 227 alone cost the NHS over £500,000 in one year. When this was extrapolated to an estimated cost for similar patients throughout London it came to £115 million per annum. That is the cost for London alone, and for the most severe form of somatic disorder. There is no estimate available for the large number of people who attend the doctor with less severe forms of the illness – possibly up to thirty per cent of GP encounters every day.

If we really want this situation to improve then we each have a contribution to make. There is room for change in all of us. Doctors should be less afraid of this diagnosis, more willing to confront it and more compassionate to the sufferers. Medical schools should teach their students about this disorder, create better doctors. Medical professionals need to stop placing this unqualified diagnosis right at the bottom of their list. Certainly, this is a diagnosis that is left over when tests are normal and nothing else fits, but why should that detract from the disability and suffering it causes? Instead of appearing as a footnote in medical textbooks, psychosomatic disorders should be acknowledged as a serious diagnosis in their own right. But most of all society, the general public – *you!* – need to stop regarding symptoms of this sort as in some way less 'real' than those associated with other diseases. That is where Charcot is to be admired. For all his faults, for all the ways in which he was wrong, he applied the same scientific rigour and the same level of interest to hysteria that he had given to every other neurological disease that he studied. That's what all of us could do differently – when we encounter somebody who is severely disabled with purely medically unexplained symptoms we should treat that person with the same respect that we would give to anybody else with any other diagnosis.

It has taken over twenty years for me to feel I am even close to an understanding of these disorders. Personally I find a strange sort of comfort in the knowledge that my body can react in this way to stress. And if my body wants to tell me something, I intend to listen. A few years ago I broke a bone in my foot and had to wear a plaster cast for a month. When the cast was removed my foot was misshapen and wasted. For two weeks I limped about as I tried to recover. Previously healthy, I could not accept that my progress was so slow – there must be something wrong. Had the fracture failed to heal? I made an appointment to see my doctor. He suggested that I go for an X-ray. The X-ray was done that morning but I had to wait until the next day for the result. I was fascinated to observe how my symptoms evolved during that twenty-four hours. I had walked to my GP surgery the previous morning, a mildly painful ten-minute stroll. Over the course of the day that followed I began to feel that my foot was weakening. My limp worsened and I ended the day hopping on one leg, only able to place the toes of the affected foot on the floor for balance. In my mind was a vivid image of a bone snapped in two, the exposed ends pushed apart by any pressure I applied. And yet, even though I struggled to walk I still clearly recall that I was not scared . . . because I had seen this before. My experience wasn't so different to what my patients have described to me. I knew there was no medical reason for my foot to deteriorate so quickly. On one level I knew that my symptoms did not make sense, but on another I reacted like any other person might. Once I had learned that my X-ray showed a well-healed fracture I made a quick recovery – I had hopped to my GP surgery but walked home.

I believe in the reality of psychosomatic symptoms, and imagining that my symptoms were psychosomatic had comforted me throughout. I was somebody who was unaccustomed to pain or any sort of disability but my knowledge had been useful to me. All along I hoped my symptoms were psychosomatic because, if they were, then I was in control again and I could hope to get better soon. There was no shame in that feeling.

For us to consider a psychological cause for serious illness it is vital that we believe that such a thing is possible, and how extreme psychosomatic illness can sometimes be. For people to accept the reality of psychosomatic illness they must accept the power of the mind over the body. We seem to be happy to accept reports of people using hypnosis in place of anaesthesia, the placebo effect, the use of sports psychologists, homeopathy and alternative medicines, the effect of meditation and cancer diets and any number of other examples of how the mind can influence the body. Why is the idea of the mind reproducing physical symptoms any harder to credit? For all the positive effects the mind can have, there can just as easily be negative ones. There is no point resisting: disability for psychological reasons is all around us, it can exist and does. It is a common problem that could affect anybody – ourselves, as well as the people we know and love.

If public perception is to change, each of us would have to accept that part of ourselves which reacts physically to the world around us. Maybe if we understood better the way our own bodies lose control, triggered only by a feeling inside, then more extreme reactions might not seem so unacceptable. Because we do all somatise our emotions, whether or not we acknowledge it. Think about laughter. When we laugh our diaphragm contracts repeatedly, air is expelled from our lungs and then drawn back in again at speed. The larynx half contracts and a rhythmic gasping sound is released. The facial muscles contract and the mouth opens. The skin around the eyes wrinkles. The head goes back. Sometimes the whole body joins in, the hands clutch the stomach, we bend forward at the middle and our whole body trembles. When the pleasurable emotion goes far enough, water gathers in our tear ducts and releases itself down our face. For a second we can barely breathe, our hearts race and our faces redden. And, even better, it is contagious. The heartier the laugh the more people around are drawn to look at us and join in. So that, even without knowing the emotion that started it, strangers are drawn into your physical concert.

But laughter communicates more than just mirth, it is triggered by a variety of emotions. Alongside humour, it can also occur as a result of social discomfort or embarrassment or it can be an expression of negative intent, such as derision. In most cases laughter is an involuntary mechanism but it can be disingenuous, it can be faked.

Nobody fully understands the mechanism by which the brain produces laughter. Many parts of the brain have been implicated but no single *laughter centre* has ever been identified. It's likely that laughter is not a single phenomenon, that different laughs have different causes and are generated in different parts of the brain. That is why a laugh of derision is not easily mistaken for one that is heartfelt, because they are related but different phenomena.

Freud believed that laughter, like dreams, could betray our secret thoughts. Most of us have laughed when we didn't mean to and in doing so inadvertently allowed people to know something of what we secretly thought. Laughter is often involuntary, so if we looked at what makes us laugh we might learn something about ourselves. Jokes allow us to laugh at things that are not normally socially acceptable and that in itself is revealing.

Laughter can be therapeutic. Pent-up anger or sadness can be converted to laughter and in doing so release an internal tension. Laughter can distract us. If we are suffering stress or fear we might feel better to suppress or deny it and seek out laughter instead.

And laughter can go wrong. Sometimes it can be a sign of illness or disease. Inappropriate poorly controlled laughter is seen in a variety of psychiatric and neurological disorders. In mania there is the raucous laughter that goes too far. Diseases affecting the frontal lobe of the brain can cause inappropriate laughter where the brain has ceased to be able to distinguish between situations that can rightly be considered places for humour and those which cannot. There is also a sort of epilepsy which manifests as nothing more than a mirthless laugh.

How easily we accept these different facets of laughter. It is a physical display of emotion, its mechanism is ill-understood, it is not always under our voluntary control, it affects our whole body, it stops our breathing and speeds up our heart, it serves a purpose, it releases tension and communicates feelings. Laughter is the ultimate psychosomatic symptom. It is such a normal part of the human experience that all its facets are universally accepted. Now all we have to do is take the few short steps to a new realisation. If we can collapse with laughter, is it not just as possible that the body can do even more extraordinary things when faced with even more extraordinary triggers?

ACKNOWLEDGEMENTS

Thank you to Kirsty McLachlan of David Godwin Associates who was pivotal in the development of the idea for this book. And to Becky Hardie of Chatto & Windus, who has taught me a great deal and whose hard work has been of endless benefit to the result.

Thanks to my parents who sacrificed a lot to give their children a good education. And to all my family, Eithne, Aileen, Paul, Barry, Oscar, Aisling, Felix, Roisin, Ciara, Chloe, Daniel and Shaun.

I owe a particular debt to the people I have worked with and learned from throughout the last twenty years; specific reference must be given to the neurologists and neurophysiologists of the Meath and Adelaide hospitals and St Vincent's Hospital in Dublin, who inspired me to want to follow in their footsteps. Also to the epilepsy teams of the Royal London Hospital, National Hospital for Neurology, and the Epilepsy Society. Thank you especially to Jenny Nightingale, Adele Larkin, Vicki Kelmanson and Charlie Cockerell, who allowed me to develop my interest in a supportive environment. Special thanks also to the neuropsychiatry teams of each of these hospitals who are a tremendous support to my patients, and to me.

But most of all thank you to my patients. I hope this book will create a better understanding of their plight.

INDEX

www.vintage-books.co.uk